**Administrative
Issues in
Developing
Economies**

Administrative Issues in Developing Economies

Edited by

Kenneth J. Rothwell
University of New Hampshire

Lexington Books
D.C. Heath and Company
Lexington, Massachusetts
Toronto   London

International Standard Book Number: 0-669-81208-0

Library of Congress Catalog Card Number: 78-174596

To
V. E. (H.) R.

Table of Contents

Preface ix

Part I   **Identifying Administrative and Management Problems**   **1**

Chapter 1   The Scope of Management and Administration Problems in Development   3
Kenneth J. Rothwell

Chapter 2   Bridging the Public and Private Sectors of Development   39
Walter G. O'Donnell

Chapter 3   Key Problems in Development Administration   47
Jack Koteen

Chapter 4   Achievement and Administrative Action in Developing Countries   69
David C. McClelland

Chapter 5   Institution Building and Administrative Problems of Developing Economies   75
William J. Siffin

Chapter 6   The Less Developed Entrepreneur   83
Wayne G. Broehl, Jr.

Chapter 7   Management Information Systems and Social Planning   95
Ida R. Hoos

Chapter 8   Aspects of Administrative Change and Reform   117
Arne F. Leemans

Chapter 9   The Myth of Alternatives: Underlying Assumptions about Administrative Development   133
Fred W. Riggs

Part II   **Technical Assistance and Training for Administrative Development**   **149**

Chapter 10   Towards New International Economic Development and Resource Transfer   151
Jan Tinbergen

Chapter 11   New Perspectives for Aid and Technical Assistance   163
Gustav F. Papanek

Chapter 12   Administrative Aspects of Education for Developing Countries   167
Jan F. Glastra van Loon and Kenneth J. Rothwell

Chapter 13 An Interpretation of Management Skills: Some Prob-
            lems of International Transferability   181
            David J. Ashton

Chapter 14 Training for the Transition from Entrepreneur to Man-
            ager: A Case Study   193
            Allan R. Cohen

Chapter 15 Public Administration in the 1970s   205
            Chi-Yuen Wu

Chapter 16 A Training Strategy for Organizational Improvement:
            A Case Study—The Development Administrators
            Training Program   229
            Vinton D. Fisher, Jr.

Chapter 17 Views on Administrative Training Strategies in Africa   247
            John H. Smith

Chapter 18 The New Design of Development and Administrative
            Change   253
            Milton J. Esman

            About the Contributors   261

            Index   263

Preface

This book presents a series of contemporary views on significant issues in the administration of institutions and organizations and the management of development in developing economies. It seeks to set out the basic problems of management and administration under conditions of hastened economic change and the ways of dealing with some of these problems, particularly through new training approaches. Special attention is given to the needs of public and private organizations relevant to the next decade of development.

The economic and social management of development cannot be considered apart from a political context, and although this broader problem presents fascinating dimensions for the decades ahead, this book is limited to an exposition of the basic concerns of administrative and management development. Political change brings organizational change and this becomes the starting point for our considerations. It is difficult to escape from the fact that in the management of national change there is no *purely* political problem anymore than there is a *purely* economic, legal, cultural or technological problem.

Both our thinking about the basic organizational and administrative issues and the training which we employ to solve these development issues require much more attention in the future. There is a need to examine new connections between established disciplinary areas of learning and to see where excesses in the application of previous learning have been detrimental to the achievement of desired results.

In particular, it is helpful to see to what extent the studies of public administration and business administration have overlaps in the context of economic and social development. Development administration, comparative administration, the application of management techniques to administration, the widening scope of national and development consciousness of managers and the blurring of the distinctions between private and public business in development are extensions of the overlapping features of the studies. Public administration and business management are seen as more closely linked in function and environment in the developing economies than they are in the developed economies. There is a greater overlapping of the public and private sectors and a greater need to provide a closer integration of training and professionalization in public and business administration—a dichotomy strongly promoted in the developed countries, but not completely applicable to the countries of the underdeveloped regions of the world. The separation of these types of training institutions in the developed countries increases the difficulties of making technical assistance programs as effective as they might be. The new approaches to technical assistance for enhancing management and administration capabilities are discussed in relation to changing patterns of needs and expectations in foreign aid programs.

The essays in this book cover a wide range of problems in management and administration development, yet their central theme is on improving the *outcomes* of developing economies. Each author seizes on a particular aspect of the administrative problem, either at the international, national or unit level, to lay down the significant issues which require attention. It is clear that one ingredient which can make considerable difference to the success of economic and social planning is more effective management and administration in the organizations and institutions which are emerging and taking new forms. The several case studies which are presented illustrate some of these particular problems in specialized situations.

The book focuses firstly on the identification of administrative and management problems, then, on ways which solutions can be implemented, particularly through technical assistance, cooperation and effective educational programs. Guides for development strategies are examined and a number of warnings on misdirected study and approaches are provided. The book contains a number of papers originally presented at a conference on "Administration and Management in Developing Countries" held at the New England Centre for Continuing Education in New Hampshire, May 1970. This conference was made possible by the cooperative efforts of a number of institutions, including:

> Whittemore School of Business and Economics;
> Harvard Development Advisory Service;
> Institute of Social Studies;
> South East Asia Development Advisory Group;
> Comparative Administrative Group of the American Society
> for Public Administration; and
> The New England Center for Continuing Education.

Because of space limitations, not all papers presented at the conference have been included in this selection, but much of the material included in this book has benefited from the continuing discussions and contributions of the numerous participants in the conference. This interchange among scholars from several academic disciplines made clear some of the overlaps in approach to the problems of planning, administration, and management and promoted new modes of thinking. Additional papers and numerous redrafts of the original papers broadened the scope of those ideas originally presented at the conference. Two of the papers have been published previously and appreciation is extended to the respective publishers for permission to reproduce the papers in this volume.

Acknowledgement is made of special interest from Ralph Braibanti, Jan E. Clee, Allan R. Cohen, Harry P. Day, Jan F. Glastra van Loon, Fred W. Riggs, Peter R. Savage, and William J. Siffin. None of these individuals or their present institutions, however, are held responsible for the final array of materials included in this book. Acknowledgement would not be complete without recognizing the patient efforts of Mrs. Elaine Vachon, and Mrs. L.P. Burgemeestre, who attended to the typing of the numerous drafts of the various chapters, and the encouragement of the staff of the Institute of

Social Studies where final assembly of the materials took place. Support from the Institute of International Economic Studies at the University of Stockholm is also recognised.

The Hague, March 1972.   KENNETH J. ROTHWELL

Part I
Identifying Administrative and Management Problems

1

The Scope of Management and Administration Problems in Development

Kenneth J. Rothwell

Approaches to Management and Administration Development

The problems of administration and management in developing economies arise from a rapid change in expectations which is not matched by appropriate organizational and institutional change.[1] Gaps are seen in the capability and efficiency of established institutions to attain social goals, and gaps are seen in established structures, systems, and functions appropriate for new human values and relationships. These gaps cannot be adequately filled by international transfers of resources, nor can they be completely removed by vast new educational efforts. Institution and system building for the public and private sectors of the developing economy, while an intrinsic aspect of the development process, contribute only a fraction of the inputs of the complex process. In this chapter the author seeks to survey the issues of management and administration related to organizational change and system building in economic development. He does not propose or expect to touch on all the problems or to assign orders of importance to issues identified, let alone suggest universally satisfying solutions to the difficulties of the "Soft State."

To a large degree, the terms "management" and "administration" are used in this paper interchangeably. This reflects a growing tendency in the literature and in practice, especially in dealing with *economic* development, to view the management and administration of the economy and change as much the same operation. Management thinking in government is increasing in both developed and developing countries. National planning and policy development is forced on administrative groups in developing economies and even managers of non-government organizations are forced to work within the guidelines of carefully defined national goals. Thus, administrators adopt managerial roles and managers become administrators in seeking to achieve development objectives.

This convergence of roles occurs despite a continuing sense of administration as an ongoing subservient role and management as a shorter-term controlling role. Administration is usually thought of as accepting goals from outside the system, as depending upon resources from other systems and

Acknowledgment is made of helpful comments by M. Faltas Mikhail and others in the Development Administration Workshop at the Institute of Social Studies, The Hague. The author accepts full responsibility for views expressed.

3

being instructed in the use of means. Management, on the other hand, is usually thought of as developing goals within the system, using resources over which the system has control, and being free in the use of means. Receiving its authority from outside (or above) and referring its decisions and results elsewhere, administration involves an instrumental relationship, whereas the manager is self-contained and acts as principal rather than as agent. The validity and sharpness of these distinctions, however, can be seriously disputed in the context of national economic development.

The need for administrative improvement in the developing economy ranges from generating a suitable polity, which helps shape the value systems of the country, to the routine relationships between individual recipients of economic progress and the private and public bureaucracies. Improvement needs to encompass the conduct of agencies of government in economic management; the administration of public enterprises charged with the pursuit of stipulated economic goals; the administration of the multinational corporation which extends disproportionate influence from a remote non-nationalized source; the administration of the indigenous small business, usually based on family ownership as much concerned with entrepreneurial development as with effective business administration; and the administration of individual finances. These are not distinctive segments of the nation-building problem since strong linkages and inter-dependencies are provided through the particular ethos and environment of national development itself.

The scope of administrative issues can also be seen to embrace the absence or prevalence of techniques used to solve administrative problems. Thus, the application of computer technology to administrative concerns, the use of sophisticated decision-making aids such as operations research, systems analysis, econometric planning, cost-benefit analysis of administrative operations, as well as the basic elements of bookkeeping are as much a problem of administrative development and improvement as are the problems of organizational structures and the relationships between the bureaucracies and political development.

Most of the traditional study of these problems of administration in developed countries have usually been within the disciplinary confines of either public administration or business administration, with greatest stress on the mechanics of the public sector. Developing countries, however, cannot always afford the luxury of multidimensional overlapping approaches—the time horizon is too short, the expense is too great, and the structural breakdown is not necessarily relevant. Broader, more problem-oriented approaches are necessary. Also a new understanding needs to be generated. As Bennis notes: "The key to the problems of knowledge utilization is collaboration between the producers and users of knowledge."[2]

Close associations between academic disciplines such as public and business administration are more strongly indicated in developing economies than in advanced countries, not because individuals perform more functions normally separated in rich countries, but because the interactions normally dealt with by separate, compartmentalized disciplines are unusually strong.

In addition, the absence of knowledge of the historical context and the psychological base of societies in the developing countries prevents the unification of findings derived from individual social science disciplines of the developed countries.[3]

Moreover, there is usually an exceptional congruency between the divisions of the social sciences and the occupational role systems in the developed countries which is not necessarily transferable to the developing countries. Experts in business management and public administration derive their solutions from interrelationships among particularized structures and organizations which have largely created the precepts and the divisions of the culture-bound disciplines. Increasingly, social action in developing countries is influenced by admixtures of the social sciences, but new research of an autochthonous nature is required.

Issues Arising from Organizational Change and Development

Political Development

For any political system there is no necessarily fixed relationship between government institutions and their functions. For the most part, present day institutions in developing countries are in their political approaches an amalgam of traditional foundations and Western legal education. Much of the superstructure which has been borrowed from abroad does not work in the manner originally intended. Connections between the institutional apparatus and other elements in society are not close. The absence of interconnections between institutions, traditional and modern, make for a cumbersome administrative and managerial operation. The stress on formalism adds further rigidity to normally divergent elements. The technological skills are easily imported, but the environment for the application of the skills cannot be easily transplanted.

A developing economy, besides being characterized by increasing economic productivity and geographic and social mobility, is also characterized by an expanding political efficiency in mobilizing human and material resources of the nation for national goals. As a simplification, we can say that for political advance to be made, national unification, economic modernization and aspirations for promoting welfare are prerequisites.[4]

The concept of political development has undergone a rapid metamorphosis in recent years.[5] There has been a widespread acceptance that economic development itself has a profound political dimension. A plethora of studies have been undertaken under the heading of "political development" producing drastic changes in analytic approaches and generating considerable terminology and numerous typologies of classification. The construction of a theory of political development or political modernization has been associated with great debates over contents, criteria, and approaches.[6]

Demands to interpret the politics of newly emerging nations and traditional societies of the Third World extended the range of variables normally considered by the political scientist so that much of what is relevant in the concept of political development has operational significance for countries that are developing economically and socially as well as politically.

A very early taxonomy of usages of the term—political development—is provided by Packenham,[7] who shows it to be a function of:

1. a legal-formal constitution;
2. a level of economic development;
3. the administrative capacity to maintain law and order;
4. a social system that facilitates popular participation;
5. the political culture in which privileges and responsibilities are recognized in established processes.

Another inventory of the use of the concept is provided by Pye,[8] who lists ten different approaches to the notion. Three core elements, however, emerge from the ten notions:

1. increasing *equality* among individuals in relation to the political system;
2. increasing *capacity* of the political system in relation to its environments;
3. increasing *differentiation* of institutions and structures within the political system.

These lie at the heart of the concept. In the list of approaches, political development is defined as:

1. the political prerequisite of economic development;
2. the politics typical of industrial societies;
3. political modernization;
4. the operation of a nation state;
5. administrative and legal development;
6. mass mobilization and participation;
7. the building of democracy;
8. stability and orderly change;
9. mobilization and power;
10. one aspect of multidimensional process of social change.

Although these notions suggest that "Western" political systems represent an optimal form, political development in Western countries has lately been more suspect as to its optimal configurations. Furthermore, despite a definite geographic boundary implied in the concept, more recent analysis suggests a global context of political change rather than an isolated nation context.[9]

Five major dimensions of political development have been advanced by the Committee on Comparative Politics of the Social Science Research Council.[10] The major issues of political development are seen in crisis dimensions as:

1. a sense of common *identity* with the territorial system;

2. *legitimacy* as the social acceptance of an authoritative structure;
3. *penetration* as the process by which the political-administrative-juridical center of a new polity becomes accepted at the periphery and develops a capacity for implementing goals;
4. *participation* as the need for creating procedures for popular involvement and stimulating engagement;
5. *distribution* as the crisis which arises from competitive claims for social and economic benefits.

With political change the varying components of the political system alter their structure and function at different rates. The major problems for the administrative system, then, are accentuated through imbalances emerging among the changing components. The major components according to Huntington are:

1. *culture*—the dominant values, orientations, and myths relevant to politics;
2. *structure*—the formal organizations which make authoritative decisions;
3. *groups*—social and economic formations with demands on structures;
4. *leadership*—individuals in political institutions and groups exercising disproportionate influences on allocations of values;
5. *policies*—governmental activities designed to affect the distribution of benefits and penalties.[11]

The public and private administrative system is both a generator of change by itself as well as a dependent system of change under the aegis of political change. It is subject to the simultaneous impacts of political and social change. The dominant features of the interrelationships between the administrative system and the political system vary from case to case depending upon the interplay of the components of political change.[12]

Bureaucracy and Organizational Change

Bureaucracy provides the continuing links of organizations, and is a powerful tool of change or non-change in developing countries. As a social invention, bureaucracy has been immensely perfected in both private and governmental forms in developed countries and transposed and modified in developing countries. For many, the study of bureaucracy is synonymous with the study of administration. Administrative capability in pursuing organizational objectives, however, means more than the perfecting of the bureaucratic system.

Bureaucracy as conceptualized by Max Weber relies exclusively on the power to influence through reason and law, and in its historical development was a reaction against subjective judgment, personal subjugation, and nepotism. Crozier has identified three contemporary meanings of the term:

1. government by bureaus by which power becomes the reign of law and order "but at the same time government without participation of the governed";

2. rationalization of collective activities which is the basic Weberian sense; and
3. the derogatory sense, which points to the slow, ponderous, routine, and complex nature of organizational activity.[13]

There are both functional and structural connotations to the term bureaucracy—or "bureaucratism" as suggested by Riggs, who advocates the need for comparative studies of the role of bureaucracies in decision-formation and decision-implementation. The basic dimensions of the "Western" Weberian bureaucratic system have been outlined by Hall as:

1. a division of labor based on functional specializations;
2. a well-defined hierarchy of authority;
3. a system of rules covering the rights and duties of employees;
4. a system of procedures for dealing with work situations;
5. impersonality of interpersonal relations;
6. promotion and selection based on technical competence.[14]

The bureaucratic machinery is modified over time through a shifting of the balance between the goals of government and the goals of the governed and between the goals of management and the goals of workers. To the behaviorist, these goals and the variables which produce them and are affected by them, are not completely mechanistically rational-legal or static elements of an economic-technical system. For modernizing states where imbalances within organizations in both functional and structural terms are more likely, governmental power is frequently greater and the range of bureaucratic authority is correspondingly greater than found in developed countries.[15] With modernization and growth, assaults on bureaucracy increase because the expansion of technological change and diversification leads to:

1. an interpenetration of government and legal-economic policies in business;
2. an increase in other-directedness in which there is greater reliance on temporary social relationships with increasing industrialization; and
3. adaptive systems of diverse specialists linked by coordinators rather than executives.[16]

The bureaucracies of developing countries although manifesting structural characteristics common to all bureaucracies, show significant behavioral variations in adapting to the particular political environment in which they function. Behavioral "deviations" however are based on classical models derived from Western experience. It is clear nevertheless, that the political role of bureaucracies is usually more prominent in developing countries than in developed countries.[17] They appear to be heavily engaged in matters of political decision-making as well as in the process of executing decisions made outside of the bureaucracy.

In terms of the sociologist, bureaucratization "is the process of rationalizing social organization, so as to improve operating efficiency and more effectively attain common goals."[18] It is an ongoing social process and refers to such activities as purposeful goal-setting, information collection and its utilization, objective evaluation and decision-making as well as social and economic planning. Rationality applies only to the ordered means used by an organization to achieve goals and not to the ends. The process of bureaucratization comes mostly in formal, large associations, although informal, small organizations such as the family or a community may not be completely devoid of some aspects of the process. Bureaucratization grows with an expansion of the organization, the formalizing of social ordering, secularization of values, norms and goals, and developments in social technology.[19] Legitimization of authority and centralization of activities enhance the power of the bureaucratic process.

While the Weberian model of organization applies particularly to business and governmental bureaucracies as well as to hierarchical religious and military organizations, it does not particularly suit organizations such as cooperatives, universities and hospitals, and political parties. For some, the nature of compliance is used as a basis for comparing diverse organizational structures and their motivations. For this purpose compliance can be considered as "a relationship consisting of the power employed by superiors to control subordinates and the orientation of the subordinates to this power."[20]

Economic Planning and Administrative
Development

The capacity to plan in developing economies has been greatly expanded on the supply side because the technique of planning and its formulation depend upon a relatively small group of well-trained individuals. Nationals for this purpose can be trained abroad in a short space of time and can be effectively assisted by small numbers of foreign advisors. The capacity to implement plans, however, cannot be expanded at the same rate as the capacity to make plans. This is because implementation involves the whole administrative structure of government as well as much of the private sector. Effective implementation is not always possible because of weak administrative structures. Nevertheless, feasible implementation is one of the tests of the realism of a plan as an instrument of development. Implementation is always a presumed objective of national economic plans: it provides an assessment of the accuracy of project and program analysis and is a test of the capacity to invest and provide improved public services.

Of all developing economies, detailed planning was first accorded a central role in the national effort of India. The demand for planning grew rapidly in the 1960s. Providers of aid have demanded more systematic planning and the acceptance of the principle of planning in international agreements such as at Punta del Este in 1961 stimulated many governments to establish planning boards and commissions. In the process, many administrators became versed in the arts and techniques of plan formulation and new administrative bodies became involved in new governmental dimensions. Plans for development were advocated in developing countries no matter what the pattern of ownership of economic resources.

Early planning efforts were concerned largely with general investment budgets. They were usually without specific provisions for implementation and had little impact on policy decisions. Frictions were not uncommon between planning commissions and ministries of finance and other branches of administration. Conflicts were frequently settled by giving planning commissions a more prominent role and involving them in policy making.[21] As the whole concept of planning has shifted away from detailed quantitative production targets to indicative prescription, planners have shifted their interests away from the drafting of abstract schemes and more towards administrative coordination.

Many strategies for economic development fail to consider the political and administrative capabilities which are necessary preconditions of success. Economic development alone can never be a viable single objective of any polity since, for one thing, it means different things to the components providing the legitimacy of the polity and, for another, the capabilities of political, administrative, and social institutions in countries requiring economic development the most are not found at levels presupposed in many national economic strategies. The economic analysis used has been largely developed for an economic subsystem of a larger social system for which typical problems of political and organizational change for developing countries have been largely solved or submerged and overcome in the rapid pace of industrialization and modernization.

The role of the state in promoting economic development is limited by the special features of the public sector and by a scarcity of critical inputs. Compared with the private sector, the public sector operates with a system of incentives and disincentives, or penalties and rewards, along with the management of information which are less conducive to creative entrepreneurship, factor mobility, and economical use of resources.[22] Hierarchical structures, the methods of remuneration and compliance, and centralization of decision making and execution compound the economic defects.

Two sets of action can be identified in the process of economic development:

1. Some state direction possible:
    a. diversion of resources from current to future-oriented use;
    b. specification of output required for economic development.
2. Role of state more difficult:
    a. transformation of inputs into growth-oriented output;
    b. economical use of all of nations' resources.[23]

Bureaucratic structures of government in developing countries do not have adequate competence, sufficient information, a relevant communications system, or enough freedom of action to efficiently contribute to product transformation. The alleged deficiencies of capital, foreign exchange, and natural resources are minor relative to the deficiencies in statistical information, inventories of natural resources, and in legal, fiscal, and administrative systems.

Despite all the problems in economic management and administration which can be listed, there have been significant improvements over the recent decades in the capacity of the developing countries to manage their economies and administer their development programs. The Pearson Commission cites as evidence:

1. the development of statistical services which are essential for sound social and economic policy;
2. control over the monetary and financial system by the central banks and finance ministries, where economic managers are becoming more acquainted with the appropriate tools;
3. improvements in the capacity to plan and implement development programs although planning capability still appears to be greater than the capability to implement.[24]

Much of development planning has tended to concentrate on selecting major policies; the plan which eventuates represents a set of major decisions. However, the preparation of development plans gives no assurance of plan implementation; there is no assurance that constructive development action will take place. Development action is not realized because of the difficulties of formulating rules and principles for the right solutions and of dealing with information feedback. Because of the complex empirical realities of development, various inputs from several social science fields are required for action programs. A framework for analysis is needed to help evaluate and improve action capability for development.

The dimensions of planning includes purposive activity directed at realizing stated development ends in various areas including economics, politics, and sociology. Another dimension is action-oriented which involves the implementation of carrying out desired actions.[25] This concerns the capability for carrying out the action, and then the assigning of concern for the consequences of action.

A systems approach entails interdisciplinary frameworks for action programs. A major problem is communication between the disciplines, each of which tends to have its own language of concepts, terms, and methodology. The significant characteristics of a system are purposiveness—a patterned arrangement of components or design—and the allocation of inputs in accord with some plan. Katz has defined a development action system "as a specific matrix of interrelated activities, directed at achieving defined development targets, according to plan, that form a coherent pattern of action, and that can be distinguished from other related matrices."[26] The major inputs for an action-systems framework are:

1. the manpower system,
2. the finance system,
3. the logistics system,
4. the participation system,

5. the legitimate power system, and
6. the information system.

In development, the administrative role is more tactical than strategic. This role derives from the importance of government as an agent of change both in respect to grand strategy and administrative tactics. The grand strategy of development includes the multiplicity of national objectives, the concerns of ruling elites, ideological mythologies, consideration of political values, and technical necessities. The tactical administrative functions for development action are: decision, specification, communication, and control.

Governmental organizations are the means for integrating and conducting the development planning process. They serve to integrate the systems with each other and with the environment in which they operate.[27] An organization is permeated by the ideology, the pattern of beliefs, values, and goals that characterize the people involved. As a technical institution, the organization, created for development, is concerned with altering existing conditions over time. But in addition, an institution involves the emotion and aspirations of its members, clients, and associates, and develops in them a concern for its continuation. National planning, then, and its successful implementation requires the building of institutions which draw upon the human dimensions of the nation as well as on its economic resources.

Administration and Management in Developing Countries

The Nature of Administrative Change and Its Obstacles

Historical legacies and forces creating static economic conditions have produced in most developing countries inadequate institutions and personnel to deal with the administrative and managerial tasks in the new drives for accelerated change. Both political and administrative institutions have to be evolved which are capable of assuring and sustaining more egalitarian values and nationally accepted political norms. The functions and responsibilities entailed in these changes are of recent origin and the traditional values and institutions face irresistible pressures for modernization, which in the simplest terms implies restructuring or replacement.

The administrative organs of society reflect the political environment and derive their legitimacy, formal substance, and methods of operation from the constitutional, legal, institutional, and prevailing sources of power in society. Administrative change is hardly possible without political change of some kind although the pace of modernization may vary as between the administrative and the political.

There is no end to the weaknesses which have been attributed to economic management and public administration in developing countries. Criticisms generally related, until recently, to organizational structural aspects, to constitutional competence, to integrity and adequacy of personnel systems, and to administrative processes. More recently, however, problems of implementation and assessment of capability, of integrating planning, budgetary and operational processes, and management of public enterprises have also come to the fore.

A summary listing of administrative obstacles in developing countries is bound to include in varying proportions some of the following:

1. Organizational and structural obstacles—these range from problems in the creation of new organizations for performing emerging functions, to rationalization of existing structures for achieving better results;
2. Administrative systems suffer from confusion over functions and responsibilities of different units, duplication of work, lack of coordination, excessive centralization, and generally inadequate organizational arrangements for administration of various functions. Centralist tendencies in administrations are particularly great and hinder performance;
3. Shortcomings in personnel systems; career services based on merit have been the objective of many administrative improvement efforts;
4. Public service personnel lack knowledge and skills required for carrying out programs of economic and social development. Many continued to be governed by attitudes developed in colonial or feudal eras when development was hardly a major concern of public administration;
5. Corruption is widespread, along with favoritism, nepotism, and jobbery. Many public services are used as welfare agencies to provide employment for educated members of society, who otherwise might become a source of political trouble. These services are overstaffed with the wrong kind of functionary and hence administrative reform measures are frequently stalemated by political decisions;
6. Members of the public service suffer from lack of motivation and low morale. Administrative leadership and supervision are of poor quality, since the discipline is lacking. In many countries the concept of full-time government employment is unknown in practice. There are special problems associated with use of scientific and technical personnel in the public services;
7. Legalistic, dilatory, and complex processes and procedures are major shortcomings. Before the advent of development, the norm was a legalistic and control-minded management, whose procedures were based on limited functions of administration, and were inadequate for the new expansions. Current procedures still suffer from ambiguities, and encourage the status quo ante rather than attending to future arrangements which is the essence of management;
8. Budgetary processes and procedures such as procurement of supplies and logistics are without a sound technical foundation. As an example, the lengthy procedures involved in land acquisition for development projects can be cited as a major factor in the slow progress of such projects;
9. Interdepartmental rivalries and cumbersome committees complicate operating procedures and dilute responsibility for results.

Paramount to the administrative problem in the public sector is the realization that planning, budgeting, and operating processes must be integrated to insure the contribution of development planning to national growth. Development planning is a joint process in which every part of administration must participate effectively. There are needs for contributions from the political scientist and sociologist as well as the economist in formulating development plans. The notions that planning and implementation are separated aspects of administration and that the private sector is sharply separated from the public sector must give way to notions of participative management and administration.

Dimensions of Management in Development

The persistent gap in managerial expertise is widely claimed as a major cause for poor performance in socioeconomic development. But it must be recognized that management operates with human elements as well as with machines. Management is a significant element in business and industrial enterprise, project development, public utility concerns, and public administration of general services. Modern management techniques require special training skills, particularly under conditions of rapidly changing technology and through the reduction of isolation in administrative systems. The identification of the managerial function helps focus on the training program as well as aiding in the selection of managers and administrators for training participation.

Managerial content differs in quality and scope according to the organizational objectives. The range of its operation depends upon the framework within which the function is exercised, within which decisions are taken, and within the extent of the environmental impact. Training for management is complicated by the nature of modern organizations, especially industrial enterprises, which function in an economic, a regulatory, and a social sphere. The enterprises control workers' access to production, yet integrate the worker into a human organization upon which the productivity of the enterprise and contributions to the economy rest. The organizational and human factors in management require delicate balance; control over workers' livelihood results in a fair measure of social control so that the organization has considerable power in regulating the behavior of individuals as well as of groups.

An organization has been described as "a group of people operating in a discrete system of physical, functional, and human relationships, differentiated from the surroundings by the boundaries of explicit tasks to be performed."[28] In contrast, Selznik has described organizations as "technical instruments, designed as means to definite goals. They are judged on engineering premises; they are expendable."[29] In the long run, nevertheless, national development depends greatly on the capacity to organize human activity, the essence of organization being the coordinated efforts of many persons toward common objectives.[30] All organizations require management: government organizations aim at contributing to the management of the economy; business organizations require overall managerial guidance as well as detailed management of financial, commercial, and industrial operations.

Management is normally regarded as consisting of a hierarchy of individuals and a set of critical functions relevant to the organization. It has also been viewed from three distinctive perspectives:[31]

1. management as an economic resource;
2. management as a system of authority;
3. management as a class or an elite.

A still broader view of management has been summarized by Chandraknant to consist of six approaches not necessarily exclusive:[32]

1. Management as a method of achieving objectives by organizing human resources. The management process school sees a management element in every function embracing planning, organization, coordination, and control.
2. The behavioral science approach to management, which focuses on the interpersonal relations within organizational connections.
3. The sociological approach to management, which seeks to identify cultural relations among social groups with the aim of systematic equation.
4. Management as a study of experience, which forms the basis for generalizing on organizational activities, and constructing principles which underlie effective management.
5. The decision theory of management which focuses on rationalizing the decision-making process to embrace the selection of a particular course of action from a number of alternatives.
6. The mathematical approach to management is based on the notion of the widespread quantification of managerial factors, which can be formed into a model that can be manipulated to demonstrate optimum solutions.

Likert in dealing with styles of management in business organizations makes a simple, fourfold classification:[33]

1. Exploitative-Authoritative,
2. Benevolent-Authoritative,
3. Consultative,
4. Participative—(group management).

He considers the participative style likely to be more efficent in the long run.

A highly important management function in development is planning which aims to rationalize the management of societies. Ponsioen has suggested four basic models of management comparable to those of Likert, but of more relevance to developing economies:[34]

1. *The imposition model*: the manager formulates an order, or a guideline which his administrators have to translate into orders. The expectation is that

these orders are obeyed and carefully executed. In the course of its trans-
mission, however, the order is sometimes changed in content by reinterpreta-
tion, partly through the interests of the receivers. The function of planning
here is to advise the manager, to propose orders or guidelines for intermediate
administrators, and to collect the feedback information to reformulate the
orders.

2. *The convincing model*: the manager produces orders or guidelines accompanied with supporting arguments. The disadvantage is that arguments pro-
voke counterarguments and execution is delayed as long as the debate
continues. The function of planning then is to produce convincing arguments
for the manager and replies to the counterarguments.

A more practical way of convincing people to follow policy guidelines is
through distributing rewards (financial ones, prestige and power) to those
who follow them in an exemplary way. In this case incentives and rewards
have to be planned also.

3. *The participation model*: managers formulate proposals, rather than orders.
Public and private reactions are solicited and taken into account when the
decision is made. An advantage of this model is that future subjects of the
orders are informed in advance, their knowledge and wisdom is used, future
resistances can be identified, and, if their suggestions are accepted, they are
committed. It also provides a corrective to the value orientation of the
planners. Planning in this model becomes largely an instrument to a societal
decision-making process. The plan in the first instance is a proposal, in the
second instance a piece for negotiations, in the third instance a compromise.
The need to execute the plan becomes a major issue in formulating the plan
itself.

4. *The interaction model*: the function of management is
   a. to identify the creative individuals on all levels of the organization;
   b. to make these individuals communicate among themselves;
   c. to pour new ideas continuously into this communication process;
   d. to have decisions taken within the frame of this communication.

   Basic tacit assumptions are:
   a. that the whole organization adheres firmly to its goals,
   b. that on all levels individuals can be found, which are creative for these
   goals.

   The function of the planning unit is that of a switchboard of communication
   within the organization; it channels all information relevant to the goals,
   received from outside or from inside a system, to the appropriate levels of
   the organization and through them into the decision-making process.

The process of modernization embraces all sections of society and has
different implications and dimensions for each stratum. The introduction of
scientific principles into management operations is a significant component
of the process of change. Considerable problems are created by the introduction of new forms of managerial skills relevant to a particular developing
country where a tradition-bound environment prevails. For the development of management much depends on the building of organizations and a
body of human resources geared to dynamic modernization processes.[35]
As in the case of planning, perhaps the most significant advances in the

application of management and administration have been in India. The government has strongly recognized the importance of sound administration and management as determinants of economic performance. When India achieved independence, the problem of national economic planning and development was given such attention. Numerous organizations, some concerned with industrial promotion and training, were established; included were the National Productivity Council, the All-India Management Association, the Institutes of Management, and the National Institute for Training in Industrial Engineering. The industrial policy statement of 1948 enunciated the respective roles of the public and private sectors.

The pattern of ownership in industry affects the nature of managerial and administrative growth. Because of strong foreign competition, Indian entrepreneurs were deterred from venturing into industry at the beginning of the century. The commercial class which had developed in India in the latter part of the nineteenth century were chiefly interested in banking, and money-lending activities; it was later strengthened by the commercialization of agriculture. The ability to make wise investment decisions became more ingrained and intuitive rather than being based on general administrative talent and managerial concern with planning, coordination and control.[36] The influence of trade and business prevented a clear distinction being made between entrepreneurial functions of an enterprise and operational characteristics of management. Government intervention in industrial development was made necessary because of the absence of autonomous institutions fostering economic development. Historically, the development of education in India was geared to the supply of capable civil servants. Furthermore, Indian society is dominated by multiple loyalties, while the societal class distinctions in which the distaste for certain types of work were common in an educational system not wholly relevant to the needs of modern development, were not conducive to sound economic growth. Technological training, which systematizes and telescopes experience, is still a low priority in higher education. High prestige in the bureaucratic system acquired by long experience is frequently the basis for selection for a top managerial position in industry.

Problems of Program and Project Management

Programs and projects are increasingly used in developing countries and represent a crucial element in both the formulation and implementation of development plans. In general, the program approach in development, its scope of operation, the nature of sponsorship, and the decision-making processes involved follow the mainstream of authority and power relationships in a society. Projects are frequently designed to overcome bureaucratic compartmentalization or to replace agencies which have become dysfunctional or counterproductive. Decision-making in a new venture involves hidden risks as well as overt advantages which almost never arise from delegated authority.[37] In brief, decisions on new programs are made at the heart of the source of authority in society and are quite distinct from routine functions of the public bureaucracy and industrial institutions.

When existing administrative services cannot handle the task directly, the need for a new program may arise because:

1. the new activity will depend upon active participation of a group of existing organizations, each eager to maintain its own identity in structure. The new program, then, can combine the strength of all participants;
2. the type of work is essentially new and the existing framework cannot absorb the staff and ideas;
3. the new job is too complicated and a separate entity must be established;
4. the activity straddles administrative boundaries, either of a functional kind— such as community development—or geographical, such as a river basin program;
5. there is a need for a new specific source of income;
6. a new activity does not yet have the support of senior officials, and the benefit of the doubt is given to a group of junior activities or individuals, or to a private organization;
7. the function and purpose of the activity is clearly defined and recognized as separate from routine operations.

Programs have various origins; the sources of sponsorship include: the head of state, the cabinet, a cabinet member, a proposal through the full legislative process, a proposal and action eminating from an ad hoc body, a proposal and action by an authority or body induced by hidden pressure from other bodies, or an international program. Foreign consultants must generally be content to leave the sponsorship to the host government although in these cases the process of induction and transfer becomes complicated.

Program organization is usually quite separated from normal routine activities. In particular, more risks are allowed and more risks are imposed, which is counterbalanced by a deeper interest and a great awareness of the organizational problems to be encountered. Programs are frequently left to be carried out by dynamic young leaders; seniority counts less and the leadership role is changed. Because there is more ability to innovate, resourcefulness and resilience are required. Training of program staff is usually necessary because of the newness of the program dimensions. Priority of resources to be used must be decided upon, which generates conflicts over priorities within the program and more especially with the routine services.

When a program comes of age in, say, three to five years, hierarchical relationships inevitably develop. There are considerable differences between excellence in initiating a program and excellence in organizing later and more structured phases of development. "Hierarchy of course, is an insidious enemy of programs."[38] Support and applause are not always available and the environment for the program may be ringed with hostility.

Administrative means for protecting a program and safeguarding its continuation include:

1. interest at the top of society—the choice of a protector is extremely important, particularly in a politically tumultuous situation;
2. interest of the public—attention should not be overdone because public authorities know by intuition when there is undue pressure to convince them of the value of a program;
3. financial semi-independence—the image of a program is best served if the outside assistance is substantial, but remains a minority interest;
4. cooperation with services—requires a broad view from the leaders of the ongoing governmental services.

It is axiomatic that in public administration as well as in business administration there is an equitable relationship between authority and responsibility for all the participants in the management system. This relationship, however, is often an insufficient model for program development and management. The most appropriate chain is, STATUS—AUTHORITY—RESPONSIBILITY—REWARD. Western biases tend to make one forget the intricacies of the whole system of attributes of management.[39] The higher rewards resulting from heavy responsibility in a capitalistic, highly organized society lose meaning unless they led to status; and the establishment is often lukewarm toward the idea of sharing status with the upstart, even in a free democratic society.[40]

In many cultures authority cannot be exercised in terms of responsibility unless status is attached. When programs operate in a non-homogenous cultural environment, the ramifications of the situation become involved. Each of the terms in the chain-link can have a different interpretation for various participants in the program. In ongoing services, the relation AUTHORITY—RESPONSIBILITY—REWARD is usually very close. There are hierarchical levels, there are decentralization and delegation, and there are consultation and reporting. Salary levels are generally linked to responsibility. In a program, however, the links in the chain may be missing, or may relate to quite different groups. For example, status attached to a program may go to the honorary chairman, or the sponsoring body, or the program may derive status and influence because it has high status sponsorship and protection. The status-bearer, however, may decline to carry responsibility and to disengage from authority. The link between authority and responsibility is consciously weakened. Responsibility is usually vested in the program manager, and top staff. They are expected to take initiatives and solve problems. The confidence of board members and of the sponsor is the main authority behind the scenes which supports the executive staff in its operations.

Rewards are of the multiple nature, sometimes expressed in salaries paid to the manager and staff, but often reward is the satisfaction and learning experiences as exemplified by volunteer workers. In developing countries, civil servants are low paid, which permits many programs to enlist part-time and part-salaried staff members.

In Western society, a person is appointed to a position with specific responsibility and a commensurate reward. Authority is delegated and the individual seeks to prove his worth of that authority. Status comes afterwards, and in the form of symbols attached to it. In Western society authority, responsibility, and reward are tangible and direct rather than symbolic. In other cultures, authority may be directly linked to visible status and not to hidden responsibility.

In many transitional societies, programs may have a brittle and dangerous existence because they do not fit into earlier societal relations. Society cannot completely lift programs out of its own transitional difficulties. In an ideal situation, also in traditional and transitional society, the key personnel in management can develop a common value, a sense of achievement, and the pride attached to achievement. Achievement can be noticed by the manager and the sense of it can be transferred to the board or other staff members; it can be acknowledged by supporting and cooperating agencies as well as by the benefiting bodies. Achievement can be measured in terms of the ethos of the program, technical innovation, in spreading service, or in publicity and attendance levels, as the case may be; it does not necessarily involve financial rewards.[41]

Administrative and managerial talents required for project and program development have numerous overlaps with those talents required in private industrial enterprise and in government departments but the institutional environment demands special considerations of its own.

The Boundaries of Administrative and Managerial Studies

The study of public administration has typically been the study of public bureaucracies, while the study of business administration has been largely the study of private bureaucracies. Traditionally, both fields have concentrated on such problems as personnel administration and financial administration. In recent years, however, the orientation of these subjects has moved in other directions such as problems of organizational behavior, information systems, and problems of decision-making. These trends emphasize the considerable overlap of the separate approaches.

Take one instance of possible overlaps. In organized decision-making two aspects can be distinguished. One is the choice of the goal objective, while the other is the choice of action necessary to achieve the objective. In public administration this distinction between the choice of ends and the choice of means provides the distinction between the study of politics and study of administration. Traditionally in business administration, where there is the assumption of only one end, the study is concerned with the variations in the choice of means. The need for consideration of alternative ends in business administration as applied to developing economies is greater than for developed countries. The choice of means to maximize given objectives is a central problem to both public and private administration.[42]

As discussed earlier, any administrative system can be treated as an analytical subsystem of political systems. As subsystems of a social system the political and administrative institutions function for governmental programs, as well as non-governmental organizations. Within this arrangement, the market system becomes an important influence on political and administrative functions.

According to Holt, the role of government and the market system in the development process has been misconstrued in economic histories.[43] Holt shows that Japan and England, which are typically conceived of as polar opposites in the manner in which they achieved economic take off, really had similar bureaucratic functions in operation. England is usually regarded as the model society which moved into the early stages of industrial revolution with the minimum of government intervention in the economy. Private capital and private management were regarded as the dominant factors. By contrast, Japan is usually regarded as the model latecomer to industrialization in which government played the major leading role. Public capital and public management were prominent features in the development process.[44]

This contrasting view arises largely from economic analyses which makes certain assumptions about the nature of government and its roles. The supporting statistics deal with relative public and private capital formation, but Holt points out that these statistics are not consistent. The English economic histories by and large ignore expenditures for military durables or exclude them from the concept of capital formation. Statistics on Japanese growth, however, show public domestic capital formation as usually including expenditures on military durables. Adjustment for these differences make the public capital formation statistics for the two countries more comparable and similar. Moreover, differences in the role of government have not been treated consistently as they might be by a scholar interested in comparative politics and comparative government. The essential similarity is that in both England and Japan, government was involved in processes of resource allocation. In Japan it occurred through direct public expenditure while in England it was through restrictions placed on joint stock companies. Both were deeply involved in allocating resources for social or government overhead capital and in the management of resources. Major differences occurred in the procedures taken. In Japan the public bureaucracy was more involved in the direct management of resources, while in England the government placed important restraints on the decisions available to private investors and business management.[45]

In the beginnings of the industrialization process, both governments were prominent in the tension-management processes which involve the influencing of individuals holding positions of potential power. Both governments later became further involved in the management of tensions through passage of factory legislation and the creation of new institutions to enforce the new industrial laws. Both governments also became more involved in the socialization process, such as public education and social control processes.

Problems associated with constructing a methodological approach to administration arise largely from difficulties of excluding normative considerations in the analysis of administrative problems. Further problems stem from the fact that the approach involves the study of certain aspects of human behavior and must consider the social setting of administrative action. It is obvious that it is not always possible to derive generalizations from the administrative action found in the environment of one country and apply them to administrative problems in a different environment. Any generalizations about public or private administration must take into account varying national and social characteristics; it is not easy to determine which aspects of administration are truly independent of the national and social setting. The study of administration therefore cannot rest on a narrowly defined knowledge of techniques and processes, but must extend to historical, sociological, economic, and other conditioning ecological factors.

Much of the comparative study of administration and governmental structure has been limited in its range of interest, essentially deriving its concepts from Western systems. It was normative because of its commitment to the values of constitutionalism and Western liberal democracy, with an underlying belief that there is a natural evolution in this direction of political organization.[46] It concerned itself largely with political expressions, and far too little with political demonstrative actions. It tended to concentrate on institutions to the neglect of processes. It tended to be too descriptive and naively empirical, too little analytically and sophisticatedly theoretical. Government was studied without the proper relations to either the motivation of the administrators themselves, or to the socioeconomic context of the apparatus of government.[47]

Attempts have been made to show the conversion of political decision making into administrative action by considering input-output systems of analysis.[48] Basically the political system is fed inputs that are processed through the output functions into policy decisions. The input functions include:

1. political socialization and recruitment,
2. interest articulation,
3. interest aggregation, and
4. political communication.

The output functions include:

1. rule-making,
2. rule application, and
3. rule adjudication.

A system can be regarded as modern by considering the extent to which structural differentiation and role differentiation have taken place. Administrative outputs can be in terms of actions affecting public or private assets.

There has been a decided shift away from normative approaches which focus on the prescription of the ideal, or the suggestion of better patterns of administratively structured action using such criteria as efficiency, or public interest. One trend is towards empirical approaches which focus on the relevancy of actual phenomena and develop descriptive and analytical information for its own insights. More recent developments in the comparative study of administration seek to underline generalizations, laws, and hypotheses that assert regularities of behavior and verifiable correlations between variables. Also there has been more emphasis on the ecological approach which necessitates not recitations of facts of geography, history, or social structure, but rather analysis of the patterns of interactions between the subject of study and its environment.[49]

Unlike public administration, the study of business administration has assumed universal uniformity rather than diversity. The study of business administration has an increasing sophistication about the organizational environment, and increasing recognition of its heterogeneity and importance. There has been the assumption that the important variables lies within the organization. There has been little recognition of the role of cultural differences in the operation of business administration. The assumption of uniformity is a commitment to efficiency, lawfulness, and rationality; in Simon's terms: "maximizing these goals becomes satisficing." The comparative study of public administration being concerned with diversity in which there is a widespread value commitment, assumes that the American or Western ways of doing things are not necessarily better or the best, or even the ideal. The theory of organization in both private and public fields has been largely culture bound, and is only gradually being supplemented by further analysis of administrative actions in contemporary societies, both advanced and primitive.

Administrative Improvement and Resource Transfer

Change and Reform

There is increasing emphasis on the urgency of administrative improvement for national development. The need for increasing national administrative capabilities has been stressed internally by national authorities and externally by international organizations and aid-granting bodies. The process of administrative change has become a theme of major importance in studies in the social sciences, as well as a significant element in the overall process of modernization. In developing countries, the forces contributing toward the upsurge of interest in administrative improvement and change include not only the achievement of national independence but also the emergence of national development as a major preoccupation.

Independence coincided with an era of changing state philosophy, in which the positive role of the state is nation building using all the national and international resources which the wielders of new power can command. Planned development imposed new demands on public administration; it increased the need for a capability to undertake multi-various tasks involved in formulating and executing national plans, programs, and projects.[50] The administrator must now act as an entrepreneur, an innovator, regulator, promoter, manager, and catalyst. These roles are in addition to traditional responsibilities of maintaining law and order, collecting revenues, and providing a system of justice. Administrative capabilities for these new tasks is obviously a scarce resource in countries devoid of a burgeoning supply of managers and administrators trained in modern techniques.

Despite these needs for change, most developing countries show a remarkably high degree of historical continuity in administrative patterns, practices, and behavior. Occasionally new dimensions and aspects were added to prevailing systems. But basically, civil service practices, patterns of field administration, and general administrative behavior continue to be influenced by ideas and practices introduced many decades ago. Historical experience suggests that administrative systems are composites of different layers rather than strictly organic growths.[51] Administrative institutions and practices were often created in response to emergency needs in the public domain, usually under pressure from the foreign or domestic private sector. These structures showed strong tendencies toward self-perpetuation, a major thrust being toward substituting personal administration of individuals by legal norms, formulated and enforced by specialized organizations and functionaries. Administrative doctrine that developed as a result of the transition emphasized stability and security, methods and procedures, routine and anticipated responses, along with conformity and caution.

Independence meant that new organizations such as foreign affairs departments, diplomatic connections, central banking systems, and defense establishments had to be immediately established. Prevailing patterns of administration were usually allowed to continue with independence. In general, a proliferation of organizations and processes, frequently uncontrolled became symptomatic of the next stage of underdevelopment. Today in every country the public administrative sector is larger than ever before. It directly consumes, or controls an enlarged share of national income and impinges more directly than ever before on the welfare and prosperity of individual citizens.

In spite of administrative expansion, there is a lag between the quality of public administration and public policy needs, and between the quality of administration in the private sector and social expectations. Most nations have appointed committees and commissions to study administrative problems and suggest solutions.

The first step of new states was toward nationalization of the public services. The emphasis here was on the transfer of power rather than the job of retooling for development. Subsequently, administrative reforms have been more concerned with the reorganizations of ministries and departments than with fundamental changes in operation. Even when genuine reorganization was undertaken, the outcome was limited because of the absence of simultaneous changes in personnel systems and other aspects of administration.

Reform efforts have aimed at the creation and strengthening of career services, based on merit, reorganization of public services to facilitate better use of scientific and technical personnel, to popularize modern management techniques, and generally to change the attitudes of the public services in terms of inventiveness and capacity to adapt. Nevertheless, constitutional and political reasons frequently make personnel changes difficult. Budgetary reforms, on the other hand, were easier to introduce and have aimed at simplifying procedures, reassigning financial powers to central and operating agencies, and adopting better accounting systems.

Reform itself has sometimes been institutionalized in the form of special agencies charged with continual appraisal of the administrative system for purposes of reform. The major preoccupation has been with internal structures and relationships of administrative functions. Significant administrative changes, particularly those involving the environment, have come through reforms basically conceived in political terms, as for example community development programs. The creation of public corporations has often been recommended as another solution in dealing with existing structures. They have been formed not only for administering public enterprises but for such traditional functions as education, health, and agriculture. This route of administrative expediency is frequently an acknowledgment of political failure in dealing with traditional agencies.

While the values sought through administrative reform are efficiency and economy, political responsibility and responsiveness provide the context for many reform measures. The system of administration reflects the balance between contending groups and values, which may not enhance prospects for reform implementation. Because of conflicts in value systems, administrative reform which also brings economy and efficiency has had limited success.

With no consensus on underlying causes or on paradigms of administrative weaknesses and with a plethora of suggestions for improvement, the basic problem is to maneuver the advice into politically feasible operations. Experimental strategies are suspect, the usual preference in administrative change being along classical structural lines with stress on order and control of organization which can be depicted in organizational charts and on principles of management which rely on written orders. Although less clearly defined conceptually, administrative improvement programs which emphasize the human element in administration and are concerned with an environment conducive to individual initiative and creativity are nevertheless becoming more significant in educational and training programs for administrators. The products of such programs are more likely to provide catalytic action for administrative improvement. A more predominant role can be played by the administrative generalist and through interdisciplinary approaches or teams comprising administrative and technical expertise.[52] A vast body of knowledge on management techniques has come into existence and awaits to be reflected in administrative rationalization and development. It seems that a major objective of central administrative reform should be to identify appropriate management techniques and to promote their adaptation.

The Transfer of Managerial and
Administrative Skills

In a world which places high esteem on technological modernization, there is a natural flow of modern management administrative techniques from advanced, high-stocked countries to developing, low-stocked countries. The flow, initiated because of basic differences in stocks, also generate effects which are not necessarily similar in the two sets of countries. There are lags in the flow and appreciation of techniques, so that the most recent techniques are not necessarily those being currently applied in the recipient country. Furthermore, there are resistances of different economic classes in different regions affecting the flows and the adaptability of the flows. The absorptive capacity for foreign skills varies among regions and regimes. It is not to be expected that the flow of techniques will make the recipient identical to the supplying country either in structure or administrative effectiveness. Techniques are influenced by the environment in which they are applied; even if the concept remains unchanged, the technique in application will bear the imprint of the environment.

In advanced countries, administrative techniques are designed to meet conditions of high labor costs and a relative abundance of capital. The impetus is to bring about economies of labor which force development through labor-saving techniques, the most significant being those concentrating on mechanization and automation. In contrast, developing economies usually face widespread unemployment of labor and a relative shortage of capital. Demands for new industries and infrastructure will frequently have greater priority on scarce capital resources over labor-saving techniques than do routine demands for traditional services. Mechanization cannot be justified simply by reference to unit-level productivity because social costs and social tensions are more significant to the decision makers than simple profitability. The focus in a developing country most usually is on an increased utilization of available physical resources, rather than effecting economies in the use of labor.

Because of the vast difference in approach, and the absence of a middle ground of administration, the importation of management technique from advanced countries frequently adds more problems than it solves. There is a need in most developing countries to nationalize or institutionalize the new supplies of management technique for the most suitable domestic application. The great differences in the sociocultural environment between advanced and developing countries makes the transfer of management and administrative techniques difficult. For example, the absence of a feudalistic system in the United States permitted the development of techniques free from feudalistic influences. In a country like India, however, these influences must be faced every day in its modernization applications. Social and cultural factors, bureaucratic systems, recent diversities, attitudes of top management, and entrepreneurial elites inhibit the rate at which management techniques can be introduced and absorbed. The attitudes of top management and the ethos of the organization can undermine knowledge already acquired in management and administrative sciences. The delay in reducing these barriers, therefore, must be counted as an extra cost in acquiring administrative and management knowledge.

Techniques for institutional change become an important aspect of management and administrative training imported into developing countries. One approach that has been used is to emphasize behavioral aspects of management and organizations, so that effective implementation is enhanced. Subjects such as human relations, organizational theory, conflict resolution, and communications become significant in training programs of this kind.

In developing countries, management operates under a wide range of controls and constraints necessitated by scarcities of raw materials, foreign exchange, and governmental management of the economy. In addition, inadequate information and poor communications skills decrease the immediate effectiveness of management techniques. Sophisticated techniques which depend upon a whole substratum of institutions cannot be applied if this substratum is deficient in one way or another.

Management and administration operations under free market conditions differ from those in economies subject to planning. Sectoral and regional differences in social cost-benefits are more likely to find correctives in the planning state than in the market economy. Management and administrative training frequently made available from advanced countries does not always take these dimensions into account. The training of economic planners, which entails exposure to the nature of market and planned economies, does not always include subjects in management and administrative techniques. There is a surprising lack of rapport and interaction between economists and administrators. This is partly attributed to the compartmentalized educational system, derived from the advanced countries whose market-oriented culture does not make interaction of this kind as feasible or as necessary.

In many developing countries there are, of course, many segments which are completely untouched by modern management and administrative techniques. In numerous developing countries, most attention is given to the improvement and application of management in the industrial enterprises. Little attention is given to the agricultural sector where the major bulk of the economic operations may be located. Furthermore, the central government, which might strongly support the adoption of management techniques for the country, frequently avoids application of modern management and administrative techniques for its own operations. Although sporadic and ritualistic efforts have been made through Organization and Methods units, strongly supported by the Public Administration Division of the United Nations, the results on management and administrative improvement have been meager compared to the growing needs. Changes in approach to the problem, nevertheless, are producing new inputs and concepts useful for guiding new development efforts.

In the developing countries, the technological gap cannot be overcome through resource transfers alone. Feeding in new technology is a slow process. Part of the technological transfer problem is the difficulty of subordinating technology to ancillary factors.[53] The mechanism of technology transfer and adjustment, however, is essential for any substantial improvement of the system. In the absence of adequate transfers, indigenous peoples must undertake the changes themselves.

More effective delivery systems are needed to enhance administrative capability in public services, agriculture, family planning, and urban affairs. The building of local private and public institutions utilizing strong management and action programs are greatly fostered by attitudinal, behavioral, and social changes which can accommodate modern technologies. The organizing and activating of constituents to interact with administrative structures will add greatly to the development effort. This involves the integration of specialized public and private agencies in rural and urban areas and their articulation with the local political process. Trade unions, business groups, and cooperatives could be encouraged through some transfer of management and administrative skills to improve government performance and the private and public bureaucracies. Transfer mechanisms that are extra-governmental in design are needed for this purpose.

Management and Administration Education

Given the serious shortages of managers and administrators as a critical bottleneck in many developing economies, efforts to supply management and administrative education are likely to produce some beneficial results, although the nature of the most appropriate curriculum is the subject of much controversy.[54] Such education, nevertheless, must be adaptive, multidisciplinary, related to changing environmental conditions and attuned to possible impacts of cultural interchange. Several basic organizational problems have to be recognized. Some overseas educational institutions in new fields of education have already been established and some are host country establishments with nationals of the host country in charge. The mission of these institutions, in line with social and economic development plans, is to provide efficient coordination of developmental efforts, to understand the variables of change in broad terms, and to provide the leadership to produce organized creative change. Broadly, the role of the administration and management school is to produce, at the university or within public or private institutions, managers capable of researching local problem areas and operating creative change in society's institutions.

Many developing countries find that the scarcest resources are entrepreneurial ability and creative talent which is mobile enough to grapple with diverse elements of change. Training for entrepreneurial development is still subject to much experimentation. Trained managers for industry, commerce, and government are few and are generally overworked and inflexible within existing bureaucracies.[55] Independent institutes of education and research provide possible conduits for forces and influences promoting economic and political change. Such developing institutions, however, need stronger ties with their clienteles in industry and government and need to expand their facilities.[56] Managers of overseas assistance programs for these purposes encounter the problem of selecting the most appropriate local institutions with which to work when the output might be critical of governmental performance.

It is generally acknowledged that management education and training in India over the past few decades has been phenomenal; and for some it might serve as a guide to development potentials. Every kind of organization, university, technical college, staff college, management association, productivity council, management consultancy, private training organization, and school of administration has shown significant expansion over the recent decade. There is still need, nevertheless, for coordination in this outburst of activity and careful direction into coherent schemes designed for meeting future requirements. The acceptance of the notion that formal managerial instruction can be part of administrative development is of recent vintage. Steps beyond the tentative and experimental approach adopted by many institutions and businesses are needed in many developing countries.[57] In India, the shortened time gap for the effective application of this training and education means that a good basis for future development has already been devised.

Increased investment in physical plant and infrastructure has not always yielded expected results because of constraints placed on the system by poor management. For a few developing economies technical skills and educated manpower are relatively adequate for the industrial sector, but competent managers continue to be scarce and impose limitations on economic progress. The major problem here is the inappropriate mix of investment in human capital rather than in a serious deficiency of overall investment. Management education has been one area where higher priority could be assigned to the allocation of investment for human capital expansion.

The benefits of management and administrative education are numerous. Its primary objective is to augment and upgrade the supply of managerial input required for the efficient production and distribution of commodities and public services to serve social goals. The benefits of a particular educational project, then, must be measured in the light of this primary objective. The quality of managerial skills may be improved by recruiting fresh graduates and developing managerial skills through on-the-job training and the accumulation of experience. Training programs for short periods can be supplied for managers with proven ability or growth potential. Additional social and cultural benefits achieved from management education lie beyond the primary objective of improving production and distribution and can be discerned in a full cost-benefit analysis. To the extent that management education generates benefits or services that cannot be valued in monetary terms, the true benefits are obviously understated. The creation of managerial inputs is accomplished by imparting education to students who are eventually remunerated on the basis of their services. The products turned out by the educational investment receive benefits or private returns. Apart from the returns measurable in money, other returns such as greater job satisfaction, a sense of prestige or well-being are part of the overall benefits attributable to the education. Far beyond these returns are the social improvements arising from the promotion of ideas of managerial efficiency and a broadening of administrative change into the subsystems of the institutional structure.

As already pointed out, many sectors of developing economies are unaffected by modern systems of management and administration. Many segments of the infrastructure are devoid of modern techniques of management.[58] If these techniques were applied, there would be significant multiplier effects on the rest of the economy. In India it is estimated that 95 percent of the training effort has been confined in its application to a very small segment of the economy. This lopsided development is sometimes caused by a lack of appreciation of management techniques in sectors which produce most.

It is increasingly stressed that techniques of advanced countries need considerable adaptation for the developing economy. In effect, the techniques have to be reprocessed for considerable parts of the educational adaptation. In the reprocessing, local environment factors, specialized government controls, labor surplus situations, and features of the planned state of the economy must be introduced.

In order to make management and administrative techniques more widely available, strong efforts have to be made by the government through educational programs to stress the awareness of the availability, relevance, and significance of these techniques. Industry-based local programs of research and application must be developed. Attention has to be given to the interaction between the environment and the process of modernization, of which modern management techniques is a significant element. The links between government, industry, and universities must become more pragmatic, with strong liaison facilities.

Examinations of management operations applied in the United States, United Kingdom, and the European countries reveal considerable differences. In the United Kingdom, for example, one study showed major weakness in British management to be the *indifference* to modern practices for improving productivity.[59] The progress of management education clearly requires a mental revolution in private and public sector enterprises. There is need for a wider appreciation of the advantages (and disadvantages) of modernized management and its attendant economic social, and technological implications. Training within industry and government has been a widely used technique for disseminating appreciation of management techniques; but to support and speed their growth they need to be supplemented by executive and senior administrator development programs, preferably in regional centers.

There is obviously a strong distinction between training and education and their respective curricula. This frequently makes for considerable separation between the types of institution. Such strong distinctions although perhaps viable for a long-run leisurely approach to development are not necessarily relevant for the immediate situation in most countries. Additionally, programs which provide a body of up-to-date practical knowledge for developing managerial and administrative competence at a faster pace must be introduced. The acquisition of tools and skills for the mastery of everyday practical situations should be developed in conjunction with learning capable of enriching the mind for dealing with new situations and examining basic human values.

Many forces operate today which alter the approach to management education.[60] Typically, one general methodology for achieving these management and administration education objectives consists of the following aims:

1. to impart a theoretical background of those academic disciplines related to management and administration;
2. to enhance the analytical ability of the participants and to acquaint them with the tools and techniques for better decision-making in diverse systems;
3. to develop a frame of reference which enables participants to perceive the complex elements and forces affecting the situations in systems of business, industry, government, and service institutions, and to handle them realistically by relating knowledge to practical situations;
4. to develop an understanding of specific functional areas of management and administration science in various levels, with particular emphasis on the interrelationships;
5. to help participants develop an understanding of organizational behavior, and to provide opportunities for increasing interpersonal skills with the aim of becoming effective executives;
6. to foster a sense of professional ethics in disciplinary approaches which are helpful for achieving these objectives.

At another level there is a need for research and training in policy-making. The importance of effective policy-making in the developing countries is emphasized by the critical range of decisions needed for accelerated and directed social change.[61] A constant improvement of the policy-making process is needed at many administrative levels. The study of policy analysis and decision-making by knowledge of operations research, simulation models, behavioral science, paradigms of the physical sciences, and insights into policy procedures in developing economies suggest only a few of the topics for education in this relatively new field of study.

Personnel needed for the management and administration of development consist of a wide range of trained individuals. Training and education can take many forms to meet national, regional, functional, and emergency needs in a great diversity of organizations and institutions. Private and public institutions need to be served by a growing output of capable administrators and managers linked to the development objectives and modifying and improving the development process as an essential part of their participation. Existing personnel in administrative operations require a continuing education, constant up-grading, and a multiplying motivation for self-development in the achievement of organization objectives.

Summary

Administrative change is inherently involved in system building for national modernization. As one of the key elements in the management of change, administrative development requires much attention, especially from an educational planning viewpoint. Fostered through the international transfer of resources and vast injections of educational development, it is still mainly dependent upon a national acceptance of political and bureaucratic modernization designed to seek the achievement of new social objectives. Available for this administrative development is a great range of recently forged management tools and methods, whose selection and rejection will be critical for the success of the modernization program.

In the main, the study of administrative and management problems has been fashioned too closely on the industrialization model of Western countries in which academic disciplines and procedures have been structured for a process of industrialization not now relevant to modern developing countries, either Western or otherwise. The occupational role systems of the developed countries which have structured the separate academic systems are not necessarily transferable to the developing countries. Similarly, the political systems developing in the new nations is to a large degree an amalgam of traditional systems and Western legal education; and Western models are not necessarily relevant. The administrative structures and institutions are not completely suited for the full range of development tasks, largely because of unfavorable ecological foundations. Institution building in both the private and public sectors is needed to meet the emerging changes in social, economic, and political goals.

New understandings of relevant political development are emerging through comparative analysis and a new orientation of social scientists to the political realities and needs of developing economies. The components of culture, structure, groups, leaders, and policy design must be incorporated in the analysis of the relationships between public and private management and the changing political system. An understanding of the private and public bureaucratic system of developing economies includes an appreciation of behavioral variations without the imposition of an ideal behavioral model.

National planning to achieve economic and social goals is a major factor challenging existing administrative systems. Since the capacity to implement plans involves the administrative structure of the public and private sector and is also a test of the realism of national objectives, suitable administrative change and the means to achieve it must be incorporated as critical elements of national planning. Economic planning without administrative planning can be a futile exercise. The capabilities of political, administrative, and social institutions in countries requiring economic development the most are not found at levels frequently presupposed in many national economic strategies. Differences in the reward and incentive systems between the public and private sectors require flexible planning and management. A concentration on the macro-economic framework, which cannot be translated into sectoral, regional, or industrial projects, conceals much of the administrative problem in national planning. The systems approach to planning, although calling for more information than is usually available, incorporates the administrative systems as a major input.

A long list of administrative obstacles to development can be constructed, but no general system is available to point out the most critical of the obstacles or which should be dealt with first with the limited resources available. Administrative change and growth also bring new problems requiring solution. There is continuous interaction between social change and administrative change. Traditional models of administrative relationships are not necessarily appropriate and each country has its particular pattern of administrative difficulty. It is obvious, nevertheless, that obstacles should be exposed and dealt with by whatever social forces that can be mustered and spared for that purpose.

Conceptually, administration and management are closely related and there is a growing tendency to use the terms interchangeably in development. The science of management which has grown chiefly around the large private business corporation has increasing potential application to problems of national management. Management tools are of increasing relevance to the understanding of public policy problems and so far have only been assimilated in minor degrees by public administration systems. The lack of adequate data systems, competent personnel, and the necessary financial resources make elaborate management systems beyond the reach of most developing countries. Moreover, the fact that many of the new management techniques are geared to tactics rather than to strategy, affect decision-making at the margin rather than bringing about structural adjustment, and bear on problems on the highly organized rather than the loosely organized institution make their full adoption less meaningful for many developing economies.

With national change, the administrator faces new roles as entrepreneur, innovator, regulator, promoter, manager, and catalyst. In addition, he operates in a context of political and institution change and reform, although rarely to the complete exclusion of traditional responsibilities and practices. This task can only be met through a constant process of education and re-education.

While the transfer from abroad of managerial and administrative experts can alleviate some of the immediate burdens and the administrator can learn about the techniques devised in advanced countries, knowledge about the particular requirements and programs for meeting the needs have to be provided by adequate research of local conditions. In some cases the importation of management techniques from abroad can add more problems than it solves. More of the technical assistance which comes from abroad might better be employed by having nationals research national problems and examine possible solutions. Moreover, the overconcentration of administrative improvement in a few centers and industries could be better enhanced through a greater dispersion of administrative knowledge. This administrative knowledge must be built on the contributions of many academic disciplines, be essentially multidisciplinary in character, be geared to dynamic processes of institution building, and be capable of testing potential contributions of the new administrative and management sciences.

Notes

1. "The entire modern world suffers from an imbalance between technological advance, on the one hand, and institutional and social change, on the other hand." United Nations *Economic Bulletin for Asia and the Far East* 17, 3 (December 1969): 19. The special conditions of the problem are suggested by the term "Soft States" as defined in Gunnar Myrdal, *Asian Drama* (New York: Pantheon Books Inc., 1968), p. 66.

2. Warren G. Bennis, *Changing Organizations* (New York: McGraw-Hill, 1966), p. 208.

3. Cf. Michael Lipton, "Interdisciplinary Studies in Less Developed Countries," *The Journal of Development Studies* 7, 1 (October 1970): 5.

4. Cf. A. F. K. Organski, *The Stages of Political Development* (New York: Alfred A. Knopf, 1965), p. 7.

5. See Samuel P. Huntington, "The Change to Change—Modernization, Development and Politics," *Comparative Politics* 3, 3 (April 1971): 283–322.

6. See in particular Martin R. Doornbos, "Political Development and Search for Criteria," *Development and Change* 1, 1 (1969): 93–115.

7. Robert A. Packenham, "Approaches to the Study of Political Development," *World Politics* 17 (1964): 108–20.

8. Lucian W. Pye, "The Concept of Political Development," *The Annuals* No. 358 (March 1965): 1–13; cf. Huntington, op. cit., p. 301.

9. Doornbos, op. cit., p. 101; cf. Huntington, op. cit., pp. 303–304.

10. Gabriel Almond and James S. Coleman, *The Politics of the Developing Areas* (Princeton: Princeton University Press, 1960), pp. 23–24. Originally, *integration* was included as a sixth crisis dimension. Its concern with the "problems of relating popular politics to governmental performance" later proved to be too nebulous a notion to handle within the scheme. See Huntington, op. cit., p. 313.

11. Huntington, op. cit., p. 316.

12. The politics of industrialization and impacts on administrative structure and function are obviously immensely different for bourgeois, Stalinist, or fascist political development. See Organski, op. cit.

13. Michel Crozier, *The Bureaucratic Phenomenon* (Chicago, University of Chicago Press, 1964), p. 3; see also Fred W. Riggs, "Bureaucratic Politics in Comparative Perspective," in Fred W. Riggs, ed., *Frontiers of Development Administration* (Durham: Duke University Press, 1970).

14. R. H. Hall, "The Concept of Bureaucracy: an Empirical Assess-

ment," *The American Journal of Sociology* 69 (1963): 33; see also Bennis, op. cit., p. 5.

15. Cf. Riggs, op. cit., p. 406.

16. See Bennis, op. cit., pp. 10–14.

17. Ferrel Heady, "Bureaucracies in Developing Countries," in Fred W. Riggs, op. cit., p. 461.

18. Marvin E. Olsen, *The Process of Social Organization* (London: Holt, Rinehart and Winston, 1968), p. 297.

19. Peter M. Blau, *Bureaucracy in Modern Society* (New York: Random House Inc., 1956).

20. Amitzi Etzioni, *Complex Organizations* (New York: The Free Press, 1966, pp. xv, and 3 ff.

21. Lester B. Pearson, *Partners in Development: Report of the Commission on International Development* (London: Pall Mall Press, 1969), p. 44.

22. Joseph J. Spengler, "Allocation and Development, Economic and Political," in Ralph Braibanti, ed., *Political and Administrative Development* (Durham: Duke University Press, 1969), p. 628.

23. Ibid., p. 629.

24. See Pearson, op. cit., pp. 43–44.

25. Saul M. Katz, *A Systems Approach to Development Administration,* Papers in Comparative Public Administration, No. 6 (Washington, D.C.: American Society for Public Administration, 1965).

26. Ibid.

27. Organizations have been conceived as having technical and environmental dimensions, see Phillip Selznik, *Leadership in Administration: A Sociological Interpretation* (Evanston, Ill.: Row Peterson, 1957).

28. See L. S. Chandraknant, *Management Education and Training in India* (Bombay: National Institute for Training in Industrial Engineering, 1969).

29. Selznik, op. cit., pp. 21, 22.

30. Herbert A. Simon, *Administrative Behavior* (New York: The Macmillan Co., 1945), p. 17.

31. Frederick Harbison and Charles A. Myers, *Management in the Industrial World* (New York: McGraw-Hill Book Co., 1959).

32. Chandraknant, op. cit.

33. R. Likert, *The Human Organization* (New York: McGraw-Hill Book Co., 1967. Cf. W. J. Reddin, *Managerial Effectiveness* (New York: McGraw-Hill Book Co., 1970).

34. Jan A. Ponsioen, *National Development: A Sociological Contribution* (The Hague: Mouton & Co., 1968), pp. 163–79.

35. Included under human resources are organization builders, top administrators, middle and supervising management and trained technical and professional personnel. Harbison and Myers, op. cit., p. 117.

36. See P. Chattopadhyay, "Managerial Revolution in India," *India Management,* March, April, July 1969; and D. L. Mazumdar, *Towards a Philosophy of the Modern Corporation* (Asia Publishing Co., 1967).

37. United Nations, *Administration of Development Programs and Projects: Some Major Issues,* New York, 1971 (E 71. UU. H4).

38. Ibid., p. 28.

39. Ibid., p. 47.

40. See Vance Packard, *The Status Seekers* (New York: David McKay Co., 1959).

41. United Nations, *Administration of Development Programs,* p. 49.

42. See Vincent Ostrom and Elinor Ostrom, "Public Choice: A Different Approach to the Study of Public Administration," *Public Administration Review*, March/April 1971, pp. 203–216.

43. See Robert E. Holt, "Comparative Politics, Comparative Administration," in Fred W. Riggs, ed., *Frontiers of Development Administration,* pp. 305–325.

44. See Robert E. Holt and John E. Turner, *The Political Basis of Analysis* (Princeton: New Jersey, 1966), Chapter 6.

45. See Holt, op. cit., p. 324.

46. Dwight Waldo, "Comparative Public Administration, Prologue, Problems and Promise," Comparative Administration Group, Papers in Comparative Public Administration, 1964.

47. See David Apter, "A Comparative Method for the Study of Politics," *American Journal of Sociology,* November 1958, pp. 221–37.

48. See David Easton, *The Political System: An Enquiry into the State of Political Science* (New York: Alfred A. Knopf, 1953), and Gabriel Almond, and James S. Coleman, eds., *The Politics of the Developing Areas* (Princeton University Press, 1960).

49. See John M. Culbertson, *Economic Development: An Ecological Approach* (New York: Alfred A. Knopf, 1971).

50. United Nations, *International Social Development Review No. 2* (E.70.IV.10), pp. 34–43.

51. Ibid.

52. Ibid., p. 41.

53. D. L. Spencer, *Technology Gap in Perspective* (London: Spartan Books, 1970).

54. Faqir Muhammad, "Use of Modern Management Approaches and Techniques in Public Administration," *International Review of Administrative Sciences* 37, 3 (1971): 187–200.

55. For an example of some of the problems see Joseph M. Waldman, "Management Practices in Pakistan," M.S.U. *Business Topics,* Summer 1971.

56. William D. Carmichael, "Challenges in Assisting in the Development

of Management Education Abroad," in Stephen A. Zeff, ed., *Business Schools and the Challenge of International Business* (New Orleans: Tulane University, 1971).

57. See David Easton, *A Framework for Political Analysis* (Englewood Cliffs, New Jersey: Prentice-Hall, 1965), p. 15.

58. The rapidly-changing range of modern managerial methods is largely academic in nature and even in the most advanced countries their value has not been tested. Note Faqir Muhammad, op. cit.

59. See VEP Report, *Attitudes and British Management* (London Penguin Books, 1965).

60. Cf. Faqir Muhammad, op. cit.; and Robert F. Miller, "The New Science of Administration in the U.S.S.R.," *Administrative Science Quarterly* 16, 3 (1971): 247–57.

61. See Yehëzkel Dror, *Public Policy Making Re-examined* (San Francisco: Chandler Publishing Company, 1968).

2 Bridging the Public and Private Sectors of Development

Walter G. O'Donnell

The main responsibility for development lies with the managers of formal organizations in both the public and private sectors. Development depends basically upon the development of the individuals who comprise the system, and particularly upon its managerial resources. These, in turn, depend largely upon education. Within the foregoing conceptual framework, the specific problem to be investigated is one of seeking bases for bridging more effectively the gap between the public and private sectors of development, with an eye to further research and management education. The accent will be on economic development, but some consideration of non-economic factors operative in the process will be included.

This bridge-building survey is not to be confused with devious linkages of the public and private sectors through graft, corruption, payoffs, unwarranted subsidies, and other forms of parasitic symbiosis. Such forms of linkage and collusion are a major source of socioeconomic waste, whether legalized, illicit, or tolerated by custom and tradition. These practices, present in all mixed economies, are inimical to a sound and extended bridging of the public and private sectors.

The Interdependence of Two Sectors

With the variety of elements in our mixed economies, the degree of dependence of one sector upon another will vary over a wide spectrum. It ranges from the extreme of a monolithic political economy with its overwhelmingly dominant public sector to the extreme of an existential philosophical anarchy of rugged individualism dominated by private emotions and impulses. Most of our mixed economies appear to manifest a central tendency toward the middle of the spectrum, with the socialized public sector tending to become more privatized or "capitalistic" and the private sector tending to become more socialized and concerned with social responsibilities. This tendency, even though it might be shown to be a trend, does not appear to warrant a prediction of complete convergence, but it does indicate a basis for more systematic interrelations between the two sectors in economic development. Moreover, the fact that in some countries, including Mexico, the public and private sectors have grown in productivity and extent side by side in an interdependent relationship supports the contention that the two sectors are not mutually exclusive with reference to development. The hypothesis is suggested that this interdependent relationship is more conducive to general economic development, especially in nations at a similar stage of economic development.

Beside this convergent tendency, and other instances of mutually supportive developmental activities in the public and private sectors, the differences between the two sectors are becoming less severe. In many advanced industrialized nations, particularly in Europe, ownership is changing in character, and private and public ownership and administration are taking newer forms of combination. Private shares eventually may be owned in public enterprises, and some publicly owned enterprises are leased to private interests for operation and administration.

The pattern of interdependence, of course, will vary with the different mixtures of the public and private sectors, but around the center of the spectrum where their relative independence-dependence approximates equipoise, some generalities of interdependence may be ventured.

The private sector depends heavily upon the public sector for the preservation of order, the administration of justice, and the enforcement of laws of property, contracts, negotiable instruments, and so on, which provide the necessary environment for private business activity. Ordinarily, much of the economic infrastructure and facilities for public use are regarded as belonging in the public sector. The control of business cycles and measures for the protection of legitimate business enterprise against adverse conditions that threaten the whole economy are generally the responsibilities of the public sector. To these could be added public education, research support, and numerous social services in the public interest. This abbreviated list of public sector functions upon which the private sector depends is sufficient to recall the dependence of the private sector on the public sector.

The public sector, in turn, depends heavily upon the private sector for productivity, generation of capital, savings, and tax revenue. The administration of the public sector, largely free from competitive pressures, usually monopolistic, with considerable assurance of tax-supported public financing, has not been generally noted for efficiency and productivity, nor generation of capital from within its operations. As a result, the public sector depends heavily upon the private sector for its financial resources, for organizations in the private sector must produce a net return on investment for growth, survival, and the payment of taxes. New ideas for products and services, along with innovations in management thought and practice, arise more frequently in the private sector, providing the inventive basis for a dynamic economic system. In this sense, the public sector depends upon the private sector for incentives, innovations, flexibility, achievement, drive, and significant dynamic elements of economic growth.

Additional interdependencies between the public and private sectors of economic development are operative, in various patterns, and economic development could be furthered more systematically if these relationships were to be analyzed, mapped out, and rendered more effective.

Impediments and Obstacles to
Administrative Bridge-Building

Standing in the way of bridging the public and private sectors of development are many impediments, obstacles, and declivities in a wide array of conceptual, environmental, managerial, and operational aberrations, shortcomings, and divisive forces. Among these is the neglect of actual or potential interdependent relations sketched in the preceding section. By overlooking or minimizing their dependencies and magnifying their assumed independence of each other, the managers in both sectors tend to engage in a tug-of-war playing zero-sum games in which both are hindered and development retarded. Of course, some sort and degree of competitiveness between the public and private sectors of development is understandable and, within limits, a mutually stimulating source of improved administration and responsiveness to public needs; but more important is their cooperation in the common interest of the development of the whole system of which they are related parts. A strategy of sub-optimization in either sector can result in a displacement of sociocultural and national economic goals of development, with resulting distortion and retardation of development.

The pseudo-independent stance and excessive pulling-and-tugging between the managers of the organized public and private sectors of mixed economies can be seen as a result of antagonistic social, political, and economic philosophies, involving a wide variety of ideologies of "capitalism" and "socialism" and various theories of social action, freedoms, and organizational and administrative behavior. Ideological and power struggles, often based on conflicts of special economic interests, are also among the obstacles to the bridging of the public and private sectors when one sector endeavors to impose its doctrine or value system upon the other instead of resorting to compromise or the creative process of integration.

There are numerous and continuing instances of one sector striving to *use* the other as an instrument for extending its power or forcing conformity to particular doctrines and interests. This is a source of chronic distrust, unrest, uncertainty, and frequent revolutionary upsets that often set back or retard development and demolish much of the bridgework between the public and private sectors. Conflicts among classes, mutual distrust between managerial and operative workers, stemming from divisive concepts, theories, and attitudes, often retard integrative development and periodically upset the cooperation of various groups in the public and private sectors of developmental collaboration.

From the experience with the upsetting effects of ideological conflicts, some have contended cogently that ideologies should be discarded. Still others strive persistently to convert or coerce the universe to accept one totalitarian ideology. None of these alternatives to ideological ferment are workable in view of the nature of man, human groups, and evolutionary society. Teleology *functions* in human and social behavior, and rational decisions without purpose are inconceivable.

Normative Foundations for Bridging the Sectors

Scientific findings substantiate the fact that persons who share goals work together at high levels of voluntary exertion. The same might apply to related sub-groups committed jointly to the more inclusive objectives of a larger group of which they are related parts. On this basis the public and private sectors can be further bridged in cooperative developmental plans, projects, and activities. International goals of world peace, support of the United Nations, armament limitations, extension of freedoms, economic welfare among nations, and human rights declarations are also being formulated and communicated. Value phenomena of this kind are usually arranged in a hierarchy of values in order of inclusiveness, with the values in each goal complex weighted, from time to time, and situation to situation, in a preference-ordering or scale of priorities. This goal-setting process, which is largely neglected in theories of administration, is mainly a function of managers of all groups at all levels in societies, nations, and formal organizations.

Further Practical Requirements

Admittedly there are gaps between ideals and actualities, but this gives meaning and function to ideals. As idealistic concepts, goals partake of this same character. The narrowing of the gap between the proclaiming of goals and their actualization in human experience is a standing challenge to scientific research, technology, and the arts and sciences of administration and management. For the public and private sectors to work effectively not only separately but together requires adjustments, accommodations, and compromises that fall short of the full reconciliation of multilevel goals and their complete achievement.

The use of the behavioral sciences in applications to these problems is urgent. New uses of the normative applied sciences are needed, along with more intense and widespread studies in comparative philosophical systems, particularly social and economic philosophy. The advancing study of comparative management in various sociocultural situations should eventually develop some general theories of organization, administration, and decision which are internationally valid. With regard to the public and private sectors of management and administration, there is already detectable a convergence of theories and practices of public administration and private corporate management, and the similarities of the public and private sectors now appear greater than their differences.[a] As in most problems and issues, the eventual resort is to education.

[a] The author presented and explored this hypothesis in Document No. 21-1, "Differences and Similarities in the Training and Development of Managers in the Public and Private Sectors of Developing Countries," at the International Seminar on Management Development in Developing Countries, at I.S.I.D.A., Palermo, Italy, June 5, 1969, auspices of O.E.C.D., I.L.O., E.A.M.T.C., and I.U.G.

Management Education

Management education will have to be accelerated and extended more widely to meet the mounting demands of increasingly complex systems within systems, and societies within societies, under augmented pressures of increasing population and the rapidly rising level of human and social aspirations. The character of this education will largely determine the general character of future managers in both the public and private sectors of development. Management is the strategic factor and change agent in the process of man-made creative evolution. As goal-setters necessarily engaged in determining values and making value judgments in managerial decisions, communications, and all of the generic processes of management, the outcomes of their decisions, cumulatively, have a major influence in determining future states of affairs.

There is no investment in the future with greater yields than that devoted to the education of the future managers and administrators of the public and private sectors of our developing countries. Moreover, practicing managers require continuing education to keep up with new developments in the applied sciences of management. One of the greatest sources of waste in foreign aid programs in the past has been a preoccupation with providing capital, technology, and equipment without adequate provision for education of sufficient managerial resources to manage developmental projects efficiently and effectively.

In the conceptual context of this presentation, it would appear that management education must be broadened to embrace the whole internal and external multidimensional environment, rather than remain preoccupied with the economic, financial, and technological. If the public and private sectors of development are to be bridged more effectively for the constructive common purposes of general development, management education needs broadening in this and other respects.

Education in public administration and business administration has too long been separated. Each educational field has much to offer the other, and both have more and more in common. Administration remains a useful organizing concept for both research and education. With future managers and administrators of the private and public sectors educated together in the same schools and management development institutes, their studies and interaction in the educational process will not only reveal the similarities of problems, processes, and responsibilities in the two sectors of development, but will enable them to understand the differences and interdependent relations of public administration and private corporate management. There could be no firmer basis for bridging the public and private sectors of developing countries.

Summary and Conclusion

An evolving community of compatible nations in a steady state of development requires widening recognition of the network of interdependent relations. Positive response to this major challenge of our times may take many forms, but the essential task consists of bridging or circumventing the obstacles that stand in the way of orderly and well-balanced international development.

National and other sub-social entities are largely dependent upon each other and the state of the whole system for their development. All of these socio-economic entities are developing at different rates and stages, and all have "mixed economies" with wide variations in the proportions of the private and public activities in the mixes. Although economic development may be regarded as basic and instrumental to the generation of human, social, and cultural values, a broader long-range pragmatic concept of development offers more assurance of well-conceived plans for economic development that will result in enduring values of general welfare.

Statesmen and managers make the crucial decisions in development both within and across national boundaries. Especially important in national development is the prevailing type of relationship between the managers of organizations in the public vis-à-vis the private sector. Development is often impeded or retarded by a largely unwarranted tug-of-war between public administration and business administration.

While there are points of interaction at which organizations in the public and private sectors compete or conflict, there is plenty of evidence to the effect that the two sectors are not mutually exclusive. The two sectors can expand the scope of their activities simultaneously in a pattern of interdependent relations conducive to development. These relationships between the public and private sectors not only can be analyzed, mapped out, and rendered more effective, but they can be planned and extended. Better understanding and arrangement of the relations between the public and private sectors of development may be accomplished in this conceptual framework.

Geo-political military strategies, wars, and autarchic nationalism, along with covert and contrived revolutionary ferment, are major obstacles to national as well as transnational development. Power struggles, social disorder, and the failures of public administration and private corporate management to gain and retain public respect and confidence create further obstacles to a steady state of development in which both sectors can collaborate effectively.

In the present and foreseeable future the criteria and goals of development in various nations had better be determined more on a pluralistic than a unitary international basis, so that eventual unifying trends will not obliterate the stimulating qualities of national and cultural diversities. It appears to be incumbent upon the leadership of developing countries to formulate comprehensive, long-range, and enduring developmental goals. In a well-balanced mixed socio-economic system, the public and private sectors—and possibly other "publics"—might cooperate in the formulation of national goals of development. Widely acceptable national goals provide the main normative foundations for bridging the public and private sectors of developing nations.

The formulation of national goals of development is only the first step. The next practical step in a mixed economy would be to have supporting sub-goals formulated in the public and private sectors, with a tentative division of labor and allocation of major projects and functional areas for each on an interdependent basis. This could be done in connection with long-range planning of development. Then organizational goals for particular public agencies and private corporations, supporting the sub-goals of the public and private sectors, would be needed on an autonomous but related basis.

The employment of science and technology, in the arts and sciences of administration and management becomes urgent, and takes on an enlarged meaning and effectiveness when used systematically in the normative context of national goals of development. Basic to all development is the potential of human resources, and basic to this is education. But instead of retaining outmoded or imported educational programs, a developing nation needs to tailor its educational system and curricula to the realities of its times and make them consistent with the currently prevalent norms and ideals of collective action incorporated in national goals. This can be done without stifling the creative powers of free inquiry and dissent. The strategic human resource is the supply of broadly educated public officials, public administrators, private enterprisers, and private corporate managers. The effectiveness of organizations engaged in development, whether in the public or private sector, depends largely upon the character, knowledge, and skills of their managers. Until the focus of public and official attention is shifted from things, quantities, concrete facilities, and statistics to the development of their people, their future leaders, and managers, through appropriate public services and education, development will lag far behind the rising level of human aspirations.

Bridging the public and private sectors of development through the interdependent decisions and actions of public administrators and private corporate managers, preferably educated together in public and business administration, and jointly committed to the accomplishment of generally acceptable national goals, offers to open new avenues to the development of our mixed socio-economic systems. It is this kind of bridging nationally and transnationally, accompanied by an expending network of understanding, interdependence, and reciprocity, from which a viable community of normally developing nations may emerge in a more orderly and peaceful atmosphere.

3

Key Problems in Development Administration

Jack Koteen

Introduction

Two decades of assistance to developing nations have produced significant improvements in administrative systems, but deficiencies in managerial capacity are greater than ever. National development programs, whether in family planning, education, agriculture, or business have too often fallen short of expectations for reasons of managerial weakness. As succinctly stated by a United Nations official, "planned development is necessarily a disequilibrium system where the 'administrative load' is continuously outpacing administrative capability."

Managerial deficiencies exist at all levels of developing economies in both the public and private sectors. They are particularly evident in the local and rural areas because talented managers, always in short supply, are better rewarded in the cities. They are also evident in the limited capacity of governments in developing countries to administer for development rather than for the established order. The prevalence of the managerial and administrative problem is sufficiently limiting to national development to warrant high priority attention.

The key problem areas in a wide panorama of deficiencies in the development administration which are presented in this paper were chosen because they were:

1. highly significant for LDC (Less Developed Countries) development;
2. widespread among low-income countries;
3. amenable to action by external donors;
4. relevant to assistance programs priorities and control staff inputs;
5. ameliorable within a 2–5 year time span.

An intensive review of the available documentation and discussions with concerned professionals, produced the conclusion that LDC development administration deficiencies meeting the above criteria fall into four problem areas. The four bring together a set of interrelated requisites for the administration of development. They are:

1. The shortage of qualified managerial manpower to cope with the demands

The views expressed are the author's and do not necessarily represent those of the Office of Development Administration, Agency for International Development, of which he is Deputy Director.

47

of development, particularly in the key sectors and at the local level.
2. The need for improvement in the relevance, effectiveness, and performance of key development institutions.
3. The inadequacy of LDC project management in terms of planning, implementation, control, and feedback.
4. The lack of capacity of local action: the critical role of local government and field units of the central government in delivering technology and services to the people and mobilizing development enterprise.

It is evident that official problem-solving efforts in development administration must proceed in close partnership with problem-solving efforts by professionals in agriculture, business, education, family planning, and other sectors. Development administration is instrumental; it cannot work in isolation from substantive development programs.

Two other themes strongly emphasized by professionals are presented in this paper. First, United States pre-eminence in management is a valuable asset in technical cooperation programs. Second, after almost a generation of assistance, the United States must proceed with new modes of partnership involving an increasing number of able professionals and institutions now available in many developing countries.

No set of generalizations about LDC problems in management can claim universal application and validity. Nevertheless, among those persons most involved there is a striking consensus about general deficiencies, although not always about the remedial measures. The deficiencies presented here must be considered as points of departure for subsequent analysis of the problem-solving effort. Selected programs and institutions in specific countries with systematic fact-finding and analysis must be undertaken so that remedial actions can be realistically tailored to the circumstances.

The Problem of Managerial Manpower Shortage

The shortage of qualified managerial manpower to cope with the demands of growth and modernization is foremost among the problems of development administration. Low-income nations are facing a marked shortage of the kinds of development-oriented managers who can handle the complex problems of technological, economic, and social change. Their absence becomes more conspicuous as development plans, programs, and promises fall short in their implementation and execution. Ample evidence exists as to the widespread existence and significance of the LDC managerial manpower shortage. It appears to be constantly growing, despite almost a generation of assistance efforts in management education and training.

Coping with the pace of change in the developing nations demands a break with tradition. In the professional community serious doubts are being expressed as to whether current programs within existing institutional patterns will make a sufficient impact upon the increasing managerial shortage. The problem is partly one of numbers; the LDCs must expand their capacity to produce middle managers in quantity. However, the quality of managerial manpower requires the major emphasis in our problem-solving efforts. The capacity of senior executives at all geographic levels of a society's key institutions to cope with the demands of growth and modernization deserves priority attention.

Thus, the general problem posed is: What more effective steps can be taken to expand the LDC supply of development-oriented managers, and assure their proper allocation and use in the key development sectors, and in institutions and programs ultimately geared to local action?

Deficiencies in the Current Situation

1. *Obsolescence of program content in overseas management education and training.*

a. Traditional Approaches. Managerial training in developing countries has typically emphasized the training of officers in the areas of established laws and authorities, rules and regulations, and administrative procedure and technique, accompanied by "principles" of efficiency and economy. This training seemed appropriate for efficient functioning of the administrative apparatus of government or an enterprise. But the laws, rules, procedures, and techniques developed during an earlier traditional period are not sufficient to cope with the demands for change imposed by population growth, technological change, urbanization, and the idea of progress. Nor do traditional approaches capitalize on the newly emerging doctrine in development administration, and the intellectual explosion of the last decade in the managerial, behavioral, and statistical sciences. Traditional approaches are certainly not adequate to cope with the complexity of delivering new technology to mass consumers to satisfy the national requirements for food, family planning, or education.

b. Emerging New Doctrine and Technique. For several decades, scholars and practitioners of administration have been turning away from the traditional forms of management education and training. They have emphasized a greater concern for program performance, in the context of policy and purpose. The underlying premise increasingly being recognized is that administration is not an end in itself; its inherent value derives from its ability to accomplish desired policy and program objectives. This recognition of administration as a vital component of policy and program performance in a framework of political, social, and economic considerations provides a useful guide for the adaptation of a series of new concepts and techniques in management. These newer ideas are widely documented and fall generally into five major areas: planning and control, the behavioral aspects of management, analytical tools for decision making, management and information systems, and the broader horizons of management—the concern for environment, social setting, and the future.

2. *The lack of qualified managers in agriculture, education, and family planning.*

Although the need for better management is becoming widely recognized in agriculture, education, and family planning, there is a dearth of institutions and programs devoted to the development of managerial competence in these fields, particularly when compared to the gigantic dimensions of need.[a] Most executives in development ministries have had little or no exposure to the concepts of management. There is extensive evidence that the state of managerial practice in these programs is inadequate.

Compared to the number of programs in general public and business administration, the efforts in sector management education and training are few. There appears to be a lack of real demand as contrasted with the growing evidence of need. If we are to meet the managerial requirements of the development sectors, we need to be able to provide a climate of acceptance for management education, sound and relevant program content, and effective institutional arrangements. Toward this objective, a whole set of possibilities needs examination. For example: How can the many institutions and programs in LDCs developing managerial manpower in the fields of public and business management, and the sixty-year stream of managerial thought, be more effectively geared to the concrete and unique requirements of the sector manager? Is it feasible to incorporate modern management components in the professional schools of agriculture, education, or health? Are national, regional, or international management service centers an effective way to upgrade or initiate efforts in many institutions by providing consultants, professors, trainers, teaching materials, and research services? How can participant training in the sector fields give more attention to managerial aspects of these technical areas? The CIC report on agriculture makes such a recommendation,[1] but the USDA reports no appreciable increase in the relatively few requests for management training for agricultural participants.

But education alone is insufficient to render a timely and effective impact on sector program practice. Education and training institutions engaged in managerial development abroad need to develop the "trinity concept" so well demonstrated in our land grant college approach of "teaching, research, and extension" of developing and adapting knowledge, disseminating it widely and actively, and taking the knowledge to where the need exists. The missionary zeal of the early U.S. agricultural schools in moving out to the arena of action is an important lesson for the managerial development movement.

3. *The lack of adaptation of Western managerial thought and practice to the specific environment of developing nations.*

Though development assistance agents and agencies have long preached the thesis, "adapt not adopt," the history of technical assistance in public administration is fraught with examples of the direct transfer of American

---

[a] See Appendix A for a chart of the relationships of training and educational needs.

or Western public administration to the developing nations with small regard to the difference of culture, politics, economics, technology, or ethics. In recent years there has been a small but growing accumulation of knowledge of the sociocultural and other environmental constraints or determinants of managerial effectiveness. The recent efforts in this direction of the Comparative Administration Group (CAG) in the public sector and the comparative management network in business need to be examined for their relevance to technical assistance efforts.

4. *Gaps among program elements of managerial manpower development.*

a. Absence of Programs for Senior Executives. It is important that a balance be achieved among the elements of management development, for an effective institution depends not only on pre-entry training for junior executives, but upon a well-trained middle management group and qualified top executives. However, most of managerial development is directed at the younger group, either in pre-entry training, or in extension type programs, or at the functional specialties of staff management. Ministries or firms cannot wait the ten to twenty years for the younger people to move to the middle or upper reaches of the structure. More seriously, most of the current crop of senior executives in the developing world have had primarily professional and technical training, but little or no exposure to the concepts and practice of management, and in consequence cannot provide the understanding or leadership necessary for managerial and institutional innovation and reform. In Turkey, for example, there is almost total lack of appropriate facilities and programs for senior executives despite the existence in Turkey of about thirty management education or training facilities.

b. Participant Training Largely Professional and Technical, Not Managerial. The AID participant program has largely emphasized professional and technical training rather than training in management, even though a number of these persons were already in managerial positions, or would assume managerial responsibilities soon after their return. In Turkey, where over 4000 have benefited from U.S. training in the last twenty years, almost all of the emphasis was on the development of professional and technical skills in such ministries as education, agriculture, industry, and transportation. But little attention was given to managerial effectiveness. In the Ministry of Agriculture, for example, of the 1166 people trained, only 21 received training in management. The urgent need for professional and technical personnel in developing countries justified a primary emphasis upon such skills. But the growing demands of development now make it critical that we equip the senior professional and technician with managerial skills.

c. Lack of Continuous Staff Development in Management: The Blend of Formal and Informal Education. For those in development ministries or enterprises who have received some exposure to management, there is little opportunity for their continuous development as managerial responsibilities increase or the nature of managerial thought and practice changes. The U.S. military management development system illustrates an advanced type of continuous staff development. Throughout an officer's career, which starts with pre-entry education, he is exposed to a sequenced blend of practical experience through duty assignments and rotation with formal education through attendance at military management schools, or at external institutions. Apart from some military programs, not much evidence exists in the LDCs of continuous, sequenced managerial development combining forms of formal education and training with informal means such as on-the-job rotation during one's entire career. The lifetime learning concept and practice of the U.S. adult education movement in general, and the management study movement in particular, deserves attention in overseas management development programs.

5. *Missing technical components in management education.*

Management development programs abroad are often hampered by the absence or inadequacy of the components that make for technical capacity: trained teachers and trainers, up-to-date courses and curricula, teaching and training materials, research, consultative activity, access to modern knowledge through libraries and reference centers, professional societies and publications, conferences, and other professionally stimulating and rewarding activities.

The shortage of qualified teachers and trainers, and essential teaching and training materials, is so extensive that consideration must be given to special programs and organizational arrangements of professional exchange to service multiple institutions and programs simultaneously.

6. *Limited institutional capacity for management education and training.*

a. **The Widening of Institutional Choice to Include Professional Schools.** A major institution-building issue lies in the proper choice among alternatives of institutions to be strengthened. In the field of management education, choices should not be limited to institutions currently involved in management education or training. The range of choice should be widened to include other professional schools (health, agriculture, education, etc.) not yet engaged in management education and consideration should be given to incorporating in their curricula a modern management component. Most of the executives in LDC governments or business are products of professional schools, and perceive themselves more often as professionals in their respective disciplines or functional areas of experience than as professional managers. Adding a solid management component to their early training, or providing middle or top management programs related to their professional responsibilities may provide a means to substantially expand the supply of managers, as well as narrow the gap of sector acceptance and relevance of managerial thought and practice.

b. **The Use of Intermediary Training Institutions Closer to the People.**

Management development programs often fail to reach the local leaders in the rural areas. To meet the need for local managerial talent, the Comilla experiment with intermediary training institutions at the "Thana" level (similar to the U.S. county) suggests an institutional device worth further exploration. The Thana training center was created as a "half-way house," where several selected leaders from the many villages were invited for training with experts from the center or external aid agents on a continuing basis. In this way, central or outside experts could meet with local leaders on neutral ground to exchange knowledge and experience.

The intermediary training institution offers several advantages. One is that outsiders are not easily tolerated within the close social structure of the villages. Another is that there are not enough outsiders to reach all of the villages, even if they were tolerated. A third advantage is that the content of training could be made more relevant to the real world in which the problems and opportunities occur, particularly as the training participant returns to his village to put his new knowledge into practice and returns periodically to discuss his problems, failures, and successes.

c. The Availability of Field-Tested Institution Building Concepts. Though we have long been in the business of building institutions, only recently have we had available institution-building research, accompanied by extensive field testing and validation, to help guide overseas institutions modernize their management education and training activities.[b] We now understand more clearly that the components of technical capacity (as discussed in section 5 above), though essential, are an incomplete prescription for guidance of management education institutions. Changes in values, functions, and social technologies, however rational or purely technical they appear to the foreign assistance experts or to some domestic innovators, are often perceived as threatening to local interests or to individual or group status. These changes may not be understood or valued by others whose perspective is different. Innovations need to be conceived as induced social change, and innovators must be aware of the complexities, resistance, and uncertainties involved.

Institution-building research informs us that the change agent needs to fulfill a dual need. He must, of course, build a technically competent and socially cohesive organization. But he must also develop satisfactory relationships with other organizations and groups in his environment that provide support and inputs for his organization or outlets for his organization's products or services.

The current research on institutional variables of leadership, doctrine, programs, resources, internal structures, and the several forms of linkages with the institution's environment are relevant and operationally useful in the process of reconstituting management education and training institutions. The research of the Inter-University Consortium on Institution Building contains several case studies of management education institutions that

---

[b] See Appendix B for several short definitions of Institution Building Concepts.

appear particularly relevant. The recent Ford financed evaluative research on three management education institutions in India adds a number of potentially useful concepts such as strategic planning, cost-effectiveness, and entrepreneurship in management education. Additionally, the CIC three-year research program on Agricultural Educational Institutions already mentioned will prove valuable as the findings are adapted to building management education and training institutions.

7. *The inadequacy of national managerial manpower planning.*

In the decade since Harbison's work in Nigeria,[2] a number of developing nations have begun to identify their long-term gap between the supply and demand of managerial manpower as part of their national manpower planning efforts. The crucial problem with managerial manpower planning, apart from such limitations as definition, classification, methodology and reliability of data, is its over-aggregation in national terms rather than in terms of sector or ministry or other units than can relate more directly to programs in management education. Country systems of manpower planning do not provide a clear projection of availabilities and requirements for different categories of managerial personnel (as they do for professional and technical manpower) that could provide guidance to management education and training institutions. Individual institutions or groups of institutions should cooperate with the national manpower planning authorities, and representatives of user institutions in refining national data to make it more relevant to their concern for (a) meeting national needs, (b) developing priorities among constituent programs, (c) relating training more effectively to the level and nature of job requirements, and (d) assuring the availability of employment for their graduates.

8. *The knowledge-action gap between education and training institutions and the problem-solving requirements of action agencies.*

Education and training institutions often stop short of helping action organizations cope with their complex decision-making, problem-solving efforts. They often perceive their responsibility as one of knowledge-building, research, and the teaching of fundamentals. But managerial knowledge does not automatically offer the practicing manager the concepts and tools in a form useful for pragmatic problem-solving action. The growing complexity of managerial and social science language, however necessary for research and analytical effort, widens the gap among researcher, teacher, and practitioner. The knowledge-action gap deserves attention on at least two fronts.

a. Need for New Organizational Arrangements and Linkages. One approach to bridging the knowledge-action gap lies in a series of new organizational arrangements and linkages between teams of specialists in the managerial and behavioral sciences and the agencies confronted with the need for managerial solutions. Such linkages of specialists with real problems in action agencies could be fostered by the creation of special institutes or centers, geared not to the building of research and new knowledge, but rather devoted to problem-solving efforts. Various experimental arrangements to foster intimate linkages should be undertaken. Operating officials could be detailed to the institute from time to time, while the institute's specialists could spend time with the operating agency, becoming oriented to the environment, conditions, and constraints essential to problem solution.

b. The Operational Conversion of Managerial Knowledge. The content of managerial thought should be transformed into relevant and understandable materials useful to the practicing manager. The production of operational guides for practitioners in selected fields like institution building, management information systems, or project management would be useful. Such guides could be accompanied by appropriately converted teaching, case study, and self-study materials that have been group tested for their comprehensibility and utility.

The conversion of knowledge into action requires individuals who possess the necessary knowledge-in-depth of major streams of managerial research and thought, and who are also able and willing to be the social engineers forging links between knowledge and action. In the choice of agents, it must be recognized that those institutions or experts most qualified at research, theory, and knowledge-building may not be the most appropriate for its operational conversion, particularly across national boundaries.

The Problem of Institution Building

The need for improvement in the relevance, effectiveness, and performance of key development institutions is the second problem area of significance. Obsolete institutions often constrain development as severely as the shortage of capital or technical talent. Effective mobilization of development resources cannot be achieved in the absence of dynamic institutions. Evidence abounds that dynamic institutions are the exception rather than the rule in the low income countries.

"Institutions" are the organized, continuing channels of action for pursuing goals and meeting needs within a society. Revised institutional arrangements are often needed to put a technology to work or translate development goals into action. Hence, institutional strategy is an essential element of development strategy.

In practical terms, the problem of institution building is this: How can the LDCs improve the productive, adaptive, and innovative capacities of key development institutions and develop networks of modernizing institutions serving broad action programs in such fields as agriculture, education, health and family planning, and revenue?

There is, of course, no magic formula for institution building. Viable institutions must be forged in nasty environments characterized by scarce resources and arrays of vested interests resisting change. Political as well as administrative factors are important, and the process is perhaps more art than science.

Institution builders may, nonetheless, learn much from the experience of others and apply existing knowledge about organizational change and institution building that is relevant to their task.

The "science" of Institution Building (IB) has been developing rapidly in recent years. Through the disciplines of business and public administration with inputs from the social and behavioral sciences, knowledge about organizational effectiveness has grown rapidly. Through research specifically directed to LDC institution building, useful concepts and case studies have evolved.

Deficiencies in the Current Situation

1. *Need for institutional change: a pervasive concern.*

An examination of recent AID and other international assistance shows that LDC institution-building problems are of great concern. Such problems are sometimes stated in terms of program needs such as secondary education, family planning, sometimes in terms of organizational deficiencies, such as the revenue service or the ministry of agriculture. In both categories, statements of deficiencies in institutional terms are very common.

Reports from developing countries have included the following observations expressing the deficiencies of IB in a variety of ways from a variety of countries:

1. comparatively little success in introducing the needed institutional improvements, especially in public administration, which would facilitate continued economic growth—Korea;
2. a major problem is the lack of effective institutional mechanisms linking the villagers to centralized bureaucracy—Thailand;
3. the development there of modern institutions is seen as "rudimentary"; specific need for widespread bank reforms and institutions to support private initiative—Afghanistan;
4. public sector agencies have proliferated, resulting in overlapping functions and responsibilities, gaps in services, and limited effective authority in policy and decision-making—Chile;
5. there is the need to develop institutions for economic integration into the international trading system—Turkey;
6. major constraints include "weakness in economic planning and policy formulation" and "insufficient managerial and technical higher and middle level manpower"; institutions to strengthen the nation's capacity for improved policy making, planning, and program implementation are needed —Nigeria;
7. a high priority need is to modernize agricultural institutions, to include attention to the organization and administration of the ministry—Morocco;
8. agriculture lacks the "physical and institutional infrastructure for a twentieth century agriculture sector."—Pakistan;

9. public agencies need reorganization and reform since many of the forms and structures of government, both national and local, have not changed since the turn of the century—Argentina;
10. there is a need for better institutional capacity to provide adequate nutrition services—Brazil.

It is clear that more attention must be directed to the institutionalization of modernization in the revenue systems of LDCs, so that the process of improvement will carry on under indigenous impetus after foreign technical advisors have departed.

The most overlooked of the technical assistance functions, has been the long, painstaking work of building central, regional, and local governmental institutions. New administrative systems are essential to break through traditional bureaucratic processes in national planning agencies, budgeting, and programing systems, operations of development banks, local administrations and, notably, universities and other educational institutions.[3]

2. Slow adaptation to new requirements.

Institutional adaptation to vital developmental needs is proceeding much too slowly. Family planning and urban growth are excellent examples, but others are evident in such areas as education, taxation, and the capacity of private enterprises to compete effectively in world markets. The most pressing requirements for institutional change must be determined on a country-by-country basis and in terms of desired functional outputs.

3. Lack of cooperative linkages among institutions.

The effectiveness of existing LDC institutions is restricted by lack of adequate cooperative linkages with other institutions. For example, it has been shown that there are inadequate linkages among research, financial, marketing, and other farm-oriented institutions. Schools and institutes of higher education lack mechanisms for technological updating and maintenance of ties with employers of graduates to assure relevant curricula.

4. Inadequate awareness of IB and organizational change methodology.

LDC institution builders often lack knowledge of analytic methods which would help them structure their task more systematically. They like foreign advisors, are often technically oriented rather than oriented toward social change. Their skill as leaders and change agents would be enhanced by training in institution-building methodology and strategies of planned organizational change.

The theory and knowledge about institutions and organizational change available in the LDCs is usually abstract and non-actionable. Legal and formal factors in organizational development are emphasized much more than practical problem solving. Pragmatic analytic tools and training programs linked to real-world applications are needed. Also applied research and experimentation are needed to determine what organizational changes are essential for the introduction of new technology. One clear need in this sphere is for knowledge about the organizational effects of introducing advanced information technology.

5. *Inadequate exploitation of research.*

Recent research has produced much useful information about institution-building methodology, but the findings have yet to be adequately analyzed for operational relevance and then widely disseminated. The costs of screening this knowledge and getting it into the action arena of LDC institution building would be modest when compared to the costs of the research effort itself.

The Problem of Inadequate Project Management

The lack of soundly conceived, well-managed development projects is a drag on the development process. Development projects are needed in the low-income countries which are better planned, implemented, and integrated for the achievement of national plans and goals. Sound projects are needed for both domestic and foreign financing.

The lack of a stream of superior projects has been repeatedly deplored by international lending agencies. In some regions there are fewer fundable projects than loan funds available to finance them. The cutting edge of development is at the project level, since it is the project that translates macro-planning and sectoral programing into units of action. Without sound projects there is a lowered tempo of development.

AID, the World Bank, the IDB, and other assistance agencies have sponsored increased training for project designers and project appraisers to meet this need. There is, however, ample evidence from field experience that the problems associated with achieving an increase in the number of sound, well-managed development projects go beyond the adequacy of trained technicians.

Deficiencies in the Current Situation

1. *Lack of top level support.*

There is a need for political executives and top administrators including ministers, the heads of planning and budget offices, and directors general of major bureaus to appreciate the analytic and decision-making process essential to sound project formulation, approval, and implementation. Some experts feel that the crucial factor is not so much the analytical methodology in developing projects as the decision making at the top levels to support project development, especially in policy and implementation follow-up.

2. *Need for an institutionalized project process.*

There is a lack of institutionalization of the process for project planning, approval, and implementation. This institutional process has to link the planning effort, budgeting and financial activities, and the technical offices that are charged with the implementation responsibilities. The institutional process refers to a viable system for relating these functions either within government or in other agencies concerned with project formulation and execution.

3. *Need for a comprehensive analytical framework.*

There is need for a more comprehensive framework of analysis for project planning and implementation. The major portion of the analytical framework for projects tends to be economic and financial in nature. This is appropriate, especially for income-generating projects, but there is a clear need to expand the analytical methodology to include the organizational and managerial manpower, civic and social development aspects. Emerging concerns for environmental impact and second order consequences create still further demands in project planning.

In addition to broadening the framework of the analysis, there needs to be a design and appraisal methodology that is realistic in terms of the data available in the developing countries and the skill levels of the project designers and appraisers. The project design must be related to the larger sector and alternative project choices available. The World Bank has found from years of experience that one of the cardinal principles of project design is to relate it to a sectoral analysis, even a rough and ready analysis of a larger systems framework within which to design and analyze a discrete project.

4. *Lack of country capacity for training, consultation, and research.*

There is an established need for trained manpower in the design, evaluation, and implementation of projects. This need extends not only to professional project analysts, but also to substantive technical people who need capstone training in project design as, for example, in agriculture, education, health, and public works as well as in the general execution of major projects.

If the capacity for project management is to be expanded rapidly, the LDCs must expand their own training of project designers, evaluators, and administrators. People must be trained to perform the underlying research and consulting services for a variety of governmental and private institutions. The IBRD reports that an increasing number of foreign officials request training in project planning but the demand currently exceeds its available training capacity.

5. *Inadequate attention to project implementation.*

Within the field of project management, there is a need to differentiate between project preparation and analysis, and project implementation, since different people skills and subject matter are involved. Too often, the phase of project implementation is neglected in favor of project design and analysis. The IBRD, for example, trains more for project preparation and analysis than for project implementation. Business schools and private consulting firms sometimes can make effective contributions in training for project implementation.

6. *Inadequate use of new techniques.*

Newer developments in project management, commonplace in much of U.S. industry, defense, and space programs should be considered for LDCs. Most common are Program Evaluation and Review Technique (PERT) and its offshoot Critical Path Method (CPM). Modern project managers are expected to know about planning, budgeting, forecasting, estimating, cost/schedule reporting, project monitoring, and project control administration. For large-scale projects, they have to know about computerized data processes of "feedback" into the revising of operations, and "feedforward" into revised planning. Systematic ways to adapt the newer concepts and techniques of project management are needed for use in the developing nations.

7. *Need for interdisciplinary and intersectoral approaches.*

Project development is complicated because, if well done, it is multidisciplinary and multisectoral in nature. Usually a project involves inputs from at least one basic technical field which is normally complemented by inputs from other fields. Projects can occur in one or more sectors and fall within the private or public sphere of activity, or both.

It is obvious that assistance to the developing countries in project management, including planning, evaluation, and implementation, is complex. Joint project approval and monitoring by several assistance and lending agencies working with the developing countries is equally or more complex. Any unidimensional approach such as supplying more trained technicians, or improving analytical methodologies, or stressing the efficiency of administration is not likely to succeed in providing an appropriate blend of factors to increase the quality of project management. A broader, better coordinated approach to the problem of improved project formulation and implementation has to be formulated.

The ultimate objective, of course, is to provide a stream of clearly superior projects that are well managed. This overall goal requires an institutional ability within the developing country to plan, evaluate, and implement such projects along with the institutional capability to undertake the necessary training and consulting services for this process. This institutional target, in turn, requires a conceptual framework within which to plan and strengthen the components of a project development system such as trained manpower, methodology, and project formulation techniques applicable to national planning, budgeting, and execution processes. Obviously, the major lending and assistance agencies can facilitate this process to the extent that they can agree on the specifications and requirements for project design and approval. An auxiliary target, therefore, is to increase the communication and the coordination among major assistance in these matters.

The Problem of Capacity for
Local Action

Local government and the field services of central government are frequently inadequate to deliver services and new technology to the people. This widespread lack of capacity for local action in the developing world creates a serious impediment to the successful accomplishment of country development programs in the key sectors: agriculture, education, health, and family planning. Because these programs are fundamentally "people" and "community" oriented, their effective execution ultimately depends upon indigenous capacity at the local level.

Despite numerous efforts to improve local capacity, the feeling persists that a more coherent strategy and more effective approaches to this vast, complex problem are urgently needed. The subject of local action appears too broad and diffuse for effective problem solving unless more sharply focused as to scope, priorities, and approach.

The range of the topic can be narrowed by an examination of the problems relevant to the capacity of rural institutions. Both public and private institutions need careful analysis, but the evidence at hand clearly indicates that severe poverty in local areas cannot be overcome without government assistance. Hence, as one part of the broader multidisciplinary examination of the problems of local capacity, we need to focus on the problems of local government and the field services of national government.

Local government and field services of central ministries are typically the least developed elements of the public sector. They are an important avenue for the delivery to the people of essential services and new technologies in the major sectors. They are typically talent starved, resource poor, and tradition bound. The core of the problem is how to shift them from traditional roles toward developmental roles. How can they act as catalytic agents to promote acceptance of new ideas, stimulate local action, and mobilize resources for development?

The environment in which decentralized jurisdictions function is often unpromising, being generally characterized by: (a) dispersed population, making communication and organization difficult; (b) lack of modern facilities, services, and amenities; (c) scarcity of development-oriented local leadership and expertise; (d) deepseated resistance to change; (e) antiquated administration; and (f) a lack of real interest in the problems of poor people.

Given these difficult conditions, it is essential to find strategies which provide opportunities for action carrying benefits directly to the people. Strategies that have already produced significant payoff are those organized action programs which are centered on limited and specific packages of technology. Medical immunization campaigns and seed campaigns are good examples. The strategies selected should make optimum use of private sector capacities so as to reduce the "administrative load" on the machinery of government.

Deficiencies in the Current Situation

1. Low priority for local development.

Decentralized development has seldom figured high in the priorities of the developing nations. The emphasis has been on centrally designed and managed development programs. These programs have in many cases benefited secondary centers and rural areas, but priority attention has been given to development in the key urban centers. Some economists hold that it is more cost-effective to concentrate development. Even if this is so, the economic costs of distributing public services more broadly throughout a country may be less important than the social and political benefits which decentralized development could achieve.

In most of the developing countries, there are strong traditional tendencies toward centralism. These may be based on historical patterns related to control by a colonial power. The Spaniards clearly left this imprint on much of Latin America, as did other Europeans in many countries of Asia and Africa. The new leaders often picked up where the colonial powers left off. Often, the government bureaucracy itself stands opposed to decentralization. National pride in the development of major cities is another cultural constraint working against decentralization. The nation is known by its large cities; therefore the development of secondary cities and rural areas is of less concern.

2. Weak national institutions for local development.

Most developing countries lack strong institutions at the center to assist local development. Pressure groups, such as associations of local governments or of municipal officials, are often weak or nonexistent. Central institutions give insufficient attention to assistance, research, and training relevant to local development needs, and often lack the professional capability to do so. National planning agencies lack the capacity to relate national and local plans, or to develop local planning capacity. The central government ministries are typically weak and mismanaged at the local level. It is common for schools to exist without teachers, clinics without medicines, roads without maintenance. There is little concerted action among the many national institutions concerned with local operations and service.

All of these phenomena are directly related to the low priority given to local development. Low national commitment to local development has led to weak central institutions to work for this cause. And, conversely, the absence of stronger institutions of this type has failed to generate more pressure for the decentralization of development.

Assistance to local government has been provided at times through diverse channels. These include (a) governmental institutions like ministries of interior; (b) autonomous agencies like national institutes of municipal administration; and (c) private agencies like leagues of municipalities or associations of mayors. Some experts claim that assistance given to autonomous or private agencies is more effective than assistance given directly to governmental institutions; others favor government channels. A comparative analysis is needed to discover which of the institutional alternatives are the more effective vehicles for technical assistance to local government in a given environment.

3. Lack of financial capacity at the local level

A basic problem confronting efforts to provide a minimum level of local service has been the inability of local government to produce sufficient revenues. Technical assistance in taxation usually emphasizes national revenue systems that focus on income and customs and neglects the potential of local taxes. Local focus is on income and customs and neglects the potential of local taxes. Local property taxes are often inadequately exploited. Many local jurisdictions do not have a complete registry of real estate. They also lack the capacity for effective and equitable real property assessments.

There is often a lack of credit availability at the grass roots. Local government typically must finance its projects from current income. This severely limits the types of activities which can be undertaken. To construct a water or sewer system or other major project, it must do it in pay-as-you-go stages, which delay the project and increase the costs. Alternatively, it can wait for assistance from a central government agency. In many countries, there is not merely a lack of credit for needed projects, but a lack of institutions to make such loans. Existing banks are unwilling or unable to provide capital; they are ill-equipped to provide the technical assistance and credit supervision needed by local governments.

Another problem frequently encountered in local jurisdictions is that accounting and budgeting procedures are so deficient that it is impossible to determine cash flows accurately, to detect misappropriations, or to coordinate local action with recognized needs. Many local jurisdictions are highly deficient in systematic means for allocating and controlling expenditures.

4. Lack of planning capacity at regional levels.

There is often a planning gap at intermediary levels between local authorities and the central government. Local authorities are not able to mobilize needed planning talent, and yet are too far removed to depend upon planning efforts at the center. Central government agencies, particularly in large, highly populated countries which administer direct services, often are ill-equipped to plan their response to local needs and problems.

A fact of life for local governments is that the forces of development and change do not respect village, town, or municipal boundaries. Local authorities acting alone cannot plan and provide adequate services. There is a need for a continuing institutional framework within which local officials can come together with central officials, discuss common problems, and cooperate in planning to solve them.

Some experts indicate the need for planning regions which lie between the central government and the local jurisdictions. Planning at the regional level could focus on a specific sector like education or health, but could also take a comprehensive view of sector interrelationships. Such planning could be better adapted to regional economic, political, and social conditions. In countries with a scarcity of first rate administrators and technical personnel, able men placed at the regional level can strengthen local planning, whereas they would add to centralist tendencies if they were stationed in the capital.

5. *Lack of managerial capacity.*

Local authorities often are unable to mobilize the talent needed to carry out development activities. Better training and staff development are needed throughout the public sector. There are crucial problems at the local level where the deficits are greater and the problems of reaching a geographically dispersed group are more difficult. Some countries are experimenting with special training programs for local personnel, using correspondence courses, radio, and mobile seminars to reach widely scattered people. Special incentives to work in rural areas, merit career and salary systems, and other aspects of field services administration and local government personnel work deserve more attention to help solve the managerial needs of local development activities.

6. *Absence of partnership between central and local authorities.*

If local needs are to be met, both local and central development institutions must work together toward joint objectives. Instead of cooperation, however, there is often a tendency for the two to work in isolation, without effective communication or understanding between them. The local authorities pursue their objectives independently and often at odds with central plans and efforts. In some cases there is open conflict between the two. For example, the sharing of revenue is an issue when both central and local authorities are attempting to tax the same economic activity.

There is an increasing need for effective partnership between local and central authorities. Schools may be staffed by central ministries, but may be built and maintained by the local authorities. Clusters of government services from central agencies or local authorities in the same geographical location may need to be consolidated and coordinated at intermediary levels closer to the people to provide a stronger nucleus for local action. In any partnership arrangement, each of the partners must be capable of carrying his share of the burden. Premature or excessive decentralization, therefore, can be harmful and wasteful if the devolution of functions is made to jurisdictions that lack the technical personnel and funds to perform them. The form and degree of decentralized partnership must be adapted to circumstances, including the capacity of the local people to discharge responsibilities.

7. *Low level of popular participation.*

Local government often neglects the dimension of popular participation in local affairs. Control by the few is unresponsive to the needs and wishes of the many. Local participation not only strengthens democratic values but provides a means for local control over government programs. Local power organized through representative local councils can make programs in agriculture, education, or family planning more responsive and better adapted to local needs. In addition, through participation, people can be encouraged to do more on their own initiative and thus make a fuller contribution to development programs.

Community development programs have stimulated many community self-help efforts around the world. Schools have been built, clinics organized, all tapping the participation potential which exists among local people. The challenge to permanent institutions at the local level is to mobilize the people to participate in the decisions and affairs that affect the quality of their lives.

Notes

1. C.I.C.-A.I.D. Rural Development Research Project, *Building Institutions to Serve Agriculture* (1968).

2. Frederick H. Harbison in *Investment in Education,* The Report of the Commission on Post School Certificate and Higher Education in Nigeria (Federal Ministry of Nigeria, 1960).

3. Note in particular Milton J. Esman and John D. Montgomery, *Systems Approaches to Technical Cooperation: The Role of Development Administration* (The Government Affairs Institute, 1969), and Committee for Economic Development, *Assisting Development in Low-Income Countries* (1969).

66

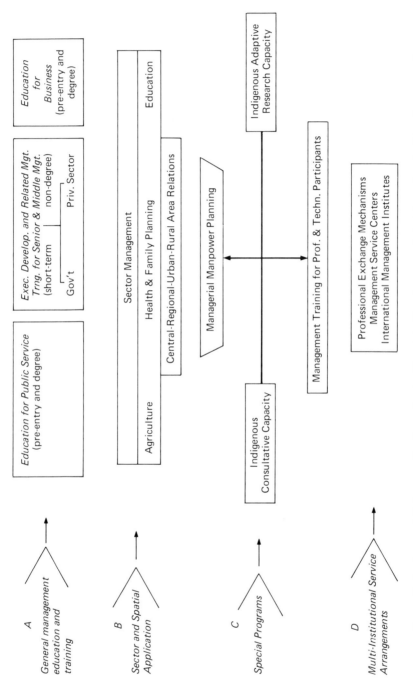

Figure 3–1. Areas of Relevance for Consultative Panels in Development Administration for Development of Education and Training, Consultation and Research.

Appendix 3B

Institution Building: Some Definitions of Terms and Concepts

1. *Institution:* A new or remodeled organization which induces and protects innovations.
2. *Innovations:* New technologies, new patterns of behavior, or changes in relationships among individuals or groups.
3. *Institution Building:* Planning and guiding organizations which induce and protect innovations, gain support, and thus become viable in their society.
4. *Institutionality:* The end-state of institution-building efforts characterized by the following conditions: (a) a viable organization has been established which incorporates innovations; (b) the organization and the innovations it represents have been accepted and taken up by relevant groups in the environment.
5. *Major Institution Variables:*
   a. *Leadership:* The group of persons who direct the institution's internal operations and manage its relations with the external environment.
   b. *Doctrine:* The expression of the institution's major purposes, objectives, and methods of operation.
   c. *Program:* The activities performed by the institution in producing and delivering outputs of goods or services.
   d. *Resources:* The physical, financial, personnel, informational, and other inputs which are required for the functioning of the institution.
   e. *Internal Structure:* The technical division of labor, and distribution of authority, and the lines of communication within the institution through which decisions are taken and action is guided and controlled.
6. *Linkages:* Patterned relationships between the institution and other organizations and groups in the environment. These relationships comprise the exchange of resources, services, and support and may involve various degrees of cooperation or competition.
   a. *Enabling:* Relationships with organizations that control the allocation of authority to operate or of resources.
   b. *Functional:* Relationships with organizations that supply needed inputs or which take outputs.
   c. *Normative:* Relationships with organizations that share an interest in social purposes.
   d. *Diffuse:* Relationships with individuals and groups not associated in formal organizations.
7. *Transactions:* Exchanges of goods and services or of power and influence.

The Institution Building Universe

Institution   Linkages

| Leadership
Doctrine
Program
Resources
Internal Structure | ←——————Transactions——————→ | Enabling
Functional
Normative
Diffuse |

4

Achievement and Administrative Action in Developing Countries

David C. McClelland

Administrative action to foster economic achievement in an underdeveloped country is not easy to identify. The problem of identifying essential action for the manager and administrator is difficult in any country. Management and administration consist of a vast array of activities for highly advanced or for newly developing countries. There are, of course, numerous administrative actions that one could select. It simplifies the matter considerably by concentrating on one type or action and one type of administrator. My focus is on the entrepreneur as one of the "agents" of economic development—one of the important contributors to the rate of economic growth.

When we use the term "entrepreneur" we must make it clear that we are referring to a type of business activity and not to the ownership of the means of production. We are not talking just about the capitalistic entrepreneur—we are talking about the man who undertakes or "enterprises" who may be in the public sector or in the private sector. My observations on this type of administrative behavior can apply to socialist systems as well as to capitalist systems.

One difference between the private and public sector has to do with the way tenure or promotion is obtained. In the public sector, it is sometimes a matter of the political process as to how you get recruited, and how long you keep your job. In my terms, there has to be some clear connection between reward or promotion and performance. If that is more difficult in a public institution than in the private institution, then the public system is simply less efficient in promoting economic development. But be that as it may, my task will be to discuss six research points that have been made in one way or another in the past fifteen years, and then to relate these to administrative action.

The Case for Achievement

The evidence that I would like to review is that a certain type of human motivation, which I call the Need for Achievement (N/A), is a link to economic development via the entrepreneur. That is, successful entrepreneurs generally have more of this human characteristic as we measure it. It should be emphasized that this characteristic has to be measured in a very particular way. We frequently fall victim to the English language in thinking that everyone understands what is connoted by the term Need for

Achievement. We do *not* mean that all great achievements are caused by the Need for Achievement. There are other human motives of great importance and it is obvious that success in politics, the army, and many other areas of life are due probably to the power motive and not to the achievement motive which is very specifically tied to economic performance.

There are six converging lines of evidence which can be presented and which lead to the conclusion that this key human motive is essential for really successful entrepreneurial performance and hence undoubtedly contributes to economic development.

The first line of evidence came from technical laboratory and theoretical work in psychology started over twenty years ago. This essentially linked high N/A in individuals to certain types of action characteristics in laboratory studies. That is, men with high N/A preferred to take moderate risks and did better when they were operating under a condition of moderate risk. They were very eager to get feedback on how well they were doing. They insisted on personal responsibility for undertaking certain actions, and they were generally more innovative. Some of these results seemed self-evident after we identified them because obviously a moderate risk situation is one in which a person interested in achievement is most likely to feel a sense of personal accomplishment.

If a person works at too easy a task and he succeeds, he will not get much achievement satisfaction. If he works at too difficult a task, he is not likely to succeed. So he is also not likely to get achievement satisfaction. You can use a utility model to predict that in fact a person with high N/A will generally like the moderately challenging tasks that are most likely to give him achievement satisfaction. Similarly he is interested in feedback because only if he gets feedback does he know how well he is doing. The particular concern is to improve performance or to improve what was done before. There is continuous concern for improvement, for personal responsibility, and for innovation. If the person does the same old dull routine, he cannot feel any achievement satisfaction; he therefore varies what he does. It seemed to us that a man who had these characteristics—the man with high N/A—should be a good entrepreneur.

The second line of evidence came from studies of achieving and non-achieving societies. We made longitudinal studies of a single country over several centuries and cross-national studies using two periods in modern times. We observed that a high concern for improvement or for doing well, as measured in popular literature, was associated quite generally with rapid rates of economic growth, both historically and among modern nations.

The third line of evidence came from the well-known historical fact that minorities have played a key role in most economic development. We demonstrated that these minorities in a number of cases were higher in measures of the N/A characteristic. Groups like the Ibo in Nigeria are measurably higher in the need for achievement and have experienced significantly greater economic success, as is well documented in an important monograph by Robert Levine (*Dreams and Deeds*). Certain groups of Jews in the West have demonstrably higher N/A and have certainly played important economic roles. In Ethiopia, it was of interest to discover that the Gurage, a small tribal group with a long-standing reputation of being successful economically also scored high on our measures of N/A.

Fourth, we have found quite generally, that businessmen scored higher on N/A than professionals of comparable education such as lawyers, doctors, priests, and bureaucrats. And within the business group, those who had higher N/A tended to do better in the sense of being promoted faster.

The fifth line of evidence was provided by a Swedish economist working in Finland. He checked to see whether firms headed by men with higher N/A in fact grew faster as we were predicting they would. The results indicated that this was the case. Among sixteen very comparable knitware firms in the private sector those that grew more rapidly were headed by men with higher N/A.

The sixth line of evidence came from our attempts to develop N/A in businessmen, a task to which I have devoted the past eight to ten years. We argued that, if N/A was so critical to economic growth, perhaps the best demonstration of its importance would be to develop it in businessmen whose subsequent activity could be followed. If we could inject some N/A into businessmen, their businesses should grow more rapidly than for comparable groups of businessmen not so trained. Our efforts in this area are summarized in a recent book, *Motivating Economic Achievement*.[1] This book reviews our efforts, largely in a few small cities in Andra Pradsh in India, in training a number of small Indian businessmen and comparing them after training with similar businessmen who had not been trained. In brief, the training consisted of five to ten day intensive courses of the management seminar type. We really adapted this approach to the particular situation despite our prejudice as psychologists that actually you could not change anybody fundamentally without some kind of an excavation technique delving into his past history and remaking his personality slowly. But we found that at least with adults and with matters such as this we could move rapidly into teaching them everything we knew about the kind of motivation, its action characteristics, and its thought characteristics. We told participants that N/A seemed to be critical for entrepreneurial success and I must say the businessmen were quite happy to learn these things as they felt it was relevant to their work.

The results of these experiments, which were hardly more than pilot experiments, although since conducted with hundreds of businessmen in several different countries, are, on the whole, encouraging. We found that those who were trained doubled their rate of activity based on some simple economic output measures. For example, using measures of new capital mobilized for investment, in two years after training we found the amount to be Rs. 12,000 on the average for the untrained group compared to Rs. 24,000 on the average for the trained group. One of the easiest things to check were employment figures. These were of greatest interest in India because they are concerned about rural unemployment. Generally speaking, in the two years after the training the untrained group added three new jobs per man per entrepreneur while in the trained group it was about six. Again training in N/A doubled the rate of economic activity.

Later, with support from EDA (Economic Development Authority) in

Washington, we repeated this experiment in McAlister, Oklahoma, and in Washington, D.C. Again the results were amazingly similar in widely different situations. In southeastern Oklahoma, in a small town with very few resources and above-average unemployment, training businessmen in N/A more than doubled the number of new jobs created by the trainees. In training black businessmen in Washington, D.C., we again doubled the new jobs created, although the level of new jobs per businessman was much lower in Washington than in Oklahoma. The untrained group in Washington added, on the average, one new employee per year per businessman trained, while for the trained group it was two a year. In Oklahoma, however, the results were more like two and five respectively.

An Approach to Training

We feel that N/A training was quite an extraordinary kind of investment for government because greater tax flows would come from the increased incomes and profits resulting from training. In this way the investment could be paid back to the government in a short span of time. The training is so inexpensive that after about seven months, tax flows generated could be paid back to the government in a short span of time; after about seven months, tax flows generated cover the initial investment. The bureaucrats in Washington, however, were unreceptive to such arguments. It is clear to me that economy, efficiency—even making money—are not good reasons for allocating public funds. The EDA had invested in this program as a kind of demonstration to repeat what we had done in India and to show, on a more substantial scale, that the training would work. I think we demonstrated it, but the demonstration had very little effect on policy makers.

What should government policy be? The head of a planning section, or something comparable in an underdeveloped country, who believes in the effectiveness of N/A training is immediately faced with the problem of credibility. As a general rule the results of our investigations are not readily believed as operable or applicable to the practical problems at hand.

If it were possible that our findings were accepted, what would be done and what use would be made of this information? Firstly, there are certain actions which should *not* be undertaken. The International Labor Organization (ILO) became very interested in the N/A training approach. They have eighty management training centers all over the world, and their idea was, "let us get McClelland to write a manual on how to do achievement motivation training and we will plug it into these ILO management training centers—the instructors are all hired anyway and they might as well give achievement motivation training as well as accounting." This is a very simple straightforward and obvious idea, but I do not think it will prove very effective.

I think the problem with the international bureaucracy is that training is pretty much divorced from the way economic activity is currently being performed in a given country. It is very much divorced from the structure of opportunities and from the planning structure. There should be a design to combine the training administratively with the planning and opportunity structures.

Motivation training is being undertaken in Uganda where we have trained a number of Ugandians using these techniques. They have proved widely acceptable. We have trained successfully in Tunisia with illiterate Arabs, as well as in India and Uganda. The training does not require a higher degree or advanced education. All it requires is usually somebody with a little business experience. The trainee should be an adult. We do not feel that you can start with children; we prefer somebody with a little experience.

Finance and N/A Training

My specific recommendation is that N/A training would probably fit best in the operations of a development bank or a similar financing institution. There are several reasons why this is perhaps the best place to introduce the training.

Firstly, it is valuable to the bank because most banks feel that capital is a scarce resource and this would be a way of getting more for the outlay. For example, in India others have estimated that for every rupee invested from public funds you mobilize about a rupee in private funds for investment: a one-to-one ratio. It is very easy to calculate that you cannot develop India at that rate. In our case a rupee of public funds invested in N/A training would have yielded 20 rupees in private investment and this is a much more feasible multiple for producing economic growth.

Secondly, banks have a natural interest in not having their loans defaulted, and N/A training should reduce the default rate and increase the regularity with which the money is raised to repay loans. Thirdly, there is an advantage to the training institution in that it gets feedback on the effectiveness of its training. One of the things that we teach in motivation training is one of the best validated psychological "laws"—that performance must be linked to rewards if it is to improve. This seems a very simple-minded idea, but behaviorists have been proposing it for years. The average professional—which includes the average teacher, business school professor, or arts and sciences professor—really has no knowledge of how effective his training is. Nor does he get paid or recognized in terms of his effectiveness. To my knowledge no study has ever been done, and perhaps it can never be done, to see whether, for example, a program at the Harvard Business School is a worthwhile investment of the student's time, in the sense that those who go there perform better afterwards than an exactly comparable control group of men and women who did not go there. Management training is also one evaluated in terms of cost-effectiveness. Lots of consulting firms give beautiful courses which elicit much satisfaction from management but produce little evidence that the investment in training actually pays off. I believe that we should check to see whether training pays off. Groups like the ILO management training center have no easy way to obtain information on whether N/A training is effective. It would require extra money—a research budget—which they do not have. A bank, on the other hand, would be able to get information of effectiveness of N/A training, at least in some minimal form, because it knows how promptly its loan is repaid and may get additional information on business performance over time.

Thirdly, I think these five to ten day seminars can be used for selection and guidance in actually making the loans, or in shaping the plan for which the loan is to be given, because one of the things that N/A training requires is goal setting for the next six months to two years. This goal setting exercise is worked out with the help of instructors and others in the seminar toward the end of the seminar. I think this improves the quality of the man trained, the way he thinks about things, and his capacity for planning correctly. To the potential businessmen, training in a bank and development institution has advantages also because it gives access to credit and inside economic information that otherwise would not be available.

We found two totally separate economic activities in India: there was a big centralized *planning* operation largely run by economists with highly competent technical people, and then there was an *implementation* operation conducted by quite different groups of people. A similar situation existed in Ethiopia where the United Nations supplied planners, at high expense, who wrote careful economic plans and ended up with what they call bankable projects, which were then put on the shelf. The government is supposed to take the projects off the shelf and get somebody to "execute" them. From a psychologist's point of view and, as a matter of fact, from everybody's experience, this doesn't work terribly well. In Ethiopia only about one-third of the bankable projects, planned at great expense, were even initiated in the first five year plan. On the other hand, in India we had businessmen, small to be sure, making plans of their own in terms of things that they wanted to do.

It is extremely important for the future of developing economies to bring the planners together with the "executers"—like these small businessmen. Having the N/A seminars conducted by development institutions and banks would be one way to do that. I am not opposed to economic plans and planning practices; I just think they need to be brought together with actual individuals who will carry them out. These people should participate in making or modifying the plans. A business plan has to be tied to a man's motivation to carry it out, and we can use N/A seminars to accomplish this objective.

Notes

1. D. C. McClelland and D. G. Winter, *Motivating Economic Achievement* (London: Collier-Macmillan, 1971).

5 Institution Building and Administrative Problems of Developing Economies

William J. Siffin

A simple syllogism is embedded in many of the strategies, plans, and programs aimed at development. It goes like this:

1. Organizational capability and effective organizations are essential to development.
2. Organizational capability and effective organizations are lacking in poor countries.
3. The establishment or enlargement of organizational capability and effective organizations is therefore necessary if poor countries are to develop.

This logic has impelled a vast amount of action and expense—with variable and often unsatisfying results. What has been wrong—the logic, or the efforts to apply it?

Pristine generalities about the essentiality of organization leave much unsaid, but it might be uncharitable for one whose living is linked to that logic to assail it. So let us turn to the question of applications. Here, too, we find some fairly simple and straightforward postulates. According to one of them: Western organization-and-management expertise and praxiology are largely aimed at "system improvement"; they do not necessarily fit the circumstances of so-called developing countries when the need is often for "system building." This type of statement can be made in various ways, all with the same import: that many of the organization-and-management problems of developing countries have been inadequately handled because they have been ill conceived.

"Institution building" is both an argument to this effect and the tender of an alternative perspective, one that promises a better view of organizational development problems common to poor countries. This perspective has acquired a certain acceptance. Properly understood, it offers utility within limitations that need to be noted. So it is worth considering what the IB view holds, how it can be used, what its limitations are, and what prospects appear to exist for shoving back those restrictions.[1] What follows concentrates primarily upon institution building as a means for identifying and attacking administrative and management problems.

The views expressed in this paper do not necessarily represent those of the U.S. Agency for International Development.

75

The Idea of an Institution

The term "institution" can be defined and used in many ways. In the institution-building perspective, an effort is made to treat the term conceptually and to apply it only to a certain category of structures: the formal, purposive, authoritative structures we commonly refer to as organizations.

The nub of the idea of "institution," when that idea is elevated to the level of concept, is suggested by two other words. One is "value." The other is "pattern." Thus an "institution" can be taken to mean a pattern—or a set of interrelated patterns—of activity which manifests, and is ordered by, some values or value orientations. In this view, any such pattern exists and persists, or within boundaries is modified, because it *ought to be*—because it is perceived as proper and acceptable by those involved.

This sort of statement can be made in various ways. Thus, C. J. Friederich, among others, has referred to an institution as "a relatively stable collection of roles."[2] The *rules* that govern the roles and the relationships among them are some kinds of "common sentiments" or "value attitudes" reflected and embedded in such things as "norms." The language that attempts to express these ideas can be tortuous and complex, depending partly upon what the spokesman is trying to say as well as upon the linguistic format to which he is habituated. But if he is talking or thinking systematically about an "institution," he is referring to a set of patterns of activity involving more than one actor and one action, guided by some sense of "how it properly ought to be."

All organizations have institutional qualities. The real questions in the IB perspective concern the kind or content of those institutional qualities. Max Weber's classic images of organizations posit a certain value orientation to be served and explore the compatibility of certain forms with certain norms. In his idealizing view, efficiency, rationality, and coherence of effort are prime kinds of norms to be institutionalized in the efficacious bureaucratic organization. A much more recent study of purposive formal organizations also emphasizes the institutionalization of certain salient kinds of norms. In doing so, the work illustrates the points at hand: that institutional qualities are acknowledged features of organizations, and that it is the particular nature of the norms that matters. James D. Thompson's potent and perceptive study of organizations presents propositions about behavioral tendencies within certain types of organization and begins many of them with the words, "*Under norms of rationality. . .*"[3]

If it can be argued that institutionality is a rather commonplace quality of organizations, then what is novel about the institution-building perspective? The essential answer is rather simple: Because persisting patterns of behavior are sustained by value orientations, it does not follow that these will be the ones posited by such scholars as Weber or Thompson. Efficiency, responsibility, and rationality may be, often are, scarce qualities in the organizational milieu of the poor countries—to say nothing of the wealthy ones. The institution-building perspective acknowledges this by implication. Explicitly it asserts the need to establish and sustain organizations that do in fact comply with efficiency, responsibility, and rationality norms and that also have a significant impact upon their environments—an impact consistent with an even higher level of rationality which the organization exists to serve and promote.

In institution-building terms, then, the problem of organizational development is one of creating relatively stable collections of roles to serve certain specified aims effectively and efficiently, in circumstances where this sort of thing is not an established way of collective action. IB asserts that the organization-building problem is essentially one of getting the right values accepted and implemented, not only within an organization narrowly viewed, but within at least some parts of a field of action that comprises the organization plus interacting elements of its environment. This problem formulation opens up new vistas, and challenges the conventional assumption that established Western technique and technology will more or less inevitably be replicated in non-Western settings, if only the appropriate skills and knowledge are made available to the actors within an organization. From the IB perspective, organization building is a lot more complicated than that.

Institution Building as Problem and Praxiology

The institution-building perspective is really two things in one: a definition or characterization of a type of problem, and the rudiments of a praxiology for dealing with the type of problem. In its latter aspect, the IB perspective tries to offer guidance for those who want to do something about a situation viewed as an institution-building problem. The appeal of this problem-praxiology formulation stems from the fact that it promises a better response to the organization-building need that is so common a part of developmental concerns.

IB Problem Formulation

To sum up the institution-building problem formulation, it is the establishment of organizations that will:

a. have different performance characteristics than those common to the organizations in the environment—i.e., will reflect and respond to different kinds of norms;
b. produce new kinds of outputs;
c. gain acceptance for those outputs;
d. produce new forms of behavior in the environment that contribute to developmental goals, and finally;
e. continue to innovate over time.

Obviously, in many circumstances, institution building is a rather heroic type of problem. It transcends the conventional or traditional Western organization-building perspective in at least two ways.

First, it posits as the core of the problem getting new kinds of norms or values built into systems of action—the rationality norms of Western purposive organization, for example. The IB view asserts that the establishment of Western forms does not automatically produce the operation of Western norms. From this it follows that the organization-building problem cannot inevitably be solved by setting up certain kinds of rules, procedures, and formal structures. Position classification, PPBS, and formal organization specifications may be necessary techniques or organization building for development, but in the IB view they are not sufficient methods.

The second basic premise of the institution-building perspective is that an institution encompasses much more than a formally specified, bounded organization: It also includes relevant elements of that organization's environment. Together organization-plus-environment compromise a system or pattern of action, and this constitutes the institution. Thus the IB perspective covers more than the conventional Weberian-type conception of an organization—the conception that has often been implicit in organization-building responses to development aims. In the IB view, the environment is seen as indifferent and even hostile. Relevant elements of that environment are not "coded" or programed in ways compatible with the desired functioning and impact of the organization. In other words, the appropriate norms and values are not much institutionalized.

IB as Proto-praxiology

Institution building, having posited the problem, sets out to offer approaches to a solution. First, it stipulates the importance of achieving a solidarity of values inside the organization, so that members will behave in ways that are on one hand appropriate and on the other at variance from the organization's normative ambience. Thus, institution building is in some ways subversive, and the beginning of a solution to the IB problem must be a degree of commitment to both the goals and the norms of the organization.[4] The organization must also obtain both support and acceptance in its environment; and to that end, it must establish an appropriate set of "linkages," or appropriate transactional patterns. To do this, those who would build the organization must know what to look for, and where to find the environmental elements with which linkages must be established. The IB perspective classifies these linkages generally in functional terms. It does not say that the linked elements must all accept or behave in accordance with the desired norms; it does posit that some clientele group must come to accept the organization's goals, and thus in some sense share in its value orientation. Other linked elements of the environment may be only important because, whatever their norms, they are supportive of the institution being built.

As praxiology, the IB perspective does have its limitations. The perspective offers only general prescriptive statements; it includes no precise formulas and indexes of effective action. Its prescriptive statements are somewhat analogous to the observation that "If a plane is flown too slow, it will stall and fall." People who fly planes would like very much to know: "What is *too slow*?" Institution building can only reply, "That depends." Yet it can be argued that this is better than not knowing about stalling at all. As praxis, institution building is heuristic rather than prognostic. Utopians will object to this limitation, but not those practitioners who find their help where they can and settle for what seems promising.

In its concern with getting resources, obtaining an acceptance of output, and generally managing crucial external relationships, the IB perspective opens up useful questions and enables people to think practically about strategy and tactics. These, of course, are the sorts of things that operators have been thinking about ever since the days of Esau and Jacob and before. To the extent that the perspective can help people mobilize this sort of knowledge, sort it out, begin to specify the conditions under which particular tactics do apply, it can make a valuable contribution.

For example, institution builders learn that one way to acquire some of the legitimation needed by an appropriately institutionalized action-system is to "buy in" to the environment. Sometimes, for example, the prospective organization can be presented as "all benefit and no cost." This tactic is used in many different arenas of action, from foundations seeking to change academic programs within and among universities to international agencies aiming to promote family planning. In many cases, this is one of the easiest and most alluring ways to penetrate a partially hostile environment. Yet this sort of tactic does not necessarily guarantee that the desired outcome will be gained. In the New Testament world of organization building and entrepreneurship, latter-day Isaacs have learned how to convert the Esau-Jacob game into a different sort of exploitation. So, the tactic of penetration-by-purchase must be linked with other forms of intervention, to appropriately socialize, coopt, and otherwise induce commitment and support.

"Technology" is a useful general label for one set of sometimes available institution-building tactics. Technologies have their own institutional features, although most technologies must be organized or enacted in structures whose institutional qualities are not merely technological. Technologies have several sorts of appeal. They are "modern." They have power; or, more precisely, they offer the promise of enhanced determinate capacities of various kinds. And the installation of a new technology is frequently an irreversible sort of change, a development whose legitimacy quickly transcends challenge.

Another important tactical term in the praxiological lexicon of institution building is "autonomy." Autonomy—not total but "sufficient"—is one way to deal with a hostile or indifferent environment. It involves the relatively closed system of inputs, conversion activities, outputs, and consumption, within boundaries protected against unconstructive exogenous interventions. The world is full of examples of such structures, ranging from self-sufficient regulatory networks that use governmental powers to both control and protect a clientele, to the professionalized elite elements of public bureaucracies.

The institution-building perspective offers an intriguing vehicle for collecting, assessing, and perhaps refining tactical knowledge about organization for social change. Not all of this has to come from the particularistic accounts of pragmatic practitioners. At the level of tactics—and perhaps even of strategy—it is, in principle, entirely possible to harness to the service of institution building a lot of fragmentary knowledge uncovered in the study of sociopolitical processes. In fact, the prospective potency of institution building as praxiology will depend upon just this sort of thing.

One of the areas in which there is a substantial latent convergence of the IB view with another knowledge string is the field of management. As James Thompson and others have noted, it is operationally useful to conceptualize an institutional level of management—a level at which the prime function is monitoring the relationships between an organization and its environment —in short, the function of institutional maintenance and development. If, indeed, the prescriptive vision of institution-building's concern with innovative organization is to become a real venture, it will have to give praxiological attention to this function, and to the factors that appear to affect tendencies toward innovation in organizations.[5]

In institution-building terms, management also faces the complex challenge of internal leadership that can elicit appropriate supportive and innovative dispositions. There is a vast amount of literature bearing on this subject, some of which offers at least the promise of utility. Institution building offers a format within which such knowledge can be selectively and judiciously mined for tactical guidance.

The Primary Limitation of the IB Perspective

As praxiology, institution building is more potential than potent, but the real limitation of the perspective does not lie in this. The limitation—and the danger—of the IB view lurks in its use as a problem definition.

During his adventures in the Nixon administration, Daniel P. Moynihan once wrote that "There is no more foul lie than an ill-defined problem." That aphorism has particular pertinence to developmental concerns. As noted, the institution-building perspective is a general prefabricated problem definition, one found appealing by a variety of practitioners concerned with administrative issues in developing countries. When the old formularies of organization building fail, people search for a better formula. Many of these people work under suppositions that the problems they attack have been properly defined in the first place—as organization-building problems, for example. Yet the IB perspective does not specify the terms and conditions of its applicability as a problem definition. Insofar as problem solvers take their problems as given, this may not matter very much. Solution rather than definition is the aim of their game. But for those who would strategize concerning economic and social development and the organizational imperatives of these things, the larger question is the more important one: Under what conditions are institution-building problem definitions and approaches likely to be sound? To return to the initial paragraph of this article, under what conditions is organization building approached in institution-building terms likely to be illogical?

If the IB problem definition is to be pursued, refined, and effectively applied, more needs to be known about this. Only part of that knowledge can come from institution-building analysis. Such analysis could, however, add some valuable qualifiers to the problem-defining aspect of the prospective. In the absence of such qualifications it remains all too possible that efforts of the sort that failed in the past, because organizational forms could not be transferred to new environments, will in the future fail because institution building is not the appropriate definition of the developmental problem either.

Notes

1. For a discussion of some of the limits and potentials of the perspective see: William J. Siffin, "Institution Building as Vision and Venture: A Critique," Ch. II, in Joseph W. Eaton, ed., *Institution Building and Development* (Beverly Hills: Sage Publications, 1971).

2. Carl J. Friederich, *Man and His Government* (New York: McGraw-Hill Co. 1963), p. 71. Among the most influential conceptualizers of the term institution is Talcott Parsons. See *The Social System* (Glencoe: Free Press, 1951), and *Structure and Process in Modern Societies* (Glencoe: Free Press, 1960). For other explications that involve conceptualization in terms of value and pattern, see Harold Lasswell and Abraham Kaplan, *Power and Society: A Framework for Political Inquiry* (New Haven: Yale University Press, 1950), and Philip Selznick, *Leadership in Administration* (Evanston, Ill.: Row Peterson, 1957).

3. James D. Thompson, *Organizations in Action* (New York: McGraw-Hill Co., 1967).

4. Philip Selznick, op. cit., is the immediate source of this element of the IB perspective.

5. Along with Thompson, see Robert C. Solo, *Economic Organizations and Social Systems* (Indianapolis: Bobbs Merrill, 1967). Also H. I. Ansoff and R. G. Brandenburg, "A Language for Organization Design," *Management Science*, August 1971. See, too, *The Conditions for Success in Technological Innovation* (Paris: OECD, 1971), esp. p. 58ff.

The Less Developed Entrepreneur?

Wayne G. Broehl, Jr.

Entrepreneurship is one of those highly respected words of the developed world, conjuring up, as it does, visions of active, purposeful men and women accomplishing a wide variety of great endeavors. Yet entrepreneurship is clearly not a quality that is uniformly distributed. Rather, it is found in some people in substantial amounts and in others in small or negligible amounts. Some countries, for example, appear to have a higher overall entrepreneurial thrust than others, and a few analysts have even been so bold as to attach entrepreneurial indices to various countries, rating them according to the degree of such qualities present in the country. Similarly, there seem to be significant variations in these qualities among various groups within a given country.

Thus differences around the world can be described on the basis of tribal affiliation, on the basis of native versus immigrant groups, on the basis of power holders versus deviant groups, on the basis of geographical areas of origin (as in the often misunderstood notion that temperate cultures are more entrepreneurially oriented than tropical cultures). In some complex combination, these and other factors accumulate to make up the total set of personal values that result in one person being an achiever and another a follower or a holder to the status quo.

A better understanding of this complicated business of comparative entrepreneurship could have a high payoff for mankind. The widening disparities between the rich and poor around the world and the heightened concern about bringing low achievers into a state of higher achievement make this concern one of the most relevant of contemporary development questions. Why are some of the countries in the less developed world in this state? Why does there seem to be a lack of achievement motivation among some of the various disadvantaged in today's life (as in the U.S. ghettos)? Are there ways to identify the seemingly non-random factor that is involved and then proceed to develop educational methods that will upgrade the achievement and entrepreneurial skills of the disadvantaged? Can the key ingredients of entrepreneurship be isolated, identified, and built into a formal system of training? If the answers to these questions are "yes," then the importance of the study of entrepreneurship turns out to be critical.

Who Are These Entrepreneurs?

The first step is to straighten out the definition. This turns out to be more than just a semantic tiff. Today, many analysts seem to confuse true entrepreneurship with other closely related endeavors. Some perspective can be gained by returning to one of the early seminal thinkers in this field, Joseph Schumpeter,[1] whose concepts have renewed relevance for today's study of comparative entrepreneurship.

Schumpeter starts with that necessary abstraction of the pure model, "equilibrium." Into this equilibrium an entrepreneur intrudes. Central to his intrusion is a critically important Schumpeterian concept, the introduction of a "new production function." This term is not used in its narrow sense but includes any one or more of the following:

1. The introduction of a new good with which consumers are not yet familiar or a new quality of good.
2. The development of a new method of production—one not yet tested by experience; this does not have to be a new discovery—it can also be "a new way of handling a commodity commercially."
3. The opening of a new market—new to a given country, regardless of whether it has existed before in other locations.
4. The acquisition of a new source of supply of raw materials or half-manufactured goods (again which may have previously existed in another location).
5. "The carrying out of the new organization of an industry, like the creation of a monopoly position (for example, through justification) or the breaking up of a monopoly position" (Schumpeter's own wording).

These new production functions are brought about by the purposeful action of an entrepreneur. This entrepreneur belongs to a distinct class—he possesses more than an ordinary degree of ability to visualize possibilities in these unproved commodities, organizations, methods, markets. The first entrepreneur in a given field must overcome all sorts of obstacles, and he succeeds in smoothing the way for others, producing a wave of business activity that runs its course and finally exhausts the opportunities for gain. From this feature of cyclicality Schumpeter developed a complex theory of business cycle activity.

Who are these entrepreneurs? It is hard to distinguish them, says Schumpeter, not because of lack of precision of their special contribution, but by virtue of the difficulty of finding the person who actually engages in this entrepreneurial activity. No one is an entrepreneur all the time, and nobody can be only an entrepreneur. This follows from the nature of the function—it must always be combined with other activities and lead to other activities.

Entrepreneurship is not the process of invention itself. While entrepreneurship is a highly creative function, it does not rest solely on original creativity. An invention sometimes does not lead to innovation (and vice versa). Both economically and sociologically, they are completely different conceptual functions.

The entrepreneur may be, but need not be, the one who furnishes the capital. It is leadership rather than ownership that matters. Therefore, risk bearing is no part of the entrepreneurial function. The capitalist bears the risk, the entrepreneur brings about the changed production function. The two may, of course, be done by the same man and often are in today's business world. Probably, there is no single more confusing distinction today than that between entrepreneurship and risk taking. The entrepreneur clearly takes great personal risk in the process of bringing about the introduction of often traumatic and upsetting new production functions. The entrepreneur may also put his own money into the new project and thereby become a financial risk taker. The first type of risk taking is directly involved in entrepreneurship; the second may or may not be present.

Today, in both the developed and the less developed world, there are men who are building great business empires and personal fortunes by clever financial and marketing skills. Some of these skills are entrepreneurial skills but not all of them. A man can develop a new corporate entity and bring it from nothing to a multimillion dollar entity by using primarily the skills of existing production functions. It may be a new firm, to be sure, and in this sense satisfies one of the criteria Schumpeter identifies with entrepreneurship. Still, in an ongoing sense, this man might not be an entrepreneur but rather a successful "trader" or a "professional manager." Today's professional manager may be a highly creative person, exhibit many special skills that bring about corporate growth and yet not be an entrepreneur. Likewise, a corporate "trader"—such as the new breed of men building the great conglomerates—might be a financial wizard or a marketing genius and in the process build a great institution from scratch; yet he might not exhibit entrepreneurial skills. It is likely, however, that he would be an entrepreneur, for a good many of these conglomerates are new production functions.

In sum, the Schumpeterian entrepreneur is a special kind of creative person—creative in bringing about growth through the process of making changes in "production functions." It is this special quality of change—innovation—that sets the entrepreneur apart from all others.

In a generalized sense, there are all sorts of "entrepreneurs" all over the world today. A man may be called an entrepreneur when he is a speculator for himself or, in the jargon of the market, "an operator"—aggressive, out for himself, making great strides in his personal fortune. However, most of these people are not entrepreneurs in the sense we use it here. They do not bring about a new production function. They are not creative in the sense of Schumpeter's concept of innovation. Using the word "entrepreneurship" in this loosely generalized sense is probably a disservice.

Less Developed Entrepreneurs?

There is ample evidence that some special features separate the entrepreneurial climate in the LDCs from that in the developed world. There has long been the belief that there is a shortage of entrepreneurs in the less developed world. In essence, this is a special form of the famous "vicious circle" pattern: the country starts out low in entrepreneurship and therefore does not have a steady flow of entrepreneurial talent upward from the lower middle class to create new businesses. The country is then thrown back to recruiting its business leaders primarily from the upper classes where both the capital and the opportunity to go into business exist. Unfortunately, these men are often conservative in ideology, believing strongly in family solidarity. Their approach is to set up family firms into which their sons are expected to go irrespective of talent or motivation. Even the small group in the country from the lower and middle classes that might have high achievement motivation find it difficult to get a start in business. There is a double negative effect—a short supply of entrepreneurial talent, compounded by serious roadblocks in utilizing the few men available.

In the past, the process of sending executives from the less developed world—often family-firm sons of little motivation and talent—to business schools in the developed world all too often misfired. As Harvard psychologist David McClelland described the situation:

Too often educators assume that an executive from a developing nation sent for a course in business administration really wants to do a good job in the sense that his concern for achievement is very high in his hierarchy of motivations. Actually, his chief concerns may be different. He may want to spend a year or two in the United States, because it is pleasant to live there, and it will give him great prestige when he returns home. His education abroad will put him in line for a key position in the government when he returns. It may even put him in touch with foreign aid officials in the United States with whom he will be negotiating contracts in the future. At the very least, it will teach him about the American mentality and thus help him in his dealings with Americans in the future."[2]

McClelland was even less sanguine about the potential brought about by management training courses when they were conducted in the less developed country. Though the courses might contain all the concepts and techniques used in the established professional schools, they appeared to McClelland to be only partially effective in increasing achievement motivation. His reasons for this are important: "On balance, exposure to partial educational influences which might increase N Achievement [McClelland's shorthand acronym for the achievement motive] does not appear to be very effective when unsupported by 'ideological conversion' of the total group in which the experience occurs. There is even some evidence that such partial exposure to other 'foreign' value systems may be destructive and even lower N Achievement."

The New Breed

Today, this seems an overly narrow view. Certainly it might have been an accurate characterization in much of the less developed world a half dozen years back. But something new is happening. A new business elite is surfacing throughout the less developed world.

To be sure, the dominant percentage of this group may still come from the upper classes, but there is a fundamental difference in the value structures involved. Carrying the earlier life-cycle story one generation further, the grandson is now coming into his own. His father had been sent abroad to an Ivy League college in the United States or its equivalent in Western Europe, probably to take a generalized course of study in the liberal arts. He ended up in the family business and brought back with him the same conservative philosophy that had typified past generations of his family.

Now it is the 1970s and his son is deciding his own career pattern. He, too, decides to go abroad to college. Here, though, a significant change takes place. The son decides to enter either a graduate business school or one of the management-oriented engineering schools, almost always located in Western Europe or the United States. No longer is he an indifferent student. He is caught up in the professionalization of the school and thrown together not only with nationals of his own country but students and businessmen from all over the world. In particular, he finds himself associated with other young men from the less developed world with the same highly professionalized career goals. While at the professional school, he is particularly fascinated by the "information revolution" he sees unfolding before him. He quickly learns computer methodology and applies to it sophisticated quantitative skills.

He is ideologically converted by the sheer believability and spirit of professionalism in the school. When he and perhaps several dozen or more of his friends return to their country, they can begin to have real influence in shifting the ideology of their more conservative fathers. Of course, if a significant segment of these men opt not to return to their countries, none of this is applicable.

When this young man returns to his country, he carries with him a new "bag of tricks" that few in his country possess. Sometimes, he tries to apply his newly acquired sophisticated techniques in situations where the environment is not ready for them (there may be computers in his country but not the requisite programing technology). Thus some slippage may intrude. Nevertheless, his way of thinking—his new "life style"—makes him a different breed of entrepreneur, not only in contrast to his father but also in contrast to his total business community.

Whether the indigenous professional management training institute can bring about this same ideological conversion within the country remains to be determined. Modest evidence in such schools as those in India suggests that some of this ideological conversion may be coming about already, and the pace of overcoming resistance to change is increasing rapidly. For the moment, however, this must remain an unsupported inference.

This new business elite beginning to permeate the developing world holds forth great promise as a potentially strong, progressive force. Central to the kit of abilities of a great many of these people is their ability to search out, grasp, and utilize the massive amounts of new information becoming available around the world. There are even a number of new firms specializing in the discovery economic opportunities and the sale of this information to others. This is a special form of "information revolution" occurring in the less developed world. It is built heavily on the discovery of new information (new, at least, to the less developed world) rather than the manipulation and analysis of existing information. There is an important new element that must be added to the Schumpeterian and other typologies: the "information entrepreneur."

The "Information" Entrepreneur

Because of the wide-ranging information revolution occurring around the developed world today, the character of entrepreneurship has changed. Today, the traditional boldness and audacity of the entrepreneur must also be supplemented by skill in scientific methods, in theory building and in problem solving. A fair proportion of today's entrepreneurs are "entrepreneurial analyst-scientists," and those who are not sometimes have such skills on their staff.

Thought-provoking ideas in this area have been advanced by a Harvard economist, Harvey Leibenstein, especially his concepts of "gap filling" and "input completing."[3] Leibenstein suggests that entrepreneurship should be defined in a new way, that it is necessary to isolate "routine" entrepreneurship—those activities involved in coordinating and carrying out a well established, growing concern in which the parts of the production function in use are well known and which operates in well established and clearly defined markets—from "new type" entrepreneurship. Generally, the production function is considered to be clearly defined, fully specified, and completely known. Where and to whom in the firm this knowledge is supposed to be available is never stated. In point of fact, there are great gaps of knowledge about the production function, and, to the extent that it is not completely defined, the entrepreneur must in some way make up the deficiency. This brings about the situation of "new type" entrepreneurship, where not all the markets are well established or clearly defined and/or in which the relevant parts of the production function are not completely known. It is this latter quality that one especially needs in the less developed world, for they are "obstructed, incomplete, and 'relatively dark' economic systems."

The reason this is so is that there are important gaps in the flow of the necessary information. Some information is simply not yet available in the particular economy. Often the information needs are subtly political in nature rather than straightforward economic information. In the politicized entrepreneurial environments of many less developed countries, business advantage is often sought (and realized) through political institutions no less than in the interactions in the market itself. This is the reason why the large, extended-family connections often give the vested oligarchy so much power.

Gaining requisite information is more difficult in the less developed world. Complicating the problem is the fact that individuals and groups (firms) generally will not work as hard or as efficiently in searching for new information and techniques, nor is this effort maintained at a constant level. Therefore, there is a considerable degree of slack, the persistence of which implies the existence of a special form of entrepreneurial opportunity— that of "gap filling" and "input completing." Most often there is a minimum quantum of information necessary to get a particular project off the drawing board. Often the gap in information prevents the reaching of this threshold. In the less developed world, says Leibenstein, this special entrepreneur is the one who does most or all of these functions:

1. seeks and discovers economic opportunity;
2. evaluates economic opportunities;
3. marshals the financial resources necessary for the enterprise;
4. makes time-binding arrangements;
5. takes ultimate responsibility for management;
6. is the ultimate uncertainty or risk bearer;
7. provides for and is responsible for the motivational system within the firm.
8. searches for and discovers new economic information;
9. translates this new information into new markets, techniques and goods;
10. provides leadership for the work group.

It is the special information dimensions implicit in this list, "the gap-filling and the input-completing capacities," that are the unique characteristics of the entrepreneur. These are the truly scarce talents. One finds a few entrepreneurs in the less developed world who connect different markets, are capable of making up for market deficiencies and create or expand business organizations. It is this special kind of entrepreneur who is the key individual in the less developed world.

Only a few indigenous entrepreneurs will be operating at this level in most less developed countries. The numbers of men coming back to a given country each year with advanced degrees from U.S. or European business schools are pitifully small. Nevertheless, they remain probably the most significant single group of nationals in terms of current patterns of entrepreneurship. There are, of course, large numbers of other men who never leave the country but still become first-rate entrepreneurs. Historically, they were very often strongly influenced by what Peter Bauer and Basil Yamey call "the foreign entrepreneur."[4] As they point out, there is an emulation pattern that follows upon entry of a foreign firm into a less developed country. Foreign entrepreneurs foster local entrepreneurship both directly by providing training and experience to employees who later strike out on their own and indirectly by creating demands for services and other collateral activities.

Enterprise Interrelation

Foreign enterprises can rarely be wholly self-sufficient and need to turn to local enterprise for various kinds of help. Bauer and Yamey note an important constraint in this process: "The role of foreign enterprise and of immigrant businessmen in enlarging the scope for indigenous entrepreneurs is rarely clearly appreciated. Instead, in political discussion, the tension tends to be focused almost exclusively on the indisputable fact that some foreign or immigrant business firms compete with some local enterprises. The complementary nature of their activities with those of the vast majority of the local population is overlooked."

In the past, this hostility toward the foreign entrepreneur was frequently visited upon the national entrepreneur as well. Past patterns of entrepreneurship in many less developed countries have left much to be desired with respect to social responsibility and concern for the country as a whole. The new entrepreneur-nationals should not only alleviate some of these antagonisms; they should also prove to be important factors for emulation. Local small entrepreneurs will be needed by these new entrepreneur-nationals just as the foreign entrepreneur needed them. The entrepreneur-nationals may also bring to the business process the best of thinking about the long-range nature of business enterprise and the need for meeting the demands of a variety of interest groups. A good case can be made that new businesses being operated on a basis of long-run profit maximization have more efficacy from the standpoint of the "emulation-pull" than do "high-profit low-volume," anti-social business firms so typical of past patterns.

Information entrepreneurship can surely be learned. Leibenstein is modestly hopeful: "It may be difficult to train people to spot economic opportunities, but it is possible to train them to assess such opportunities once perceived. Similarly, managerial skills are trainable. . . ." This leads Leibenstein to an interesting conclusion about the supply of entrepreneurship in the less developed world, namely, that "while entrepreneurship may be scarce because of a lack of input-completing capacity, some entrepreneurial characteristics may, in fact, be in surplus supply. That is, they are unused simply because of the lack of input-completing capacity." As a consequence, even a small change in the reduction of market impediment and an increase in information may turn an entrepreneurial scarcity into a more adequate supply.

Up to the present, the generation, sorting, and evaluation of information in the less developed world has tended to be limited. Yet it is easy to see how these lacks could be remedied once the need is perceived. One does not have to envision mass shipments of computers to the less developed world (though this is coming more rapidly than many had guessed). The computer in the developed world can generate information rapidly and make it available to the rest of the world with far less difficulty than has been true in the past. Lying behind the computer is a whole range of new quantitative techniques and information-systems concepts that have revolutionized the analytic art.

Further, it is not just the quantitative information that fills gaps and completes input. Obviously, one cannot "grow" an entrepreneur merely by filling him up with new information and the methods of treating it. Along with the information that the son obtained in the graduate business school, he was also caught up in a pattern of motivation and development that characterizes these schools. In McClelland's terms, he was treated to a concentrated dose of the "language of achievement" developed out of an achievement-oriented pattern of "goal setting" and pushed along by "cognitive supports" and "group supports," all designed to foster the notion of high-caliber entrepreneurship and high-caliber professional management.

Thus a whole range of qualitative information and conceptual thinking makes the entrepreneurial cycle "complete." For example, such hoary teaching techniques of the U.S. business schools as the case method are startlingly and unsettlingly new when applied to business education and executive education in the less developed world. In the early 1960s, the Graduate School of Business of Columbia University embarked upon a substantial cooperative teaching program with the University of Buenos Aires in that latter city. Several of the professors participating in this program took with them the case analysis and role-playing methods they had used in their classes for a number of years. According to the Dean of the Business School at the University of Buenos Aires, ". . . Professors Walton and Broehl used a role-playing technique in 1962 that was completely new to the faculty. This plus other innovations brought from Columbia (case studies, panel discussions, essay assignments, et cetera) generated a minor revolution in teaching methods which spread to other departments of the faculty."[5]

One need not be perhaps as pessimistic as Leibenstein even in the training of people to "spot" economic opportunities. Can there not be put together an imaginative combination of McClelland's achievement-motivation training, the case method and other devices of the business school and some of the work of the "sensitivity/creativity training" groups to provide a form of entrepreneurial training that will inculcate an information-search concept? If Vilfredo Pareto is right that there is an inherent "instinct of combination," then man's eternal search for the materials of combination would seem to make the training for this perhaps difficult, but nevertheless realistic and possible.

Within the special dimensions of "information," three identifiable "characteristics" of entrepreneurship as they are applied in the LDCs seem to be prominent.

The Early Risk Taker

There is a special quality about risk taking as it is applied in the less developed world. This is the "earliness" of the actual risk taking. When one moves from the developed world to the less developed world, there is a clearly identified time lag in a great many of the happenings between these two worlds. What is "old hat" in the developed world may well be startlingly new in the other. If one thinks of the risk-taking process for a given innovation as having a time-dimension continuum, one can see that the first innovators in the developed world have the highest incidence of risk. Those who adapt this particular innovation along the time line clearly have less. Then when the innovation is carried across to the less developed country, there is a discontinuity in this time line. The incidence of risk moves back up to a level perhaps even higher than the first application in the developed world, as the first new entrepreneur in the less developed world begins to apply the innovation within the confines of a new and less certain situation. Thus, there is a vernal quality about the first entrepreneur for a given innovation in the less developed world. It becomes important to identify that person who has the special entrepreneurial skills and to recognize the point on the time continuum that is "Spring" in the less developed world.

The Information Adaptor

The reason this entrepreneur is the first to recognize that "Spring" has arrived in the less developed country is due in considerable part to his unique ability to pull together the necessary information—necessary in the context of the less developed country. He is Leibenstein's "gap filler" and "input completer." The reason that he is able to fill these gaps and complete the various kinds of inputs is in part that he has the requisite information to do so. He may well be the first person in the less developed country who recognizes the special situation where it has become possible to apply a developed-world concept in the less developed country. He is a discriminating empiricist, using a derivative process. His ability to adapt and combine developed-world information for use in a less developed country allows him to be the early risk taker.

The Mock Innovator

The central point will become even clearer in adding the third member of the trilogy. Sometimes an innovation in the less developed world is a true innovation in worldwide terms. The wheat and rice miracle seeds are in this category. Yet one is hard pressed to think of equally significant innovations in industrial management. Innovators have come from the less developed world but have made their innovations within the confines of the developed world.

Nevertheless, there are a whole host of other types of innovations in the less developed world. These are the innovations of adapting a developed-world concept (itself probably an innovation at an earlier stage) to the special constraints, difficulties and opportunities of the less developed world. Without denigrating the importance of these special adaptations of earlier innovations, they may be termed "mock innovations." James Berna, in his study of entrepreneurship in South India, called these men "humbler entrepreneurs," as distinguished from the "Schumpeterian innovators" of the developed world. This interpretation misses a crucially important distinction, namely that an innovator operating on a "small" scale does not necessarily make the process "humbler" than that same application in the developed world. Seen in these terms one can think of dozens of examples of highly innovative adaptations. An excellent example of the combination of these three special characteristics may be found in the operations of the International Basic Economy Corporation (IBEC).[6]

Moving into Latin America right after World War II with a number of projects never before tried in that environment, IBEC was an early risk taker. It introduced large-scale, centralized food marketing through supermarkets in Venezuela, Peru, and Argentina. The company insisted on the widest possible dissemination of information about its development techniques and projects and encouraged emulation. In just about everything it undertook (food processing, housing, mutual funds), the technology was known. IBEC's "mock innovation" was to adapt the technology to Venezuela, Peru, and Argentina.

It seems apparent that these special characteristics—timeliness of activity, use of information, adaptive innovation—are not only unique but critically important to the process of entrepreneurship in the less developed world. A better understanding of them will enhance our knowledge of the particular dimensions of innovation and entrepreneurship in the developing countries.

Notes

1. Joseph A. Schumpeter, *The Theory of Economic Development* (Cambridge: Harvard University Press, 1934).

2. David C. McClelland, *The Achieving Society* (Princeton: Van Nosstrand, 1961).

3. Harvey Leibenstein, "Entrepreneurship and Development," *American Economic Review, Papers and Proceedings,* May 1968.

4. Peter Bauer and Basil Yamey, *The Economics of Underdeveloped Countries,* Cambridge Economic Handbooks (Chicago: University of Chicago Press, 1957).

5. William Leslie Chapman, "Experiment in Argentina: The Bitter and the Sweet," *Columbia Journal of World Business,* Fall 1966.

6. Wayne G. Broehl, Jr., *International Basic Economy Corporation* (Washington: National Planning Association, 1968). See also my article summarizing this study, "Company with a Cause," *Columbia Journal of World Business,* July-Aug. 1968.

7 Management Information Systems and Social Planning

Ida R. Hoos

The management information system, long regarded as a vital element in big business operations, has also become a *sine qua non* for government planners at all levels, from local to national. A manifestation of advanced technology, and variously acclaimed as a powerful tool, management information systems are bought and sold extensively not only for use in the United States but for application abroad as well. The export of information experts, especially to developing countries where lack of progress is largely attributed to technological backwardness, constitutes a little-explored but fast expanding dimension in foreign relations. With McKinsey & Company, Booz, Allen & Hamilton, Inc., and Arthur D. Little, Inc. deeply involved in the management of British and European industry and public services, and serving such clients as the Shell Petroleum Combine, British Broadcasting Corporation, and the Schweppes Beverage Company, the importation of brain power from abroad is by no means an exclusive phenomenon of less developed economies.[1] A real danger lies in the possibility that nations not ready for such high powered ministrations may be beguiled into providing the foreign market sought by the rapidly growing "think industry."[2]

Through an interesting confluence of historical trends, technological developments, and political circumstances, public officials the world over have come to believe that their mandate is to plan rationally and that utilization of computer hardware and software will supply them with a wealth of data that will enable them to achieve efficiency of operations and effectiveness of programs to an extent never before attained. Dangled before them is the prospect of planning procedures imbued with a measure of scientific precision long sought but beyond reach until now.

Considerable amounts of time and money have been invested in the development of management information systems. Not surprisingly, this has swathed them in an aura of indispensability. The designers, vendors, and tenders extol their enormous capabilities. Their buyers, public officials, visible and vulnerable to attacks of extravagance, follow the sage advice of Abraham Lincoln to cleave all the closer to a bargain when it is bad. In a world of interests so vested, the voice of candor may not be altogether welcome, but it should be given an audience lest the panegyrics over the "rational approach" and "powerful tools" so dominate the social planning scene that only the adherents and advocates will be heard.

In order to understand the status of information technology and to assess realistically the state-of-the-art, reference must be made to its historical development, for the management information system is a link in a chain reaching from the electronic data-processing system of the past to the cybernated government of the future. The management information system concept in current usage will be considered as a separate entity and as a component of a larger system. Here, we will investigate the premises on which information systems have been accepted as adjuncts to the public decision-making process, the way in which they have been conceptualized and rationalized, and the uses to which they are being put. The experience of a number of public agencies provides illustrative case materials. Whether the information system stands as an independent unit with its own goals, objectives, costs, and benefits, or functions as part of a larger system, the assumptions embedded in it reflect the philosophical orientation and methodological predilections of its designers. Particular attention, therefore, is focused on the role of the expert. The evolution of the systems expert, and especially the information systems expert, as a profession constitutes a fascinating chapter in the sociology of occupations. Finally, we concern ourselves with the social implications of advancing information technology, for it is increasingly apparent that the individual's right to privacy is being undermined by dossiers and data banks that make possible cradle-to-grave surveillance—all rationalized by the cult of efficiency that once dominated business practices and now pervades government.

Developmental History of the
Management Information System

Electronic data-processing was introduced into the business world in the mid-1950s amid a fanfare of promises for faster record keeping, better data flow, and reduction of clerical personnel and concomitant costs. In other words, the primary objective of office automation was improved management of information. Fifteen years and two computer generations later, the promises are still unfulfilled. Records move faster but their volume has increased exponentially. Data flow has become a flood requiring the services of technical specialists. While content and environment of office work has undergone metamorphosis, electronic data-processing has not delivered the promised economies. If greater efficiency of operation has been achieved through EDP, the savings have not yet reached consumers or taxpayers.[3]

Clearly evident, by contrast, has been the effect of EDP on organization structure. No longer a service function within the organization, EDP assumed a determinative role, affecting division of labor, personnel requirements and practices, work techniques and scheduling, communication up and down organizational and across departmental lines. The demands of the system imposed radical changes on decision patterns and operating methods with attendant shifts in procedures and bureaucratic relationships as information came to be regarded as the corporate nervous system.[4] Its handling of information became the prime criterion by which a company's efficiency was judged. The bank that compounded interest daily or the company whose up-to-the-minute inventory assured prompt service enjoyed immediate advantage over its laggard competitors. It was thus that management of the *information* became, in the business milieu, equated with and tantamount to management of the *enterprise*. Management of information has remained an important function, but with growing sophistication of hardware and software, the mode has changed to management *by* information. The science of management—to a great extent the science of managing information—is basically the science of managing *by* information. These prepositional changes, which occurred through the fusion between management science and computer technology, brought about the Management Information System (MIS).

Books on the MIS abound;[a] the business journals are full of articles on the subject; high level and higher-priced how-to-do-it seminars have proved to be a bonanza. And yet, a curious situation persists: (1) there is no generally accepted definition of an MIS; (2) there is considerable doubt as to where any exists; and (3) there is a conspicuous lack of realistic cost/effectiveness measures for MIS. Definitions range from the hardware concept, which concentrates on mass-random access storage and on-line terminals, to software, which emphasizes methods and language for the organizational data base, to management usage, which constitutes the purposes for which the MIS is to be designed. In the absence of firm definition, distinctions between an MIS and an advanced information system, such as an airline reservation system, become unreliable. According to one authority, far fewer MISs than the sales and professional literature would have one believe have been put into operation, and evidence of failure and poor performance is common.[5] As for cost justification for the move from conventional data-processing to the technologically advanced and very expensive realtime system with all the requisite hardware and software, calculations of payout potential seem largely to be based on faith.[6]

Nonetheless, the notion of the MIS has persisted, and in the business world, MISs have gained acceptance and prestige beyond their accomplishments. The aggressive sales campaign promises of computer manufacturers and software salesmen have not been realized. Clerical costs remain high; paper problems plaguing management persist. A survey by the Research Institute of America of the experience with computerized systems of about 2500 companies is cited in the once enthusiastic columns of *Fortune* as indicating uncertainty as to appreciable return from even the routine operations. One author described widespread "misguided euphoria" and found considerable confusion over the meaning and purpose of the MIS.[7] Systems reviewed in a survey reported in *Dun's Review* were criticized for inundating managers with data, the overabundance of which obscured what might have been important.[8] Lack of demonstrable results is deplored by an experienced data-processing specialist, who cites "development times, agonizingly long costs woefully underestimated, systems ill-conceived and poorly designed"

---

[a] The Society for Management Information Systems and the MIS Research Center of the University of Minnesota jointly sponsor an MIS bibliographic project. To date, over 2000 citations have been compiled.

as some of the common shortcomings.[9] Estimates of investment in electronic systems vary. The *Fortune* article calculated that some 60,000 computers had been in use during the preceding fifteen years and that in 1969 alone over $7 billion would be spent on computers and peripheral equipment with an additional $14 billion for operating costs.

Despite vast expenditures by U.S. industry, there is no unequivocal evidence that managers have been helped to make better decisions nor even that profits have been favorably affected. Herein lies an anomaly, in that the clever calculations of computers have not been able to establish a favorable cost/benefit ratio for themselves at a time when this kind of justification is mandatory for survival in many budgets. For all the alleged sophistication of record keeping, computerized systems have yet to provide a convincing accounting for themselves. International conferences have been devoted to the problem of ascertaining the precise advantages of computerized information systems, but no method of quantification has emerged.[10] A Rand study, reported by Sharpe, brought wildly inconsistent ratings when only two systems were compared.[11] With precise quantification the main *raison d'être* for computerization, this lack is all the more flagrant; such information would be of vital interest not only to the organization paying for the system but to the purveyors of computers and software in substantiation for their long iterated claims.

Cost-cutting, having eluded capture through computerized quantification, cannot legitimately occupy a place in the credit column. Neither can the claim of labor-saving, justified only by spurious comparisons with hours of manual work during the gaslight era. Ever since the introduction of electronic data-processing, the proclivity to sorcerer's apprenticeship has been apparent. Notwithstanding occasional accounts of disenchantment, however, a mythology has evolved, and each succeeding generation of information technology has been enveloped in it—the computer, the electronic data-processing system, and now the management information system.

The MIS in Government

When the management syndrome moved into the public sector, it carried with it all the inherited myths of methodology. To the rationalization that big government is big business, there was appended the ready corollary that application of management science would insure efficiency and economy of operation. Consequently, as in industry, information became the crucial factor, for did not better management of information assure better management of the enterprise, i.e., more expeditious achievement of its organization objectives? Assumptions, even though sometimes proven questionable, became ground rules for public planners: (1) if officials had more information, they could plan more rationally, make better decisions; (2) more and faster moving information would improve operations, perhaps cut costs, surely provide better service; (3) efficiency of operation is identical with service to community and society; (4) this efficiency can best be achieved by application of more sophisticated technology to the accumulation and utilization of data; (5) a technologically advanced information system is a highly technical matter requiring the specialized skills of an "information expert."

A ready welcome awaited the advent of sophisticated management science techniques into government operations. Adoption of "smart business practices" was especially desirable to public officials in whom the role of whipping boy had instilled a deep-seated inferiority complex. Perennially the target for accusations of organizational rigidity and bureaucratic ineptitude, public officials at every level from county to Congress have demonstrated readiness to welcome any technique, however untried and untrue, that might lend their operations the semblance of order they prize but rarely possess. Aware that public planning has neither the pretension of being a science nor the excuse of being an art, managers have eagerly accepted as consultants those who would tell them what to do and as experts those who would tell them how to do it.

Similarly susceptible to the claims made for the techniques and technology of planning, especially the information system, are the developing countries which seek to emulate their prosperous and industrialized neighbors. They, too, suffer from feelings of inferiority. Their paralyzing red tape, long the butt of international humor, their "backwardness" a stigma in a world where "progress" has a special connotation, many small countries have sought the services of the jetset consultants. The authoritativeness of this flying squadron of mini think tanks often increases in direct proportion to the distance traveled from home. Small entrepreneurs, whose base is a Cambridge, Massachusetts, or Falls Church, Virginia, post-office box, search out contracts on their own or through the Agency for International Development, their "expertness" a movable talent defined more by the task to be funded than by demonstrated skill and experience.

In so favorable an environment, here and abroad, the notion of the management information system as the first logical step in the rational planning process and as an indispensable component of any planning model flourishes. The wide-ranging purveyors of systematic planning have easily convinced their clients that the information gathering phase is crucial. In fact, this is how they set about their business and often, finding it so *gemütlich* an activity, they never move beyond it to another stage. And precisely because the information system may eventually become the basis for policy formulation or program evaluation, it is indeed crucial. Far from being routine and mechanical, its design demands searching inquiry, for there are presuppositions and assumptions embodied in its conception. These ultimately determine the uses to which it will be put and its validity as a tool in social planning, where the current vogue is to rely on cost/effectiveness ratios to devise programs in the short run and social indicators for anticipating long run needs. The vital input in all the calculations is data, supplied, gathered, generated, and dispersed by the system.

The Ends and Means of Information Systems

The primary item for consideration in the information system is, of course, information. *Information* is used interchangeably with *data*, generally confused with *facts,* widely associated in the military with *intelligence,* and even endowed with an honorific correlation with *knowledge*. We who live in a computerized age have become receptive to the inherent authority of "hard facts," and the more the better. We accept the "data bank" as indispensable to public planning and even imbue it with a virtue never accorded its predecessor, the dreary and dusty archive, the dead record office. The allure of a bank full of data, available on command, is practically irresistible to any public administrator, who may not know what he needs to know and hopes that technology, in typically cargo cult fashion, will deliver it.[b]

Despite protestations to the contrary, usually in professional journals far from the scene of application and action, the notion prevails that information, data, or facts exist in a pristine state and need only to be captured to serve as input. Herein lies an interesting transformation in the etymological concept of *data*. *Datum*, the singular form, is, by origin, something *given*. *Data*, the plural form now used, signifies something *gotten*. When recognized as such, *data* are divested of the qualities of objectivity and accuracy and become subject to scrutiny. Who gathers the data, for what purpose, how to be used and how interpreted become questions that must be answered. And they elude simple, obvious answers, for embedded in them is the fundamental unresolved issue of the relationship between management science and MIS. Known as the chicken-or-the-egg debate, disagreement centers on which comes first—the information system or the total organizational model. Some argue that the MIS should be determined by the requirements of the larger system it is to serve. Others maintain that no meaningful model for the total operation can be developed without the MIS. It is difficult to find in either position much clarification for and improvement of the present state-of-the-art. By definition, data are the system's input and, therefore, once engineered into it are virtually unassailable.

Lacking theory, which Kaplan reminds us determines the way in which we conceptualize facts,[12] and experience, through which, Churchman tells us, we learn that data cannot be accurate and objective, especially in the context of social policy,[13] information technologists have, nonetheless, demonstrated a proclivity to approach the design of any information system as though the desiderata were purely technical, with input the unequivocal data waiting to be gathered and processed and subsequently to provide the basis on which decisions can be made no matter what the field—urban develop-

---

[b] A modern version of the cargo cult has been attributed to inhabitants of a remote Pacific Island, used during World War II as a base. The natives, having observed that at certain intervals, after landing space was cleared, great silver birds descended from the skies and unloaded bountiful supplies of food, clothing, blankets, etc., continued to hack out runways and await similar landings long after hostilities had ceased and the planes' missions were directed elsewhere.

ment, health, education, or transportation. Conceived in this fashion, the information system has its own objectives, *viz.*, efficient storage and access of data. Its own costs and benefits can be rationalized economically, even though, with the exception of important seminal work within a narrow framework by Stigler,[14] no rigorous methods for analysis and calculation have been developed.

Generally deprecating the "information explosion," some economists have, perhaps unwittingly, provided impetus to it. Arguing for the economics to be achieved through mass production, for example, Marschak uses the telephone directory and the Sunday newspaper to justify what might be considered an oversupply of useless information.[15] In the case of each, the user is forced to purchase information sources that would be wasteful to him were they not so cheap. This kind of "economic" reasoning has provided the information technologist with ready-made justification for ubiquitously sweeping into the system anything that can be weighted, counted, or measured, almost irrespective of social costs and consequences and certainly without regard for the intangible, non-material considerations. Here, then, is the making of an archive approach, more burdensome than older forms, in that discrimination of that which is pertinent and useful is made difficult by the very system presumably designed to ease the tasks of the users. How to keep the congested channels of information free from spurious traffic is a problem studiously avoided in this frame of reference. It would be unfair to economists to imply that their profession limits its interest to narrow cost calculations of information. Marschak expresses the need for attention to what he calls the "socially optimal allocation of resources to informational goods and services,"[16] but he does not elucidate how this can be ascertained. Determination of what is "socially optimal" is a value judgment, outside the ken and beyond reach of the tools of the economist. Even if such calculations were possible, they would be of little help in assessing the social costs and benefits of information systems as a means of achieving improved government planning.[17]

Accepted as a necessary step in the rational planning process, the information system is often conceived as though it were itself a kind of problem solving mechanism. This phenomenon occurs whenever and wherever lack of information has been singled out as the root problem. For information technologists, this occurrence is, not unexpectedly, almost universal; for public planners, whose profession has no real discipline upon which to draw, it is a convenient form of optimization or at least satisfying. Under such circumstances, the information system is treated as a self-contained entity, with its own *raison d'être*, its own justification. It operates as a surrogate for, rather than an adjunct to, intelligent social planning and program management.

Substantiation for this high regard for and unique function accorded to information can be found in the usual places—the hard selling campaigns of vendors of hardware and software, the thinly veiled sales presentations by "experts" wherever associations meeting in serious professional deliberation provide a podium. Less easily dismissed is such high level endorsement as that which is embodied in the widely disseminated report, *Technology and the American Economy*. Because of the prestige of the National Commission, pronouncements contained in its various studies have been assured a receptive and generally unskeptical audience. It is useful, therefore, to review in detail the recommendations vis-à-vis information technology so as to ascertain precisely what urban planners mean when they talk about data and information systems. In one section of the report, the following statement appears:

Information (interpreted data) is the universal common denominator in metropolitan problem solution; it is the core of any metropolitan growth-management scheme, guidance mechanism, booster campaign, or research effort, both private and public. A tremendous range of metropolitan-oriented undertakings, private and public, operational and research-development oriented, founder for lack of data.[18]

Specifically, basic data were required for "increased community understanding" and "development of appropriate management tools" and were identified as "people, automobiles, workers, levels of skills, housing available, number of unemployed, salaries, taxes, routes traveled, structures, land characteristics, utilities *ad infinitum*." Noteworthy here are the lumping and dumping of categories and characteristics, a not uncommon practice of planners who are vague about their needs and prone to rely on some consulting information expert to formulate the problem for them. As noted elsewhere, dependence on the technical specialist introduces a certain bias and influences the entire operation thenceforth. Lack of meticulous attention to detail is reflected in items poorly conceptualized, such as *structures, automobiles*; overlapping classifications, such as *people, workers, number of unemployed*; and downright nonsense, such as *routes traveled*.

On the supposition that in this gallimaufry of discrete and heterogeneous items, routes traveled referred to transportation, we should mention that a "never-mind-the-why-and-wherefore"[c] approach to information gathering seems to be especially prevalent in this field. A typical example is the activity of the (San Francisco) Bay Area Transportation Study Commission, created by the California State Legislature and instructed to prepare a master regional transportation plan. BATSC set about its task by acquiring data from a multiplicity of sources and through a variety of techniques, including aerial photography. Personnel using origin-and-destination Home Interview Survey methods covered a 5 percent sample of the region. Gathered were items about household characteristics, such as rent and income; individual members, such as education and employment; and notes on each trip taken by members of the household, such as origin, destination, purpose, and mode of travel. Persons responsible for this data-gathering exercise list as their accomplishments a total of 10 million pieces of information, converted to 1.5 million punch cards, which were then recorded on 1100 reels of magnetic tape which require one and one-half hours of IBM 7094

---

[c] Song from Gilbert and Sullivan, *H.M.S. Pinafore*.

time to reprocess. This is the end of the road. Interpretation of what added up to a three-million-dollar agglomeration of indigested data has not occurred, probably because the simple question, "So what?" was never asked or satisfactorily answered. Transportation in the area remains the same hit-or-miss affair, with no signs of improvement. In like fashion, vast sums of money continue to be allocated, not only in California but elsewhere in this country and abroad, to transportation information systems that are ultimately an accumulation of data that get us nowhere.

By strange coincidence that defies explanation at this point in our experience, the data-gathering step which in transportation leads to a dead end becomes, in other areas of public planning, so useful a device that it is imbued with a purpose *sui generis*. Especially in the field of public welfare, management-minded officials eyeing mounting costs of aid to the poor have been prone to concentrate on the information flow and paper-processing as though this would in some way reverse the trend toward higher welfare budgets. Far more palatable politically and much less likely to stir up protest than overt acknowledgment of the handicapping social and economic conditions which contribute to dependency, reorganization of the information system has become a popular bureaucratic diversion.

The advanced information system is made an end in itself by assigning to information handling procedures a key role in the so-called "welfare problem." Proposed information systems hold out the promise of correcting the failures and deficiencies of the entire welfare system. For example, an information system designed for Nassau County (New York) stated as its ultimate objective: "to aid the Welfare Department in optimizing programs, services, and resources to satisfy community needs." Specifically, an information center proposed for the County was intended to accomplish the following:

1. establish Welfare Department goals and objectives;
2. define information requirements and managerial techniques;
3. establish information requisition requirements;
4. establish information distribution requirements;
5. develop information feedback techniques;
6. develop decision-making techniques; and
7. develop computerized information system.[19]

Items (1), (2), and (6) are especially noteworthy in that they presume that it is the function of an information center to establish welfare department goals, define data requirements, and prescribe managerial techniques. Review of the proposal indicates that its architects assumed that Nassau County's poor people's lot would be materially improved by computerized information flow. In point of fact, a County Planning Commission study revealed that the poverty-stricken inhabitants of the area suffered not because their records did not move but because they personally could not. Recipients of public assistance, with an annual income of less than $5000, were trapped in pockets far from jobs and without adequate transportation facilities.[20]

In California, a team of consulting information experts hired under a quarter-of-a-million dollar contract to provide "technical management" and "tools for program implementation and evaluation" in the state's multi-million-dollar welfare system selected the Aid to Families with Dependent Children program as the object of a system study because, they said, this portion of the welfare system "offers some hope of reduction using the techniques of systems analysis."[21] With orientation no better than their grammar, the experts focused their activities on the information handling, as though it, and not socio-economic factors and statutes regulating eligibility and amount of aid, accounted for the huge welfare load. Juxtaposed against a detailed list of shortcomings of present data-handling methods was the following set of "design goals" for a proposed information system:

1. to increase the flow of information in order to promote better service and management control at all levels;
2. to minimize administrative cost and improve efficiency;
3. to provide research and statistical data for state planning and program evaluation purposes;
4. to provide inquiry service for questions which cannot now be anticipated;
5. to provide fiscal data for state planning and evaluation purposes;
6. to provide a system sufficiently flexible to accommodate changes in needs, volume, policy, and/or data demands; and
7. to reduce the cost of operations below that of the present information system.[22]

Even cursory reading of this table of particulars shows that it is a stretched-out serialization of overlaps and contradictions rather than a thoughtful paradigm. Items (1) and (2) are variations of the same theme; the information system proposed could not accomplish them *and* (7). Assuming that it could achieve (1) and (2), it would accomplish (1) only if "cost of operations" were construed to mean unit cost, a figure as nebulous and elusive here as is a workable definition of "efficiency."

Item (3) implies that the welfare system itself generates the information needed for program evaluation and particularly for planning. This is not the case. State planners are greatly interested in the population-at-risk, i.e., those persons who are likely to become dependent. The "research and statistical data" that might be helpful in making projections should be sought in areas other than the welfare system per se.

Another important factor affecting the need for public assistance is, of course, the state of the economy. The ripple effect of sharp cutbacks in employment are felt in local welfare offices. For example, retrenchment at Boeing hit not only Seattle's aerospace engineers but the grocers and gardeners, cobblers, and house cleaners who provided them with services. Persons marginally employed and precarious financially had to apply for relief. Another factor affecting welfare expenditures is the statutory regulation of eligibility. For example, a Senate Committee reported widespread deprivation and recommended expansion of Food Stamp programs and other forms of public assistance.[23] Legislative changes redefining eligibility often account for steep rises in relief rolls and reflect what actually may be the political response to the urgent problem of persistent poverty in an affluent society.[24]

Information generated by planned systems may not always be as useful for projections and predictions as data already in use in smaller quantities. Whenever design by quantity is the rule, the danger of fallacious causality increases. Research for "program evaluation purposes" must deal with the determinative aspects of the broader social fabric. Because there are no accepted criteria for judging the efficacy of any given program, value-laden judgment based on personal, social, and political bias prevail, notwithstanding the trappings of technical jargon to cover this fact. Moreover, since only machine-processable data are "usable," it may well be that essential information is systematically ignored. The importation of information experts to amass data indiscriminately has frequently caused the research function to be bypassed and become atrophied, while the true nature of the information becomes subservient to political manipulation. The mass production of information and the propensity for profuseness of detail irrespective of relevance are in many cases heuristic fumblings in the hope of stumbling upon something worthwhile.

Much of the money spent on elaborate EDP systems in welfare programs fosters the defensive bookkeeping intended to keep poor people honest. The adoption of a different philosophy, with less emphasis on possible fraud, would substantially lower paperwork and costs of administration. A more "efficient" system in public service, however, which was based on a sophisticated information system, would most likely increase operating costs because investigative and certifying procedures would be speeded up and more eligible persons located and placed on welfare rolls.

Information Systems as Components of Larger Systems Designs

The information system is often conceived as a component of a larger system design and suits the flow chart technique. In practice, however, this kind of information system suffers from most of the defects discussed earlier, with a few added. Presumably, this type of information system should be a means toward attaining the objective of some larger system. The fact that it does not contribute to attaining the objectives implies either delusion or deception, neither of which is consistent with the "rationality" touted as an attribute of these powerful decision-making tools. What we find repeatedly is that, although portrayed as a box with arrows going in and out and upward, the information system becomes the dead end of the system; nothing happens beyond it. Perhaps this occurs because the information system with its ubiquitous appetite has consumed all the resources. But observation of information experts at work in unwonted areas suggests another explanation. Comfortable in the data-gathering and processing phase, they and their techniques are simply not adequate for the larger tasks ahead. The goals that looked good and easy on paper elude the simplistic approach that flowed so smoothly across the fold-out charts in the proposal. Faced with the reality, the technical experts fixate on the information system; it becomes the total system. There are a number of areas of public concern that have provided happy hunting grounds for such information experts. Environmental protection, with land, seas, and the sky the limit; delivery of medical service, with nationwide federally sponsored programs a bonanza and special programs such as drugs and alcoholism a bonus; land use and management from Tennessee to Timbuktu —these are only a few instances where "rational planning" stopped at the information stage, where profusion brought paralysis.[25]

Consider as an example, the Criminal Justice System, the ultimate objective of which, we are informed, is "control of crime." To that end, the State of New York "took a major step" in allocating hundreds of thousands of dollars of special federal grants in addition to large sums from the Law Enforcement Assistance Administration, under the Safe Streets Act, to create the New York State Identification and Intelligence System (NYSIIS), described as the nation's first statewide criminal justice information system, and the prototype for many to follow.[26] Its director justified it by claiming that a large portion of the problems of law enforcement and criminal justice were due to "cultural lag in embracing the scientific method" and would persist until the "dawning of the age of science in criminal justice."[27]

NYSIIS, attributed to the "special vision" of New York's Governor Rockefeller, who saw in it the realization of a "grand dream,"[28] houses more than seven million criminal and non-criminal fingerprints and corresponding identification and case history data, available for dissemination through a communication network to some 3600 law enforcement agencies in the state. The NYSIIS computer prints out "rap sheets" at the rate of 1040 lines of record information per minute from a computerized data base containing over 400 million bits of criminal history information. This cornucopia and speed, according to statements from the Public Relations Office of the Burroughs Corporation, which had a hand in the design, have helped make significant strides toward the two-fold ultimate objectives of NYSIIS; viz. (1) improvement of criminal justice administration through systematic computerized information sharing, and (2) protection and enhancement of civil liberties.[29]

A New York State Controller's report, issued December 11, 1971, exuded less enchantment. A five year audit of NYSIIS revealed that it inadequately protected individual rights, provided easy access to unauthorized personnel to search its confidential files, and maintained such slipshod security of its own premises that its most sensitive division, the Bureau of Organized Crime, stored its data behind doors the hinges of which were on the outside, and, hence, easily removable.

Aspiring to achieve a peaceful population through its own war on crime, the State of California engaged the services of Space-General Corporation to design a system for the prevention and control of crime and delinquency. A crucial item was to be "the development of an information system linking together various agencies of criminal justice and capable of evaluating program and system effectiveness through collection, storage, and processing of appropriate data."[30] The information experts' notion of "appropriateness" became immediately apparent: they regarded "criminals" as certain types of persons with characteristics that set them apart from the population at large. Disclosing the simple, closed-minded notion that crime is that which gets punished and the criminal, the person who gets caught, the analysts used the statistics of convicted offenders as the basis for their calculations. Culling records of arrests, they devised a Neo-Lombrosian taxonomy,[31] in which the crucial factors were sex, age, ethnicity, education, employment status, and geographical location. Their scrutiny of California correctional institutions revealed that the major portion of inmates were (1) male, (2) between 14 and 29 years of age, (3) black or Mexican-American, (4) poorly educated, (5) unemployed, and (6) from heavily populated, low income areas. Actually captured here was the shared haplessness that renders certain groups, under certain conditions, more susceptible than others to the embrace of the law. The poverty syndrome, mentioned earlier, i.e., poor education, lack of work, a slum address, a dark skin, were the accepted indicators of propensity for a life of crime, within the information technician's concept of the term. Ironically, the system of criminal justice designed on such a basis would catch those sectors which are least protected and most need protection from and by the law .

These cases show that the "system of criminal justice" turns out to be little more that a technological game of cops-and-robbers, with such crucial elements as "criminal" undefined and "justice" forgotten. Reliance on arrest and conviction records as the data base and as an index to criminal behavior revealed the naiveté of the system's designers. Authoritative estimates have placed figures on offenders, i.e., persons arrested, at 25 percent of total crimes known to have been committed.[32] The unreliability of crime statistics as indicators of criminal activity was underscored in a study submitted to the President by the U.S. Commission on Federal Statistics on December 10, 1971. Crime bulletins issued by the Federal Bureau of Investigation were criticized for increasing the reported volume of crime so as to justify expansion of its budget. Moreover, statistics show concentration of law enforcement activity rather than incidence of lawlessness. Much depends on the discriminatory enforcement of law, which is a manifestation of community tolerance, or on the enforceability of laws. The deeper social implications of the information system as a tool for social control are ignored in the zealous application of technology.

Information Systems and the Invasion of Privacy

With benefits calculated in terms of efficient operation and dollar and social costs submerged or ignored, information systems concerning everything and everyone have become the first order of business, public and private. Storage of records for rapid interrogation, search, and retrieval, through constantly advancing mechanization and computerization, has developed its own image, that of the "data bank." To the private organization and the government agency, the first in pursuit of its affairs, the second in discharge of its duties, the data bank has become a *sine qua non*. With management science rationalizing the data base and technology facilitating its utilization, there is quietly emerging a state of Big Brotherhood unprecedented in and unhealthy for a democratic society.

As the administration of public affairs becomes more encompassing and more complicated, the areas in which controls must properly be exercised expand. Government means regulation, and, in order to regulate, the government needs to know. But there is no clear-cut line of demarcation between the official liberty to know and the individual's right to privacy. With computerized files, the official appetite for information expands in Parkinsonian fashion. The inevitable result is the emergence in ordinary government affairs of a phenomenon once associated with spy stories and high treason. I refer, of course, to the dossier. So numerous have government dossiers become that they defy inventory, but mere mention of the highly compartmentalized agencies such as the National Security Agency, Defense Intelligence, Central Intelligence Agency, Federal Bureau of Investigation, State Department, and Atomic Energy Commission will suffice to suggest the magnitude of personal information compilation going on. The fact that the new FBI building in Washington, D.C., is designed with space and facilities for 200 million files, equivalent to one for every citizen of this country, the hap as well as the hapless, indicates the extent of electronic surveillance likely and the possible intent of that watchful agency.[33] A congressional investigation into the federal government's personnel practices resulted in disclosures of detailed dossiers, censure for perpetrating "one of the most subtle invasions of privacy,"[34] but no changes in policy and no protective measures. Four years later, with a different administration, a Senate Subcommittee on Constitutional Rights was still uncovering evidence that "intelligence collection" was widespread standard procedure and that, in the absence of regulatory mechanisms, almost any activity could become grist for some official mill.

Police networks stretched across the land link together and into the FBI not only items about car thieves, murderers, and drug peddlers, but also the biographies of persons observed to have participated in "civil insurgency." This broad category includes civil rights activity, community action, church group affairs, Earth Day observances, and even the political posturing of members of the loyal opposition. The American Civil Liberties Union has filed a law suit in Philadelphia, accusing the FBI of gathering information that relates exclusively to lawful and peaceful activities protected by the First Amendment, for the purpose of harassing and intimidating persons from exercising their right of free speech and association. On the ground that it might some day be called upon to quell violence, the army has deployed 1000 intelligence agents across the country to ascertain in advance "the wellsprings of violence and heart and nerve causes of Chaos." Special targets for the information gathering are peace marches and anti-Vietnam war protests, with the findings lying in a computerized data bank at Ford Holabird, Maryland. So great has been the Pentagon's preoccupation with domestic intelligence that Senator Ervin, chairman of the Subcommittee on Constitutional Rights, referred to it as "overskill" and recommended that the Army regroup, redefine their strategic objectives, and re-identify the enemy. "Under our Constitution, that enemy is not the American citizen."[35]

Assiduous tracking of the dissident in pursuit of peace and domestic tranquillity is not limited to the army, nor are peace demonstrations the only source of information. Until recently, the U.S. Treasury Department assigned some of its Internal Revenue Service agents to the task of searching the circulation files of public libraries. To be sure, the object of scrutiny was borrowers of books on explosives, but it is conceivable that official interest could embrace other areas, to the point where a serious threat to the individual's freedom to read might become involved. With police agents not necessarily known for fine literary discrimination, readers might find themselves on suspect rosters for a myriad of reasons. Depending on the political and social climate, practically any book or magazine could excite suspicion, and, with *Winnie-the-Pooh* now found to have deep psychiatric implication, Bemelman's Madeleine living in the dubious shadow of a "little house all covered with vines," and Mary Poppins and Dr. Doolittle considered sexist and racist, the range of innocuous reading becomes severely circumscribed.

Instead of guarding the privacy of the public, many government agencies make personal information available for a fee or without charge. Some departments charged with the duty of licensing pilots, ham radio operators, boat owners, etc., sell lists of the names and addresses to commercial users. State and local governments sell automobile registration lists, complete with license numbers, age, and type of vehicle, etc. In California, a Senate Committee buried a proposal to prohibit the Department of Motor Vehicles from selling driver license application information, a department spokesman having testified that the information was of value to private enterprise.[36]

The Internal Revenue Service, under pressure, has ceased to distribute the names of gun collectors, but still, under the Freedom of Information Act, sells for $140, or less than one-tenth of a cent each, the 143,000 names and addresses of persons registered under the 1968 Gun Control Act.[37] Withholding names, the Internal Revenue Service supplies data on comparative wealth of taxpayers, neighborhoods, and the like by zip codes to business firms.

Just as every military and civilian agency and every official bureau at every level is busily gathering and disseminating information about individuals, so also is every religious, social, and fraternal organization. Information about people is big business, too. H&R Block, Incorporated, which claims to prepare income tax returns for eight million Americans annually, was accused on June 30, 1971 by the Federal Trade Commission of using financial information supplied confidentially by customers in compiling lists of names and addresses to be solicited for life insurance, mutual investment funds, and other sales.³⁸ The Associated Credited Bureaus of America maintain credit files on more than 110 million persons. The publisher of 1400 different city directories advertises that for almost 100 years the company has been "in the business of keeping track of people— who and how many they are, where they live, where they work, and what they do." This big brotherly concern takes the form of city-wide, door-to-door canvasses in about 7000 American communities.

The National Data Center

Although the National Data Center, as conceived and recommended in 1965, was officially quashed in 1968, the history of the development and demise of this ambitious undertaking deserves attention, for it contains valuable lessons about the pervasive cult of efficiency, the high level naiveté that trained incapacity nurtures, and the fragility of social and moral defenses against the overpowering appeal of technology.

On the grounds that the present federal statistical system is both inadequate, in failing to do the things that should and could be done, and inefficient, in not performing at minimum cost, the Bureau of the Budget (Office of Statistical Standards) appointed a special committee to consider "measures which should be taken to improve the storage of and access to U.S. government statistics." Known as the Kaysen Committee, the Task Force examined the current system, found it widely decentralized as to function, duplicatory in operation, and enormously expensive. Their recommendation: a National Data Center, with responsibilities summarized as follows:

(1) assembling in a single facility all large-scale systematic bodies of demographic, economic, and social data generated by the present data-collection or administrative processes of the Federal Government, (2) integrating the data to maximum possible of the original information content of the whole body of records, and (3) providing ready access to the information, within the laws governing disclosure.³⁹

The official documentation of support for the National Data Center contained a report to the Bureau of the Budget, November 1965. Its conclusion reflects the advocacy position:

In sum, the main purpose of a Federal Statistical Data Center is to create a better integrated information network, for use by Government, industry, and the research community which will provide better understanding of interdependencies within our pluralistic society, leading to better informed choices among alternative policies and programs, and more effective program implementation.⁴⁰

The logic here was little better than the syntax; the assumptions were shaky, the conclusions unwarranted: (1) that the Center would improve the quantity, quality, or availability of reliable data; (2) that decision making in and functioning of government agencies supplying and being supplied by the Center would be improved by the centralization and integration of information gathering and processing; and (3) that the Center would be a cornucopia of worthwhile social and economic data for research purposes.

On the first point, the Task Force assumed improvement without devoting adequate attention to the quality control aspects of information flow. Nowhere mentioned were the statistical techniques needed if data were to be acceptable. The mere mass of data, without specific consideration of time frame, meaning of terms, sampling variations and major sources and amounts of bias would, according to the precepts of R.A. Fisher, have dubious value. One of his basic rules, *viz.* that the interpretation of data must be made in terms of the physical arrangements under which they were generated and gathered, was violated. The divorcing of the interpretation of data from the explanation of how they were gathered and processed has been seen as "a fatal defect" of computerized systems to date.[41]

Secondly, equating integration of information gathering and processing with efficiency was not only fanciful wish fulfillment, but counter to the currently approved prescription of decentralization as promising antidote to unwieldy government. Overlooked in the enthusiasm for "efficiency" was the intrinsic value of statistics gathering as a function within a given agency. With existing agencies assigned specific purposes by Congress, their respective data needs are bound to be dissimilar. Centralized, computerized filing, which would require reconciliation of noncompatible categories and coordination of the statistical function, far from reducing total processing costs and streamlining operations, would entail an elaborate and expensive system of liaison for communication and feedback. Worth pondering in this context are Landau's arguments in favor of redundancy, for the safety factors it supplies, and for duplication, for the flexibility it allows.[42]

Thirdly, the Federal Data Center was supposed to serve as a reservoir of worthwhile social and economic data. The chairman of the Task Force claimed that a beneficial outcome was "the real improvement in understanding of our economic and social processes . . . with all the concomitant gains in intelligent and effective public policy that such an understanding could lead to."[43] Inherent in this statement is the presupposition that the data residing in the Center would be useful as significant research material, that the missing ingredient for "improvement of our economic and social processes" is more information and that, understanding of those baffling processes somehow achieved, there would follow "concomitant gains in intelligent and effective public policy." This scenario conforms to the simulated, optimized world of the formal model-maker; the stuff and substance of intelligent and effective public policy demand far more than data manipulation.

The intent of the Task Force, made up of highly respected specialists in economics, statistics, and similar fields, was to improve public service by the utilization of information technology. If the conceptualization of this data bank had been the outcome of engineers' thinking, one might better understand the enthusiasm for efficiency through technology and the lack of sensitivity to the wider social consequences and implications. But, it appears, trained incapacity is not exclusive to any profession, and the Task Force was so imbued with the "payoff" that they neglected the social costs.

In response to public concern aroused by and expressed in Congressional Hearings, the chairman of the Task Force reviewed the recommendations for the Federal Data Bank and the arguments advocating it and stated a credo:

> . . . with full recognition that a government too feeble for the welfare of its citizens in some matters may be too strong for their comfort or even liberty in others, it is possible to believe, as I do, that the present balance of forces in our political machinery tends to the side of healthy restraint in matters such as these.[44]

Reliance on the political system to operate with "healthy restraint" may be just as naive and more dangerous than expecting to achieve efficiency through the technological system to provide safeguards against the invasion of privacy.

With political science avowing faith in a situation where skepticism might be healthier, and the law stressing a certain kind of social order when justice is at stake, investigation of technological locks on data systems as a means to insuring privacy can add little more than a ritualistic post mortem. Nonetheless, an examination should be made of the widespread naive assumption that the information stored in computerized files is somehow protected. The intellectual architects of the National Data Center, for example, took comfort in and used as defense for their "gigantic oversight" the argument that their proposal was for a *statistical* as contrasted with an *intelligence* system. Presumably, the distinction here was between aggregate and individual data, but this differentiation was proved illusory by computer experts who developed an algorithm for compiling a dossier from a statistical bank.[46] The fatuity of relying on computer confidentiality is demonstrated further by a number of data bank breaking experiences and methods.[47]

In addition to the earlier reference to the relationship between privacy and law-and-order, it should be noted that in general the law is notoriously laggard with respect to technology, and no redress is forthcoming until after damage has been claimed and proven. The legislative process can be of little help, for it requires a great deal of lead time, while technological developments move at a rapid pace. Moreover, legislatures mirror the times; their law-making reflects more than it leads. When the technology, such as the computer or data bank, is in use, vested interests influence usage. It is to be expected, therefore, that the framing of protective statutes will be governed by economic and political factors.[48] Moreover, with privacy a "nonlegal concept"[49] and American law "in the worst possible shape to deal with information processing and privacy,"[50] the prospects for individual freedom, even in a democracy, evanesce.

Conclusion

Information systems as a manifestation of advanced technology and as a tool for improving public planning are not, by any means, an American phenomenon exclusively. The agenda of international meetings and the contents of books and journals attest to the widespread use and interest. Far from unique, the American experience in all its dimensions must be viewed as prolepsis, an anticipation of what is ahead for the countries of Western Europe, where computerized data systems lag about three to five years, and in developing nations, where the time interval is still longer. For the industrialized nations of the world, the pattern of problems is much the same as has been described in this paper; only the details differ. Nonetheless, the push toward technology, the predilection for computerization, the persuasion that information technology is to be equated with efficiency —these are universal.

For the developing countries, the situation in the United States and other industrialized countries carries a message of *"sum quod eris."*[d] And there are additional dangers: (1) the possibility of an "oversell," deplorable in big countries with big budgets, but disastrous in poor countries; (2) the "technological imperative" which might impel developing countries to adopt techniques not appropriate to their actual needs; (3) the potential for abuse by dictatorial leaders in nations where the power balance is unstable and government volatile. Oppression in the name of efficiency, with information technology providing the means and "rational planning" the justification has already been perceived in the industrialized countries of the world. It remains to be seen whether the developing nations can get the best of the Faustian bargain by reaping the benefits of technological progress without paying the costs.

Notes

1. D. G. Greenberg, "Consulting: U.S. Firms Thrive on Jobs for European Clients," *Science* 162 (November 29, 1968): 986–787.

2. Paul Dickson, *Think Tanks* (New York: Atheneum, 1971).

3. Ida R. Hoos. *Automation in the Office* (Washington, D.C.: Public Affairs Press, 1961).

4. Ida R. Hoos, "When the Computer Takes Over the Office," *Harvard Business Review* 38, 4 (July-August 1960): 102–113.

5. Russell L. Ackoff, "Management Misinformation Systems," *Management Science* 14, 4 (December 1967): B-147.

6. Robert V. Head, "The Elusive MIS," *Datamation* 16, 10 (September 1, 1970): 22–27.

7. Tom Alexander, "Computers Can't Solve Everything," *Fortune,* October, 1969, pp. 126–129, 168, 171.

---

[d] "I am what you will be," inscription on a headstone found in a Boston graveyard.

8. Arlene Hershman, "A Mess in MIS?," *Dun's Review* 91, 1 (January 1968): 26–27, 85–87.

9. George Glaser, "Computers in the Real World of People," *Datamation*, December 1968, pp. 47–56.

10. Second International Conference on Mechanized Information Storage and Retrieval, London, September 2–5, 1969, as reported in *Nature* 223 (September 20, 1969): 1205.

11. William F. Sharpe, *The Economics of Computers* (New York and London: Columbia University Press, 1969).

12. Abraham Kaplan, *The Conduct of Inquiry* (San Francisco, Calif.: Chandler Publishing Company, 1964), p. 313.

13. C. West Churchman, "Real Time Systems and Public Information," Fall Joint Computer Conference, San Francisco, California, 1968.

14. George J. Stigler, "The Economics Of Information," *The Journal of Political Economy* 69, 3 (June, 1961): 213–25.

15. Jacob Marschak, "Economics of Inquiring, Communicating, Deciding," Richard T. Ely Lecture, Papers and Proceedings, 80th Annual Meeting of the American Economic Association, *American Economic Review* 58, 2 (May 1968): 12.

16. Jacob Marschak, "Economics of Information Systems," Chapter 2 in Michael D. Intriligator, ed. *Frontiers of Quantitative Economics* (Amsterdam: North-Holland Publishing Company, 1971), p. 35.

17. Uwe Thomas, *Computerized Data Banks in Public Administration* (Paris: Organization for Economic Cooperation and Development, Informatics Studies, 1971): p. 13.

18. Richard D. Duke, "Urban Planning and Metropolitan Development —The Role of Technology," *Applying Technology to Unmet Needs,* Appendix V, *Technology and the American Economy,* Studies prepared for the National Commission on Technology, Automation, and Economic Progress (Washington, D.C.: U.S. Government Printing Office, February 1966), p. V–8.

19. Sperry Gyroscope Company, *A Proposed Demonstration Project for a Nassau County Welfare Information Center,* Sperry Publication No. GJ-2232-1116, May 1966, p. V.

20. Nassau County Planning Commission, "Study of Constraints on the Poor of Nassau County," conducted under grant from U.S. Office of Economic Opportunity, November 1969.

21. Space-General Corporation, *Systems Management Analysis of the California Welfare System,* SGC 1048 RG, March 15, 1967, p. 1.

22. Ibid., pp. 4-2, 4-3.

23. U.S. Senate, Select Committee on Nutrition and Human Needs, *Seattle: Unemployment, the New Poor, and Hunger,* November 28, 1971.

24. Frances Fox Piven and Richard A. Cloward, *Regulating the Poor* (New York: Pantheon Books, Inc., 1971).

25. More complete discussion on these areas is to be found in Ida R. Hoos, *Systems Analysis in Public Policy, A Critique* (Berkeley and Los Angeles: University of California Press, 1972).

26. Robert R. J. Gallati, "New York State Identification and Intelligence System," in *Information Technology in a Democracy,* Alan F. Westin, ed. (Cambridge, Mass.: Harvard University Press, 1971), p. 40.

27. Ibid., pp. 42–43.

28. Ibid., p. 46.

29. Burroughs Corporation (Business Machines Group, Public Relations Office), "New York State Identification and Intelligence System," *Datamation* 20, 3 (March 1971): 31–32.

30. Space-General Corporation, *Prevention and Control of Crime and Delinquency,* Final Report, PCCD-7, July 29, 1965, p. 4.

31. Cesare Lombroso-Ferrero, *Criminal Man, According to the Classification of Cesare Lombroso-Ferrero* (New York and London: G. P. Putnam's Sons, 1911).

32. William H. Kruskal, "Mathematical Sciences and Social Sciences: Excerpts from the Report of a Panel of the Behavioral and Social Sciences Survey," *The American Statistician* 25, 1 (February 1971): 30.

33. Stanton Wheeler, *On Record: Files and Dossiers in American Life* (New York: Russell Sage Foundation, 1969).

34. U. S. Senate Subcommittee on Administrative Practice and Procedure, 90th Congress, First Session, *Government Dossier, (Survey of Information Contained in Government Files),* November 1967.

35. Quoted in *Modern Data,* May 1970, p. 44.

36. *Datamation,* May 1970, p. 59.

37. U. S. Congress, Committee on Post Office and Civil Service, 91st Congress, Second Session, *Mailing Lists,* July 22 and 23, 1970, p. 69.

38. John D. Morris, "False Advertising Laid to H&R Block," *New York Times,* July 1, 1971.

39. "Report of the Task Force on the Storage of and Access to Government Statistics," *The American Statistician* 23, 3 (June 1, 1969): 15–16.

40. E. Glaser, D. Rosenblatt, and M.K. Wood, "The Design of a Federal Statistical Data Center," Appendix C in *Statistical Evaluation Report No. 6,* issued by the Office of Statistical Standards, Bureau of the Budget, Executive Office of the President, Washington, D.C., December 1965.

41. This and many points of incisive criticism are suggested by A. S. Rosander, "Analyses of the Kaysen Committee Report," *The American Statistician* 24, 1 (February 1970): 20–25. (Dr. Rosander has been for thirty years a supervisory mathematical statistician in the Bureau of Labor Statistics, the War Production Board, the Internal Revenue Service, and the Interstate Commerce Commission.)

42. Martin Landau, "Redundancy, Rationality, and the Problem of Duplication and Overlap," *Public Administration Review,* July-August 1969, pp. 346–58.

43. Carl Kaysen, "Data Banks and Dossiers," *The Public Interest,* No. 7, Spring 1967, pp. 52–61.

44. Ibid.

45. Edgar S. Dunn, Jr., op. cit., p. 23.

46. Lance J. Hoffman and W. F. Miller, "Getting a Personal Dossier from a Statistical Data Bank," *Datamation,* May 1970, pp. 74–75.

47. Caxton C. Foster, "Data Banks—A Position Paper," *Computers and Automation* 20, 2 (March 1971): 28–30.

48. Alan F. Westin, *Privacy and Freedom* (New York: Atheneum, 1967).

49. Clark C. Havighurst, "Foreword," *Law and Contemporary Problems* 31, 2 (Spring 1966): 251.

50. Alan F. Westin, "Civil Liberties Issues in Public Databanks," in *Information Technology in a Democracy* (Cambridge, Massachusetts: Harvard University Press, 1971), p. 305.

8 Aspects of Administrative Change and Reform

Arne F. Leemans

The Problem of Administrative Change

Extremely ambiguous opinions are held regarding the machinery and operations of governments of developing countries. Some feel that the government bureaucracy is the raft on which society is kept afloat and saved from political and economic collapse. With the exception of a few countries with strong military or one-party organizations, government machineries are by far the largest and best equipped of organizations. They have most of the natural resources at their disposal and form the hotbeds in which the overwhelming majority of intellectuals are brought to fruition, or—not exceptionally—to frustration. Under such conditions, the natural conclusion is that a government bureaucracy should play a major role in the development of the country, if indeed not the primary role.

Governmental organization, however, also shows a less favorable countenance. It can be clumsy, ill-organized and badly coordinated, pedestrian, autocratic, or corrupt. The apparatus may be unable to adapt to modern needs or to adjust to a development orientation which requires dynamic and innovative behavior. It may tend to dominate all political organs and to stand remote from the people.

The first view may be inspired by high expectations, perhaps unfounded in the light of prevailing conditions; the second may be due to an excessively critical attitude; or perhaps both are based on a sound evaluation of the situation for parts of the government machinery. Undoubtedly, some of the criticism of bureaucracy's unsatisfactory contribution to development is unfair. Politicians have set targets, and professionals have designed plans and programs which are unrealistic, given the scarce resources and the environmental obstacles to their achievement. Nonetheless, the administrative machinery is often made the scapegoat for any failure. In many countries, an inefficient administration is unjustifiably regarded as the cause of the government's inability to meet development expectations or to realize the objectives set out in its economic and social plans. In other cases, however, there is ample evidence that the root cause lies in inefficient

This is an amended version of an article which appeared as "Administrative Reform: An Overview," in *Development and Change* 2,2 (1970–71):1–18. An enlarged version with several case studies will be published in a volume on Administrative Reform by the Institute of Social Studies.

117

machinery of the government. In developing countries particularly, the dominating role played by the government in social and economic development makes this all the more serious.

Conditions in these countries have been frequently unfavorable for administrative development. Former colonial territories have been administered by the "iron frame" of the colonial service, usually composed of foreigners whose principal tasks were in the realm of law and order, although developmental activities were certainly not lacking. Most independent countries in Asia and Africa and, in a different context, in Latin America, suffered from equally autocratic and order-oriented regimes. Former colonies experienced turbulent change in the pre-independence and transitional periods; high expectations were raised which for some time were remarkably absent in most countries of the other category. Independence caused the departure, almost en masse, of the expatriate administrators, disrupting the government machinery while its tasks rapidly escalated. Not only was expansion necessary, but also complete reorientation.

Fundamental social changes in both groups of countries make new demands and create new tensions. The rapid spreading of urbanization and secularization and calls for the democratization of government and administration, heavily burden the government machinery and make adaptability essential.

All these changes and transformations create tension between old and new values, traditional and modern. This is reflected not only within the government bureaucracy, but also in its relationship with the society. Compared to most sections of the society, bureaucracy is frequently modern, although the educated young may stigmatize it as conservative and authoritarian. In most countries, the bureaucracy is undoubtedly of a strong elitist character, only too likely to adopt an authoritarian attitude and to lack open communication with the general public.

Administrative Reform: Its Scope and Nature

While the need for change and adaptation of the government machinery is obvious enough, the problems involved in bringing about change are overwhelming. It is inevitable, therefore, that administrative reforms in developing countries usually claim widespread attention.

"Administrative reform" is used to describe activities which actually go far beyond its evident meaning. It can imply any reform of the administrative machineries of national and lower-level governments, being thereby conceived as directed action. Dror speaks of "directed change of the main features of an administrative system."[1] Caiden defines administrative reform as "the artificial inducement of administrative transformation against resistance."[2] He distinguishes administrative reform from administrative change, which is a self-adjusting "organizational response to fluctuating conditions," saying that the need for the former arises from the latter because of the malfunctioning of the natural processes of administrative change.[3]

Although it is agreed that directed action is an essential characteristic of administrative reform, concepts are not sufficiently crystallized and defined. For instance, can any directed change in government administration be considered administrative reform? Dror limits the concept to changes in the main features, specifically changes "either . . . of at least medium comprehensiveness plus high innovativeness, or . . . of high comprehensiveness plus at least medium innovativeness."[4] These terms are naturally subject to different interpretations; according to Dror, however, administrative reform clearly excludes minor changes in administrative organization and procedures. The advantage of this qualification is that it allows the study to concentrate on major reforms. This may conceivably cause minor change efforts to be neglected, although they may be useful to a better understanding of reform characteristics and problems.[5] Many behavioralists contest the feasibility of achieving this type of reform suggested by Dror. They argue that organizational change can only be realized by affecting bureaucratic behavior and relationships. Although a general organizational change of policy may be designed, its effectuation is a matter of individual and small group approach, which is strongly opposed to "grand" reform. Moreover, behavioral change can only be "internalized" by an organization over a long period of time.[6]

The idea that organizational change and reform can only be properly studied and undertaken within a wider context is gaining increasing recognition. With the exception of minor changes of a technical nature, reforms can only be effective when designed with proper attention to the environment in which the organization operates. In fact, reforms are often directly or indirectly occasioned by events in the world around the organization. In an extreme form, administrative reform can be considered part of societal reform,[7] government organization and bureaucracy being parts of or related to other systems, political, social, or otherwise. Changes in the governmental machinery and in its mode of operation may occur under the impact of other systems and may also affect these. Most authors reject a cut-and-dried "general principles" approach to administrative reform and stress the need that reform efforts be adapted to the particular case, conditioned as it is by numerous factors.

Allegations of Failure in Administrative Reform

Experience with administrative reform in developing countries gives rise to justifiable pessimism. Complaints are manifold, while causes for satisfaction appear only too infrequently.

Causes of Failure

Methods and approaches followed have been frequently too narrow and one-sided. They have inclined towards excessive concentration on changes in structure, administrative methods, and techniques, neglecting the behavioral aspects of organization and administration, with the result that the change tended to be purely formal and to have little effect on the actual operations of the administrative organization. In many other cases, notably when foreign organizational systems or methods were taken as examples, the newly-designed organization was ill-suited to the environment in which it had to operate.

Transplantation has usually been unsuccessful, except perhaps where it has been imposed with the aid of coercive measures over a considerable length of time, as under colonial conditions. In these cases, there has obviously been little recognition of the fact that governmental reorganization cannot be severed from its environment or from other systems within which it operates and with which it interacts; administrative reform is a dependent variable.[8] Birkhead emphasizes this point very strongly: administrative reform can only be successful when associated with social, political, or economic reform.[9] The cultural restrictions of administrative reform have been stressed by Milne.[10] Cohen, however, who advocates a group dynamics approach, is more optimistic about the possibilities of overcoming cultural barriers in order to establish new organizational relationships.[11] Strong emphasis on the conditioning of the government machinery by ecological factors incurs the danger in static societies that this will impede innovative efforts.

There may be many other reasons for failure, including reasons of a political nature. It has been often observed that politicians are not truly motivated to press for administrative reform programs. Moreover, political stability is lacking in many developing countries, enabling non-continuity in programing and executing administrative reform.

Feasibility of Administrative Reform

The justification of many complaints notwithstanding, there is yet need to critically evaluate the generally pessimistic view of administrative reform feasibility.

Firstly, to what does an acknowledgment of failure refer? Is it the degree to which targets set by the reform initiators were achieved? The proposals which were put up for final decision? The plan which was ultimately adopted? The original targets may have been utterly unrealistic and the plan therefore almost doomed to failure. On the other hand, the plan which is actually adopted may be the outcome of long deliberation assisted by considerable feedback of information from relevant groups and with recruited support; this results in a compromise which is perhaps likely to be implemented, but which nevertheless represents a failure in view of the original intentions. Were the original plans nipped in the bud, or did they prove insufficient during their implementation?

Secondly, although some reforms laid down in the final plan may not be implemented, they may still have some impact on organizational reality. Weak spots in the reform schemes may become apparent during the implementation phase, necessitating considerable revision to the plan. New and unforeseen circumstances may also cause revisions to be introduced. Although perhaps far from the original objectives, the results may thus be more effective. Even if the implementation of the reform program is abandoned altogether, it may have some unanticipated yet positive impact on the organization. For example, a program of structural change intended to make the government machinery more development-oriented may be dropped sometime during its implementation, but may nevertheless give rise to a new dynamism under the civil servants which is just as effective.

Thirdly, the time factor, to which we shall refer again later, is very important. This time-dimension of change in bureaucratic organizations is too often disregarded, causing unrealistic expectations and plans and consequent unnecessary feelings of failure and frustration.

Finally, some specific cases are indicative of conditions under which administrative reform may be quite successful, and in fact has proved to be so. In principle, these fall outside what is generally considered to be the heart of the administrative reform movement: efforts to improve the administrative organization and practices, or to inculcate a different bureaucratic behavior in order to increase the efficiency or effectiveness of the government machinery. Negative criticisms in particular seem to refer to this type of administrative reform.

Positive Bases of Reform

There are several other situations, however, which are not always recognized or cited as administrative reforms, but in which considerable successes have been recorded.

Firstly, administrative reform has been introduced in many developing countries as a result of and concurring with changes in the political system or, in some cases, with a change of ruler. Braibanti speaks of "the adjustment the administrative system makes to the political system."[12] In Brazil under Vargas, in the U.A.R., Ghana, and Tanzania, direct action brought about considerable change in the bureaucratic machinery. It is difficult to assess the extent to which the effectiveness of intended reforms was furthered by changes in personnel,[13] or reduced by environmental conditions (the Egyptian government machinery bears enormous strain because it is the nation's principal employer, and also because of the conditions of armed conflict which exist in the country).

A second category of reforms which have proved quite effective are those connected with change in governmental institutions. A striking case is that of the amalgamation of states in a federal country, as for instance in India in the period of 1948–57, with the subsequent merger of administrative institutions. Gorvine mentions the sheer weight of details in the administrative changeover incurred as a result of the consolidation of the provinces of West Pakistan into one unit in the mid-fifties.[14] Similar situations have frequently occurred at lower levels of government. Although many local government reforms undertaken in developing countries have undoubtedly failed to reach their objectives, some have had considerable effect on the organization and operation of the administrative machinery.[15] The Indian Panchayat Samithi is an example.

Although the malfunctioning of government administration in developing countries is widely recognized, this does not imply a corresponding plenitude of reform efforts. Quite the contrary, in fact. In the majority of developing countries and in some of the more advanced, there is little probability of bold administrative reform programs being introduced, whether at random or after thorough preparation. Not only is there a "high tolerance of maladministration,"[16] but the potential initiators or supporters of reform: political leaders, civil servants, and other, are faced with many adverse factors.

Initiation of Reform

Governments and political leaders in developing countries generally give little priority to administrative reform, being more concerned with substantive development programs or with maintaining and consolidating their political power. Only inasfar as it is considered crucial for these purposes, will they be prompted to undertake reform efforts. In analyzing the relationship between the type of regime and administrative reform efforts, Groves reaches some rather distressing conclusions with regard to the effective governmental concern for reorganizing the governmental machinery. Lee mentions the improbability of political leaders initiating administrative reform.[17]

Two concepts are useful in this context. Montgomery uses the "annoyance" concept in analyzing the problems of administrative reform.[18] Only if the working of the government bureaucracy becomes so annoying to the political leaders, either as a result of arrant malfunctioning or of inclinations towards independence or domination, will the government be induced to change the machinery. This kind of annoyance sometimes assumes such proportions that it creates a situation of crisis. In fact, it has often been claimed that administrative reform is most likely to occur in such a situation.[19]

The second concept is that of risk, made up of two opposite poles. Firstly, there is the risk faced by political leaders or government in maintaining the existing machinery. This is again related to the annoyance factor mentioned by Montgomery. This risk may be particularly great for political leaders who have recently come into power and who may consider the bureaucracy to be inimical or obstructive to the execution of their policies. The new rulers may use various methods to counteract these risks: top personnel may be changed, and loyal elements (military colleagues, party members, etc.) infused into the higher bureaucratic strata; the role of the (one) party and its position with regard to the bureaucracy may be strengthened; the administrative machinery may be reformed, perhaps in combination with one or both the other methods.

Political leaders are therefore only likely to undertake reforms if the risk involved in continuing the existing situation is large or if considerable gains may be expected. The greater the significance of such action to them, the greater will be their insistence. If increased loyalty is a major reason, they are likely to attach great value to reform efforts. Changes in personnel rather than structural changes will then probably be undertaken, but the latter together with reforms in procedure and communication may also be undertaken, although at a later stage. However, in some cases political leaders may consider large-scale structural reforms essential for consolidating the nation. The creation of a major administrative unit in West Pakistan, for instance, was a political action in which all administrative obstacles were considered minor in the light of the political objective of national consolidation.[20]

The reluctance of political leaders to engage in administrative reform programs is very understandable. The risks involved, or the possible "costs" of reforms are considerable. The danger of antagonizing the government bureaucracy may be very real, especially if leading groups in the bureaucracy represent a major source of power, or if the government is weak and politically insecure. The power element is therefore an essential determinant of administrative reform probability. Administration reform also tends to create temporary disorganization, insecurity, lack of continuity, and other features which the government may consider harmful to the proper conduct of its affairs and therefore to the achievement of its goals.

The bureaucracy forms the second major group which may initiate reforms: it may also be a principal source of resistance.[21] The measure of annoyance tends to conform to the degree of professionalization of the civil service and to its penetration by members of different social classes and by innovative young intellectuals. There is considerable evidence that dissatisfaction with the existing structure and operation of a government organization and bureaucracy increases with the degree of exchange of personnel between government and other organzations. The detection of signals of maladministration is thereby increased. Lee has analyzed the probability of innovation on the basis of three categories of bureaucracy: closed, mixed, and open. He concludes that bureaucracies in developing countries are usually combinations of mixed and closed, and thus give relatively little support to administrative reform programs.[22] Deviance is rejected by the social system *in casu* the bureaucracy,[23] deviates being either forced to conform for the sake of personal security, or confined to inferior and harmless positions, or ejected from the system.

There are several other causes of mediocre bureaucratic initiative. Resistance to change is universal in organizations, an inherent inertia often leading administrators to wait for events to justify further action rather than to anticipate future demands. Moreover, members of an organization are often unable to act as signals or detectors of administrative ill-health,[24] even if they are aware of organizational defects, they feel powerless to act.

Thirdly, reform may be initiated by external organizations or persons. In developing countries where international organizations and foreign governments are actively concerned with reforms of government administration through their technical assistance programs, this is particularly significant. Dramatic mistakes have resulted from transplantation of methods and from lack of appreciation of specific ecological conditions.[25] These lessons have undoubtedly caused a less dogmatic and more realistic approach to be adopted by foreign consultants who, together with national counterparts, can play an important role in planning, programing, and implementing administrative reforms.

Objectives of Reform

The setting of objectives is of primary importance in administrative reform as in any public policy or decision making. It is essential in the first place for the determination of reform strategies as these are to some extent dependent on the goals.

The degree to which objectives are attained is a principal yardstick in judging the success or failure of administrative reform programs. Proper evaluation of the effectiveness of reform efforts therefore requires that objectives be adequately set. This need not imply that evaluation should disregard any side effects which were not taken into consideration in designing the reform.

Administrative reform programs are rarely designed with a single purpose in mind. Even if only one objective is specifically earmarked, others may be tacitly or unconsciously adopted. For instance, administrative efficiency may be the primary or only stated objective; nevertheless, there may be even more important latent political or power objectives such as increasing bureaucratic loyalty to the regime, or attempts by top civil servants to strengthen their position vis-à-vis the political organs or other government departments.

Traditionally, administrative reform has been equated with efforts to increase organizational efficiency or effectiveness. In this narrow sense, the predominant and sometimes only objective is to improve the administration. Caiden, who holds this view, terms it alternatively the cure of maladministration. However, he gives this a wide interpretation, quoting Mosher who identified four sub-goals; change of operating policies and programs, improvement of administrative effectiveness, higher quality personnel, and anticipation of outside criticism and threats.[26] The first and last objectives may naturally also have a political undertone. Lee emphasizes the same general objective which he specifies as improved order, improved methods, and improved performance.[27]

Others emphasize the multiplicity of goals. Dror considers reform basically a "multi-goal oriented endeavour," distinguishing six goal clusters: three intra-administration directed and primarily concerned with improving the administration, and three dealing with societal roles of the administrative system. Among the latter, he refers to the power element in administrative reform, often particularly important as an impetus or impediment to such reforms in developing countries.[28] The struggle to strengthen the position of persons or groups involved undoubtedly inspires many reform efforts. According to Montgomery, many administrative reform plans "reflect the competition for power and privilege."[29]

The structuring of administrative reform goals is usually complicated by the fact that various parties are involved, each with its own objectives which may concur, differ, or even contradict each other. These objectives are likely to be more or less subjective in nature, especially if those engaged in reform plans or their implementation will be favorably or adversely affected by the results. A well-defined set of objectives for which sufficient support can be recruited may be hard to draw up. However, failure to do so will mean that plans become stifled at birth or thoroughly emasculated. Alternatively, the objectives will become so obscure as to be detrimental to an efficient reform development and implementation.

The Scope of Reform Strategies

Administrative reform strategies have only recently been given any systematic attention, and this by scholars of different orientations. Firstly, scholars concerned with problems of organizational change included the public organization in their studies. Secondly, public administration scholars of different genre and disciplinary backgrounds became interested in the various aspects of change and reform of the government machinery. Political scientists have studied changes in government bureaucracies as an aspect of change in political systems, institutions, and processes. Finally, a newly emerging area of study, that of policy and decisional science, is giving attention to problems of administrative reform.

The whole question can be broken down into a series of strategical dimensions,[30] frequently expressed in terms of sets of polar approaches. This has the disadvantage of stressing unrealistic extremes, but also promotes analytical clarity. The opposites in these polar sets should be therefore interpreted not in terms of "either-or" but rather of "more of the one–less of the other." Moreover, the poles, such as micro-macro or adaptive-innovative, are essentially subject to individual interpretation, so that the terms may be used on different wavelengths: a strategy may be considered micro or adaptive by the one, macro or innovative by the other. Perhaps the most hotly debated polar set, to which I shall give special attention here, is structural versus behavioral. This is possibly the most pervasive issue in organizational change and reform, and one which affects most other strategical dimensions.

Behavioral concern with the organization developed around the beginning of the 1940s, the tide of behavorialism later becoming so strong that it almost expunged structuralism from theory building. Strangely enough, the latter still prevails in practice where its frequent failures serve to strengthen the behavoralist faith. The main weakness of the structural approach is its static character and inclination toward organizational dogmata. However, after an initial period in which it groped to acquire some substance, part of the behavioralist school has also tended to become static[31] and to assume general traits in organizational behavior without which it was difficult to operationalize behavioralist theory.

Opinions as to the relative utility of the structural and behavioral approaches still conflict, although the former seems to be gaining new recognition. According to Braibanti, "institutional change appears to be increasingly more effective than attitudinal manipulation, even as an internal means."[32] Irrespective of whether this judgment is correct or not, such a trend might be explained by the greater appreciation shown by the structuralists of the behavioral dimensions of administrative reform. The major defect of behavioralist, on the other hand, has been probably their failure to recognize the structural dimensions of reform or, as Pye expresses it, "strangely enough the overwhelming burden of behavioral studies of institutions and organizations has been in trying to explain how the individual adapts his behavior when he joins or acts within an established institution and we have done almost nothing on the problem of how behavior can create (or change) an institution in the first instance."[33] Institution building should therefore be of greater concern to behavioralists.

The ineffectiveness of the one-sided behavioral approach with regard to bureaucratic reform partly results from the size of the government organization and the problem of reorganization involved. As already suggested, behavioral change tends to focus on the individual and the small group rather than on the organization as a whole and therein to emphasize a micro approach. However, a macro approach is often needed, particularly in government organizations in developing countries. The whole machinery is antiquated, disorderly, and badly coordinated, and its growth has mushroomed, necessitating complete or considerable overhaul. Structuralists are generally more inclined to accept a macro approach in certain cases. They examine the organization as a whole, and its relationships with superior, lateral, and subordinate organizations. They have become aware of the limitations of structural efforts and so tend to consider the behavioral dimensions of the problem. They realize that structural change will have but limited impact if no effort is undertaken to influence the behavior of the members and groups of the organization. Moreover, the significance of the impact of the environment on the organization, its operation, and on changes therein, has been almost universally accepted.

A particular reform strategy of mixed structural-behavioral character is increasingly advocated as an alternative to administrative reform. This suggests the creation of new organizational units, possibly outside the existing organizational framework. Downs terms this "break-out."[34] Such units will not only be relatively free of the ills of existing organizations and their behavior, but their organizational form and the select top personnel assigned to them will tend to make them dynamic and innovative. The new units may thus be regarded as competitors to power and influence, prompting other organizations to achieve a higher output.

This strategy evidently relies on the conflict theory which has of late received increasing support in organization theory.[35] One of its most outspoken advocates is Lucian Pye, who recommends its application to bureaucratic development: "The new bureaucracy must be built around conflict and competition."[36] Braibanti adheres to the same idea when advocating the creation of "countervailing loci of power, each with enough authority to be resilient and gently resistant, and each maintaining boundaries of insulation rather than merging ignominiously into a haze of interlocking structures.[37] Such new units may have a shock effect as well as a demonstration effect, to which Dror and Cohen refer in different contexts. Many developing countries have adopted this strategy by creating numerous organizational units such as special purpose organizations, special authorities, public corporations, etc. In many cases, these units have indeed proved to be among the most dynamic and innovative sections of the government machinery. Their major problem has often been the struggle to survive in the face of older government departments, and this has frequently drained their energy. Downs, who states that such a unit's productivity is extremely high and its "breakout" from the regular bureaucracy, initially at least, quite effective, also points out that these units tend to degenerate fairly quickly.[38]

The pace at which substantial administrative reforms can be achieved is conditioned by various factors. Time is a crucial element and a major strategic issue, affected by the following conditions:[39]

1. The designing of an adequate administrative reform scheme necessitates that the weaknesses of the existing organization and their causes be analysed, and that insight be developed into alternative solutions for increasing the capacity of the government machinery to perform the role assigned to it and to realize governmental targets.
2. Dependent on the strength of the government, particularly vis-à-vis the bureaucracy, political support will have to be recruited. This will require negotiation and compromise. A government is only likely to press through a substantial administrative reform scheme if its necessity is obvious, the political feasibility of acceptance great, and sufficient support for its implementation forthcoming.
3. The implementation of a reform scheme requires that members and subgroups of the organization be informed and made familiar with the purpose and content of the reorganization. Inertia and resistance must be overcome and organizational behavior adjusted to the new needs. These changes are likely to be time-consuming.
4. Inasfar as reform of the government machinery is dependent on environmental conditions, the pace of change in the environment is largely determinant of the pace at which reform can become effective.
5. Finally, the need for continuity in government proceedings may require that reform schemes be implemented at a moderate rate.

As a result of these and other factors, fundamental change of the administrative system or large parts thereof is a lengthy process. An interesting case in point is the implementation of the Northcote-Trevelyan reforms in the British civil service. These were started in the 1850s and in retrospect can be seen to have considerable influence on the operations of the government bureaucracy even in the present day. Although submitted in 1853, decades passed before the intentions of the report were implemented to any considerable extent, partly because of legal and judicial barriers, but fundamentally because the political and social environment resisted the new social relationships which resulted from the reform.

In view of the time involved, continuity of effort is essential for the success of any substantial reform. The government must show enduring interest and consistency in its long-term views. Lack of such continuity as a result of political instability is a principal cause of failure in developing countries.

Continuity and consistency do not imply rigidity in reform planning and implementation. Although long-term reform planning is essential, plans should be flexible; moreover, continuous reevaluation should be made during the implementation process. Rigidity can also be avoided by using the approaches by Cohen in his organic-adaptive organization, in which the organization should develop its own corrective process.[40] The danger will thus be avoided that a new status quo develops which will be strongly defended by the reformers who designed it, thus creating new stagnation, while new pathological rigidities are substituted for old.[41]

Constructing Theoretical Approaches to Reform

Caiden's statement that administrative reform rests on the assumption (or belief) that there is always a better alternative to the status quo in an organization[42] goes right to the heart of our subject. The addition "or belief" underlines the tacit theory and its source of inspiration on which many hypotheses and generalizations in administrative reform theory building are based.

This assumption has a strong appeal in a world to which change has become an idol, and thus incurs the danger of becoming a dogma. Although it is improbable that an organization can achieve optimal status at any moment of time, there being a natural lag of organizational adaptation to changing external and internal conditions, this basic assumption has yet to be proven. We are faced here with a major weakness in the mother discipline of public administration which so far has been unable to develop satisfactory criteria for evaluation of the structure and operations of governmental and administrative machineries. A fortiori, there is as yet insufficient theoretical basis on which to judge when administrative reform is desirable and the direction it should take, or to evaluate administrative reform efforts. At least three approaches to this evaluation may be conceived:

1. The extent to which the objectives of the administrative reform program have been attained. This is in some respect a rather poor criterion: firstly, for whatever reason, the program may have had serious defects; secondly, it is generally agreed that administrative reform should never be an end in itself. To a certain degree, therefore, the end product is irrelevant. However, the better the reform scheme is programed, taking into account the purposes of the organization and the conditions in which it operates, the more reliable this criterion of evaluation is likely to be.
2. An administrative reform program is evaluated in terms of the greater degree to which the changed organization attains its objectives. Here we become unavoidably involved in the debate on the various decision-making theories. Should a "greater degree" of ultimate goal attainment be the aim of administrative reform? If so, should this be judged on the basis of the level of aspiration, i.e., be satisficing in its orientation (Simon), or of incrementalism (Lindblom)? Or should "optimal" goal attainment be the target and consequently the measure for evaluation? And in that case, what should be considered optimal? Should the reality of administrative reform constraints thereby be taken into account?
3. Dror rightly recognizes the difficulty of using such primary criteria; in many cases it will be hard if not impossible to evaluate the net output of public policies, particularly the real output, i.e., the effect of the policy on social reality.[43] He consequently advocated the additional use of secondary criteria for ascertaining the quality of public policy, these criteria to be based on such aspects of the process as its pattern, substructure, input. If evaluation of the reform scheme is confined to its immediate target, i.e., the structure and operations of the organization, this approach is likely to suffer the same defects as the first mentioned above.

Undoubtedly, a more systematic approach to evaluation may help to trace successful administrative reform efforts or the causes of unsuccessful attempts. Although in the ultimate resort the second approach would be desirable, it seems yet too vague and unverifiable a basis for evaluation, except for public service or productive organizations in which an improved input-output ratio can be ascertained. A complicating factor is that, apart from the reform, many factors whose weight is difficult to estimate may adversely or favorably influence the degree of goal attainment. At this stage of public administration research, the first and third approaches, or a combination of the two, generally seem more reliable.

The development of a descriptive-explanatory theory of administrative reform still requires a great deal of research.[44] Case studies can provide an invaluable information basis for this purpose. Although there is some truth in Caiden's statement that the "universals" deduced from case studies may be no guide to action if cultural diversity is of much greater importance and the universals change over time,[45] this does not necessarily gainsay their significance. Rather it reflects the deficiency of work done in this field and the rashness of the conclusions sometimes drawn from case studies.

The inadequacy of case research is located in the frequent lack of attention given to environmental factors, although developments in this respect are encouraging.[46] Moreover, data collected by case researchers are rarely comparable, as their research designs differ—if the research can be said to be systematically designed at all. This greatly hampers comparative research and the development of assumptions with the wider applicability essential for theory building.

A basic weakness of administrative reform efforts has been the use of assumptions of a rather universal nature without previous testing of their applicability to the reform situation in question. Case research should be used to develop a typology of reform situations on the basis of such indicators as political, social, and cultural environment, the objectives of the reform and its scope. "Universal" assumptions might then be developed for each type. Lee suggests such a typology of closed, mixed, and open bureaucracies and their effect on feasibility and methods of reform; Groves analyses different political conditions and their effects, including dominant political leadership, regimes of military government, governments under single and multiple political party systems, as well as elitist bureaucracy; while Cohen, on a lower organizational level, suggests that some situations require a collaborative, others a non-collaborative reform strategy.[47]

It would be unrealistic to assume that such a typology could be easily construed. In fact, even in public administration theory only slight progress has been made toward the development of descriptive, analytic models. Riggs has long been one of the foremost advocates of this type of analysis.[48] Some political science typologies may also be useful as they provide different patterns of the political environment within which public administration operates and which, as we have seen, is also an important factor for administrative reform.

Descriptive-explanatory theories form an indispensable basis for the development of normative theories, i.e., those concerned with a prescriptive future state of affairs, as well as for instrumental theories concerned with "how" and "when."[49] In fact, most administrative reform efforts have primarily concentrated on these instrumental aspects of the subject, although consciously or unconsciously influenced by certain norms. The descriptive-explanatory analysis of reform situations has frequently been the weaker part of reform efforts; as a consequence of this weakness, only a meagre foundation was available for decisions on the instrumental aspects.

Notes

1. Yehezkel Dror, "Strategies for Administrative Reform," *Development and Change* 2, 2 (1970–71): 19–35.

2. Gerald Caiden, *Administrative Reform* (Chicago: Aldine Publishing Co., 1969), p. 65.

3. Ibid., pp. 57, 58, 65.

4. Dror, op. cit., p. 29.

5. See Hahn-Been Lee, "Innovation and Administrative Reform in Developing Countries," *Policy Sciences* 1–2 (1970): 182. Caiden, however, correctly hypothesizes that "size alone may preclude some approaches to administrative reform that are employed at lower levels of administration." op. cit., p. 77.

6. Allan R. Cohen, "The Human Dimension of Administrative Reform: Towards More Differentiated Strategies for Change," *Development and Change* 2,2 (1970–71): 65–82.

7. Caiden, op. cit., p. 4.

8. Ibid., p. 11.

9. G.S. Birkhead (ed.), *Administrative Problems in Pakistan* (New York: Syracuse University Press, 1966).

10. R.S. Milne, "Mechanistic and Organic Models of Public Administration in Developing Countries," *Administrative Science Quarterly* 15, 1 (1970).

11. Cohen, op. cit.

12. Ralph Braibanti, *Political and Administrative Development* (Durham: Duke University Press, 1969), p. 83.

13. See Roderick T. Groves, "Administrative Reform and Political Development," *Development and Change* 2,2 (1970–71): 36–51; and Lee, op. cit.

14. Albert Gorvine, "Administrative Reform: Functions of Political and Economic Change," in Birkhead, op. cit., p. 192.

15. Arne F. Leemans, *Changing Patterns of Local Government* (The Hague: IULA, 1970).

16. Caiden, op. cit., p. 132.

17. Lee, op. cit. This is also illustrated by V.V. Moharir, in "Administration Reforms in India," *Development and Change* 2, 2 (1970–71): 83–97.

18. J.D. Montgomery, "Sources of Bureaucratic Reform; A Typology of Purpose and Politics," in Braibanti, op. cit., pp. 427–71.

19. Cf. for France in Michel Crozier, *The Bureaucratic Phenomenon* (Chicago: University of Chicago Press, 1964), pp. 196ff.; also Braibanti, op. cit., pp. 75–77; Leemans, op. cit., p. 178.

20. Gorvine, op. cit., p. 193.

21. See Montgomery, op. cit., pp. 465ff.

22. Lee, op. cit.

23. cf. Caiden, p. 133.

24. Caiden, p. 130.

25. See Groves, op. cit., with regard to Venezuela; and A.G. Samonte, "Administrative Reform in the Philippines," paper presented to the EROPA Assembly, Kuala Lumpur, 1968, which deals with the efforts of the Filipino government to change the personnel classification system.

26. F.C. Mosher, (ed.) *Governmental Reorganizations* (New York: 1967), pp. 497–98.

27. Lee, op. cit.

28. Dror, op. cit.

29. Montgomery, op. cit.

30. Cf. Dror, op. cit.

31. Cf. Lucian Pye, "Bureaucratic Development and the Psychology of Institutionalization," in Braibanti, op. cit., p. 401.

32. Braibanti, op. cit., p. 67; cf. also Caiden, p. 154.

33. Pye, op. cit., p. 403.

34. Anthony Downs, *Inside Bureaucracy* (Boston: Little, Brown & Co., 1967), p. 160.

35. See N.P. Mouzelis, *Organization and Bureaucracy; An Analysis of Modern Theories* (London: Routledge and Kegan Paul, 1967). Among others, Moyzelis refers to Whyte (*Patterns of Industrial Peace*), Crozier (*The Bureaucratic Phenomenon*), and Dalton (*Men Who Manage*).

36. Pye, op. cit., p. 415.

37. Braibanti, op. cit., p. 85.

38. Downs, op. cit., p. 161.

39. See Dror, op. cit.; Caiden also mentions a number of factors which determine how quickly a reform can be integrated, op. cit., p. 6.

40. Cohen, op. cit.

41. S.K. Bailey, "Objectives of the Theory of Public Administration," in J.C. Charlesworth (ed.) *Theory and Practice of Public Administration: Scope, Objectives and Methods* (Philadelphia: ASPA, 1968), p. 132.

42. Caiden, op. cit., p. 23.

43. Yehezkel Dror, *Public Policymaking Reexamined* (San Francisco: Chandler Publishing Company, 1968), p. 48.

44. For the typology of theories used here see Bailey, op. cit., pp. 128ff.

45. Caiden, op. cit., p. 118.

46. This trend is evidenced in many of the reports submitted to the EROPA conference in Kuala Lumpur in 1968 and reproduced in H.B. Lee, and A.G. Samonte, *Administrative Reforms in Asia* (Manilla: EROPA, 1970).

47. See special issue on Administrative Reform in *Development and Change* 2,2 (1970–71).

48. Fred W. Riggs, "The Structures of Government and Administrative Reform," in Braibanti, op. cit.

49. Bailey, op. cit., p. 135.

The Myth of Alternatives: Underlying Assumptions about Administrative Development

Fred W. Riggs

Introduction: Thesis and Antithesis

During the 1950s a widely held view, especially in the United States, was neatly expressed by President Harry Truman in a famous State of the Union message under the caption: "Point Four." It attributed to the science and technology of the West the superior levels of productivity, efficiency, health, education, and stability which the non-Western world, by contrast, was believed to lack and to desire. Consequently, in a philanthropic mood, the United States, he said, would offer the benefits of its superior knowledge and experience to the underdeveloped countries of the world.

During the 1960s, after many programs of bilateral and multilateral technical cooperation and economic assistance had been launched, a general mood of disenchantment began to spread around the world. The less developed countries, if and as they developed, found that many of the practices and institutions which had apparently worked so well in the West failed to achieve their hoped-for results in the non-West, and with the rise of newly awakened and militant nationalisms, Westernization in its many forms came increasingly to be repudiated and resented. Concurrently, the chief supporters of the technical assistance and foreign aid in the West, and particularly in the United States, became increasingly disillusioned. They began to think, as failure after failure followed their best efforts, that, somehow, what had apparently worked so well in the West often worked very badly or not at all in other countries. They began to search for clues to explain this apparent paradox, to understand when the knowledge they possessed might usefully be exported, and when it would do no good.

Some arrived eventually, and with great misgivings, at the conclusion that the experience of the West was largely irrelevant to the problems of the rest of the world, that each country would have to find for itself the solution to its own problems, based on its own history, culture, and experience. As a general mood of pessimism and self-criticism in the 70s began to creep over the Western world, pummeled as it was by crisis after crisis and a growing fear of disasters ahead, foreign aid programs came under increasing attack.

In a spirit of disillusionment, it was argued that if Western knowledge, institutions, and practices could not solve the problems of the West itself, they could scarcely be expected to meet the needs of non-Western countries.

133

Moreover, since the West was finding it increasingly difficult to solve its own problems, it could ill afford to spare the resources that would be needed to make a significant contribution to the solution of the problems of the rest of the world. Indeed, some observers in the West began to say that the ills experienced by the non-West were perhaps largely the result of Western intrusions—if so, the biggest favor the Western world could do would be to withdraw and permit non-Western societies to follow their own historical and cultural norms which, after all, might well give them the most appropriate solutions to their own problems.

Of course the two contrasting points of view outlined above did not, historically, separate out as neatly as the foregoing statement suggests. Even in the 50s there were sharp critics who challenged the naive assumptions of the Point Four Westernizers, and during the years of disillusionment in the 60s, there have been plenty of hard core enthusiasts who maintained an optimistic front in the face of growing disaffection and relativism.

A Possible Synthesis—Alternatives?

If we regard these two contrasting orientations as a kind of "thesis" and "antithesis" in a dialectical confrontation, can we perhaps discern in the first years of the 70s any early signs of a synthesis that may, by the end of the decade, provide a coherent and intellectually valid reconciliation of these apparently contradictory underlying assumptions?

One idea that has begun to attain some popularity parades under the heading of "alternatives." In one of its most popular manifestations we read of "alternative futures." A variety of possible future destinies are postulated, for each of which a scenario is constructed. Reading backwards into the present, the proponents of these alternatives then urge us to select those policies or strategies which will enhance the likelihood that desired futures can occur and the more dismal potentialities can be avoided.

At a more prosaic level the notion of opportunity costs, as developed in economics and decision theory, has also spread. Rational choices are supposedly based on consideration of all the alternative uses which might be made of a given set of available resources, the course selected being that alternative which leads to the most desirable set of consequences as compared with the other alternatives that might have been selected. Under the rubric of PPBS (for program planning and budgeting system) the programing and budgeting officers of complex organizations are asked not only to describe and cost out proposed courses of action, but also to explain all possible alternatives and consider whether they might be more acceptable than the recommended course of action.

This general posture toward the analysis of alternatives as a basis for choice is now being applied also to development theory, at least by a few proponents. It seems to offer a synthesis for the Westernizing versus anti-Westernizing formulae identified above. One of the alternatives would, of course, be a Westernizing one, another might be called "neo-traditional."

One can also visualize choices between a "socialist" model of development and a "capitalist" model, between a capital intensive and an agriculturally based model, or between a strategy designed to maximize economic growth and one intended to distribute wealth and power more equitably, or to promote the goals of "liberation" and of "revolution."

The idea of alternatives is, of course, often a myth in the sense that the proffered choices are not real, they presuppose a capacity to choose between fundamentally different courses of action. Insofar as choices are realistically possible, they are usually incremental or marginal, and very often the unintended consequences of a choice far outweigh the intentional in their long-run significance. Environmental constraints, moreover, severely limit the degree to which free choices are possible. One of the salient characteristics of development, if not its defining essence, is an increasing capacity of social systems to make choices. Thus the less developed a society, the less able it is to choose between alternatives. The concept of alternatives, insofar as it has relevance, is relevant to the most developed social systems, but scarcely applicable to the least developed.

An Ecological Alternative

In my opinion we must look in quite a different direction for a synthesis. Or perhaps we should look for a new set of assumptions in which the question of Westernization or non-Westernization can be discarded as irrelevant and misleading. Let me suggest such a frame of reference: an *ecological* view according to which decisions can be taken by any social system only within narrow limits that are environmentally constrained, and a contextual framework in which the real choices that are possible rarely involve the need to select between Western and non-Western alternatives. Indeed, the whole question of what is "Western" and what is not tends to dissolve when alternatives are viewed ecologically.

Taking the field of public administration and bureaucratic organization as a theme, let us inquire into the domain of Westernisms. Can we assume that bureaucracy, as we now find it in the Western world, is characteristically "Western" and that the bureaucracies of the non-Western world are typically "non-Western." To put the matter in a paradoxically exaggerated form, I suggest the following extreme hypothesis: "the characteristic bureaucratic structures of non-Western countries are Western, and the typical bureaucracies found in the West are non-Western."

At least superficially, this paradox is as plausible as its opposite, unless we want to deprive the term "Western" of all substantive content, giving it only a geographic meaning. But then we would be driven to say that Western bureaucracies are, by definition, Western because they are found in the West, whereas any bureaucracy found in a non-Western country is necessarily non-Western because it is located in the non-West. This reduction of the idea to a tautology suggests the absurdity of trying to use the term "Western" for any substantive meaning.

If you ask what characteristics found in the bureaucracies of Western countries are "Western," you are likely to come up with a strange mixture of traits. One student who used Monroe Berger's definitions, based on Max Weber's description of bureaucracy, to compare the attitudes and practices of officials in Tennessee to those of Egyptian civil servants found that bureaucratic behavior in Tennessee was less Western (!) than in Egypt. The argument seems to be a reductio ad absurdum, but if so, why follow it?

If bureaucracies in the West are thought to have particular characteristics, then why not refer to them by descriptive labels, M, N, P, etc. We could then ask whether bureaucracies in the West—or in Tennessee or America—tend to rank higher on scales M, N, P, etc., than do bureaucracies in the non-West—in Tanzania or in Afghanistan. When we do this, of course, we discover not a single complex of tightly linked traits or structures, such as may be implied by a portmanteau word like "West," but rather a series of variables, each of which may vary independently of the others, generating a multivariant field within which an infinite number of differentiations become possible.

The absurdities in the traditional argument can be seen clearly if we substitute "North" and "South" for West and non-West (or East?). Consider the proposition that bureaucracies in Northern countries are relatively Northern, whereas those in the South are more Southern. Since the words North and South carry only geographic, not substantive, meanings, these statements become obviously tautological. A Northern bureaucracy is, clearly, only a bureaucracy found in the North, whatever its characteristics might be.

It is possible to argue, however, that the substantive content of geographic-directional terms, like East and West, can be meaningfully applied to origins, even though irrelevant for characteristics. By this definition, anything is Western that was invented or begun in the West, and conversely Eastern if it can be traced to Eastern origins. Accordingly, Chinaware is Eastern, having been invented in China, and automobiles are Western because they were first built in Western countries. However, no American gourmet feels any incongruity in eating his rib roast off a China plate, nor does a Nigerian or Indonesian driver feel alienated because his car was built in Germany, the United States, or Japan.

Why Western Is Non-Western

Actually, it is when we trace origins that we discover why modern bureaucratic institutions are essentially non-Western. They came to Europe by way of India from China. We still call our numbering system "Arabic." Why not similarly call our civil service examination system "Indian" or "Chinese"? Certainly the Chinese were the first to establish written examinations as a basis for selecting public officials, an institution that long ago became very well established in China, making it possible for this traditional civilization to establish a remarkably effective machine for administering one of the world's largest and most long-lasting empires.

As to India, Westerners often think of the Indian Civil Service as a British export to its imperial domain, yet anyone who studies English bureaucratic history knows that the patronage system survived in the "mother country" long after the Indian Civil Service had been established as a relatively rational bureaucratic structure. Actually, it was the East India Company, operating in India—and administering many of its activities through offices whose structure had been established well before the British arrived, notably under the Moghuls—which created overseas a system of governance that had no real counterpart in England. Since the company had factories in Canton, it was quite familiar with Chinese bureaucratic structures and administrative theories, including the principles of pre-entry education for officials, and recruitment through examinations. No doubt it took a long time for these ideas to be accepted and implemented by the East India Company, but eventually, during the first half of the nineteenth century, they were.

Subsequently, it was from India that the same ideas about the improvement of bureaucratic performance percolated into England, affecting the administrative reforms accomplished during the second half of the nineteenth century. From England, of course, the notion that examinations for the public services would improve administration seeped into the consciousness of American reformers who, after making some fundamental changes in the design of the examinations, were able to introduce them, but only during the last quarter of the nineteenth century.

And Non-Western Is Western

Actually, the influence of Chinese experience and ideas in Western administrative practice is deeper and more pervasive than this illustration suggests, but it is not important for the argument made here to press this subject further. Rather, we can look at the opposite side of the coin: the extent to which Western administrative ideas and practices have already seeped into the non-Western world. The experience of countries formerly under colonial rule may seem to be exceptional, but few would deny that the metropolitan powers deeply shaped the patterns of governance in the countries they occupied. The structures of the Philippine government today are clearly American, just as the forms found in Ghana are British, those found in Indonesia are Dutch, and the bureaucracies of Chad or Algeria are typically French.

Despite this, of course, much of the continuing substructure of bureaucracy in Vietnam is Chinese, with a French, and now an American, overlay, and we have seen that the Indian system of administration was a composite of Moghul and Chinese ideas, mixed and remolded by Englishmen. One might argue of course that the system of administration which the British took with them to Africa was developed in Calcutta, Madras, and Bombay more than in London. The point is, however, that the structures of bureaucracy and the patterns of administration which one finds today in the many states that are post-colonial have already been shaped by Western influences to such a degree that it would be virtually impossible to re-establish forms of governance along truly indigenous lines. Throughout Latin America one could scarcely find any forms of administration not shaped essentially and permanently by Iberian precedents and practices.

One may well argue that not all of the non-Western world was subjected to colonial rule, pointing to countries like Japan, China, Siam, Egypt and Turkey, Iran and Ethiopia. No doubt pre-Western symbols and institutions survive in these countries, but one may doubt whether they are more decisive in the actual practice of government than they are in the ex-colonial countries. As far back as the Meiji restoration the fundamental structures of Japanese administration were revamped along Western lines, strongly influenced by German, French, and British examples, and since World War II American influences have added another overlay.

The ancient Chinese structure of bureaucratic rule was, essentially, destroyed by the revolution of 1911, and the new bureaucratic institutions which emerged later were influenced in far-reaching ways by American and Russian precedents. The Thai system of government is quite eclectic, showing a wide variety of influences, but the residue of truly traditional institutions is minor in importance compared to the patterns built on Western models. The late Ottoman Empire reshaped its administrative system in fundamental respects, following French precedents, establishing new institutions which survive to the present day in the Turkish republic, subject only to secondary modifications drawn from American and other Western sources during the last few decades.

In short, the actual institutions and practices of public administration in virtually all of the non-Western countries have already been institutionalized rather firmly on lines imported from the West, subject to variations derived from differences between the French, British, Dutch, Russian, Spanish, and American models. As a consequence, the alternatives which are effectively open to the new nation-states of the non-Western world do not involve, at the bureaucratic and administrative level, real choices between Western and non-Western patterns of organization and operation.

Choices and Levels

Choices no doubt can and must be made between alternatives, and the more developed a society becomes, the greater the range of choices continuously open to it. But choices always arise within constraints, the number of real alternatives that can be chosen are limited, and many hypothetical possibilities are not, in fact, real possibilities at all.

What, then, are the kinds of choices which can and could be made? At the ideological level, a very high level, there are no doubt choices to be made on a scale of policy alternatives, the values to be embraced by any polity. These concern, for example, the degree to which priority may be given to increasing the national output as compared with a more equitable distribution of the available goods and services. The more developed a society and polity, the more it can, assuredly, have its cake and eat it too: it can both produce more and assure more equity and social justice in the allocation of increasingly available goods. For poor countries, however, this may be an area of agonizing choice, since efforts to widen the distribution of goods may reduce the level of savings required for investment if production levels are to be raised. Contrastingly, of course, stress on productivity may well impair the ability of a country to provide, simultaneously, for more distributive justice.

As this example makes clear, the values in conflict are universal. They are equally Western or non-Western. The choices to be made involve the rank ordering of highly prized values. There is no dispute about the purposes to be sought, but there may be disagreement about which should be sacrificed if either of two fundamental goals can be achieved in the short run only by compromising efforts to achieve the other. The need to choose between greater equality and greater capacity has been a long-run universal dilemma of traditional civilizations and developing pre-industrial societies, as it continues to be in the modern, relatively industrialized and developed countries—there is certainly no difference between North and South, on these criteria.

Nor is there a difference in these values between capitalist and socialist systems, for both in practice seek to promote greater production and better distribution, although the ideology of socialism no doubt lays greater stress on equalitarian values while free enterprise norms pay more attention to productivity. If the history of the Soviet Union can be taken as representative for "socialist" practice rather than theory, then clearly its great drive for industrialization under Stalin's five-year plans gave far higher priority to production than to distribution, and in the United States, the social policies launched by the New Deal and maintained more or less since then have given great weight to distributive values. In both cases, however, there has been a continuing emphasis on distributive and productive values, and with increasing affluence, a growing ability to achieve some success on both fronts simultaneously.

For poor countries, however, this value choice is more difficult to make, and more critical. However, from the point of view of public administration and bureaucratic organization, the same machinery of government can be used to implement either value choice. Thus the ideological debate, the struggle over the relative priorities to be assigned to fundamental values which are shared by all, but may not be achieved simultaneously, is not a conflict about different ways of organizing a government, but rather a political or policy choice which needs to be made at a higher—or at least a different—level.

Turning from the highest levels of public policy to the more immediate and "practical" proposals of administrative reformers, we think of such items as the introduction of performance budgeting (or PPBS) in place of line-item budgeting, the modernization of personnel administration by the introduction of a position classification system, the creation of Organization and Methods units in the government, or the establishment of Institutes of Public Administration as relatively autonomous centers for research and training.

Without questioning the intrinsic importance of such reforms, it should first be pointed out that these proposals grew out of efforts to improve administrative performance within the West itself—that is to say, the practices to be changed or replaced are as Western as the new institutions which are proposed for adoption. Thus the line-items budget system is as Western as performance budgeting, and it continues to be widely used in the West, even as it has spread from the West to most if not all non-Western countries. Consequently the choice between performance budgeting and line-item budgeting is not a choice between something Western and something that is non-Western, but between two ways of budget planning, both of which are equally Western—or rather, now that the issue has been globalized, they are both equally non-Western, in the sense that we find among non-Western administrators passionate adherents of both approaches to budgeting, just as we find the same controversies among Western administrative practitioners and theorists.

A Deeper Issue: Salaries

If we want to find issues which could more realistically be posed as alternatives between Western and non-Western modes of organizing governmental operations, we would have to go back to questions which might have been agitated in the nineteenth rather than the twentieth century. Such an issue, for example, might be the question whether public officials ought to be compensated on a full-time salaried basis, or authorized officially to collect fees and gifts for their services. One could consider this issue as a part of the much broader question of secularization of sacred societies, or the marketization of relationships hitherto governed by principles of reciprocity.

The issue has, of course, been almost universally resolved in favor of the official salary system. Civil servants and military officers are now, in virtually every government of the world—non-Western as well as Western, capitalist as well as socialist—paid official salaries in exchange for which they are expected to work exclusively for government and not to be paid by, and hence to be in the service of, private citizens, interest groups, or business firms.

If we look at this issue more closely we will see, however, that the marketization of public employment is not really Western as contrasted with non-Western, except perhaps in the sense of historical origins. When we think of European history, we immediately recognize that under feudalism public officials were not paid salaries but, as fief-holders, maintained themselves from their lands and followers. Although the creation of public offices whose incumbents were salaried no doubt has antecedents reaching far back into European feudalism, the prevalent Western system of government has certainly been based for a very very long time, not on the payment of salaries, but on fiefs, on the possession of "livings" and on other prebendary sources of income. The secularization and marketization of government was as much a revolutionary transformation in the West, achieved for the most part during the eighteenth and nineteenth centuries, as it was later to become in the non-Western world, during the nineteenth and twentieth centuries. Thus the salary system in public bureaucracies is much more "modern" than it is either Western or Eastern.

Actually, of course, one can find antecedents for the salary system of compensating public officials in the non-Western world, notably in China, whose procedures for examining candidates for employment in the public services, already referred to, were accompanied by modest "salaries." However, in China as in pre-modern Europe, public office was typically worth much more to the incumbent (because of non-salary income) than the official salary attached to his position. In seventeenth century France, as elsewhere in Europe, the sale of public offices was widely practiced—this says a lot about the income public officials derived from sources different from the public payroll, but it also underlines the marketization, and secularization, of office-holding.

There is no reason why, in principle, the effective use of a salary system for public bureaucracies could not have evolved in China much earlier than it did in England, France, or the United States. It was not the idea or the institution that basically distinguished between the Western and non-Western administrative practice, but rather the level of national income, augmented in the West by the industrial revolution, which made it economically possible to pay officials enough to cover their essential living costs, and hence to make extra-official income unnecessary, even though in practice, even in the West, bribery and other illicit forms of fees-for-services rendered continued to be practiced.

This illustration should help us to understand the essential differences in public administration between the situation as it exists in much of the Western world and what can be found in a good part of the non-Western world. These essential differences are not to be found in the institutions, or perhaps even in the values, which prevail, because these resemble each other to an amazing degree around the world, in the structure and avowed purposes of government. There are, however, great differences in the way these institutions work, and hence in the functions which they actually perform. Moreover, the reasons for these functional differences, for variations in achievement or performance levels, are to be found in ecological variables, not in the essential institutions and practices of formal government.

Achievement and Performance

Poverty and Administrative Performance

Among these ecological variables particular weight must be given to the level of economic performance achieved by a society. In poor countries, for example, the resources available to be channeled through public treasuries for the payment of salaries to officials are severely limited. This means that salary levels cannot, in the nature of things, be high enough to enable military officers and civil servants to live on them, within the prevailing standards of living of their own societies. Moreover, the rising demands for enhanced social mobility—another obvious consequence of the demonstration effect of Western industrialization—means that an increasing number of college graduates in each non-Western country clamours for positions in government. The typical and virtually unavoidable response has been overstaffing, the employment of more office holders, and the multiplication of official positions. Given the inadequacy of public revenues, salary levels have been further depressed to accommodate the swollen registers of public employees.

In other words, it is not essentially the institutionalization or the practice of placing public officials on a salaried basis that distinguishes Western from non-Western administration, for the essential structures are similar, if not identical. Far more decisive differences are found if one reflects on economic and social factors affecting administrative performance. One of the key reasons why administrative performance in poor countries is low, therefore, is quite simply the persistence of poverty. Moreover, low standards of public administration adversely affect the conduct of public programs designed to raise production levels. In short, poverty leads to inferior administrative performance which, in turn, may well impede growth and perpetuate poverty.

The Political Context of Bureaucratic Achievement

Economic and social factors are not the only ecological considerations that affect bureaucratic achievement. Perhaps equal weight should be given to the political context in which bureaucracies operate. To explain this point we need to recognize a distinctive institutional form which is found in all modern governments, although, strangely enough, the form is often not recognized, even in the West. The components of the form, are, however, very familiar: they include an elective assembly, an electoral system (without which an elective assembly could not, of course, be constituted), and a system for nominating candidates to be elected to the assembly. Since all these components are inextricably linked to each other, and since the dynamics of a political system can be understood much better if one can refer to this whole structure rather than only to its components, I believe it is useful to have a name for it. Our present situation is confusing in the same way that it would be confusing if we did not have a name for automobiles, although we had names for engines, bodies, and wheels. We could then only talk about the components of automobiles, or refer to "that thing" which is made up of an engine, a body, and four wheels.

I call "that thing" which is made up of one or more elective assemblies (we have two in the United States—a Senate and a House of Representatives), of an electoral system, and a party system (which includes both the Republican and Democratic parties, and various "third" parties in the U.S.) a "constitutive system." I shall not try to explain here why this particular label was chosen, and readers can use any other expression they prefer, but having defined the "thing," let us see how it helps us understand the political ecology of administrative performance.

First of all, the constitutive system is a common element in modern Western polities, although there are great variations in the way constitutive systems operate. In the Soviet Union the constitutive system is dominated by its party system, whereas in the United States the elected assemblies play a far more important part. Both in both systems, there are generated through the constitutive system important constraints upon, guidelines and incentives for, bureaucratic performance. No doubt public bureaucracies also play an important political role in any government, and their influence is decisive in many. But it is difficult to imagine any modern government, whether socialist or capitalist in its basic ideology and economic structure, which does not have a more or less effective balance of power between the executive branch of government, centering on a public (military and civil) bureaucracy, and a countervailing constitutive system.

I have deliberately said "modern" rather than "Western" because the type of government which has prevailed in the West for most of its history did not have a constitutive system. It was only during the eighteenth and nineteenth centuries that constitutive systems developed and became institutionalized in the West. During the nineteenth and twentieth centuries almost all non-Western countries have also created constitutive systems. Many of them do not work very well in these countries—as indeed they often do not fulfill expectations in Western countries. The point is that this institutional form, which evolved rather recently in the West, has already spread throughout the non-Western world. The decision whether or not to try to establish a constitutive system, therefore, is not an open one—it has already been made.

From Monarchy to Constitutive System

The impact—actual or potential—on administrative performance of constitutive systems can be seen fairly well if we reflect on the institution which it replaced, namely absolute monarchy. Pre-modern governments, in non-Western as in Western countries, had come to be organized around the institution of a hereditary ruler. It is true that there have been republican forms of government in city states and villages in traditional societies—both in the Western and non-Western worlds—but all of the larger polities which had organized governments at the supra-urban level were able to do so only because they succeeded in creating relatively competent centralized bureaucracies. In my judgment a necessary condition for the creation of such bureaucratic systems was an effective ruling institution which traditionally took the form of a king (or emperor, chief, kaiser; the name is not important) who was recruited by hereditary principles. An apparent exception was the Papacy, but we are dealing here with the government of a church, not a state, except for the very small area of the Vatican itself.

Monarchies provided the necessary pivot for political centralization and control which welded bureaucracies together and continuously reinforced the principle that offices should be filled by appointment rather than by inheritance. In short, a prerequisite for the maintenance of any monarchy as a center of power filled by inheritance was the ability to prevent most of the offices in the supporting staff of that monarchy from being filled by inheritance. Whenever, as under feudalism, bureaucratic offices became hereditary, the effective power of monarchies was undermined, and power became increasingly localized.

Because of the industrial revolution, however, the problems confronting government in the industrializing societies became too complex to be effectively solved by public bureaucracies subjected to control only by a hereditary ruling house. A new secular institution, far more responsive to the interests affected by governmental policies, and far more ubiquitous in its ability to penetrate the domain, was required. Such an institution was discovered when constitutive systems first evolved, following a rather long period of trial and error. It succeeded in taking the power of governing a state bureaucracy away from kings.

Of course, monarchies persisted and, I am inclined to think, those countries which have succeeded in modernizing and retaining their ruling houses have indeed been fortunate. Constitutional monarchies—i.e., monarchies in countries where effective power is exercised by a constitutive system—tend to be more stable than policies in which the head of the state is elected or seizes power by violence. Unfortunately, once a monarchy has been discredited, it has proven virtually impossible to reestablish a kingship, no matter how desirable the institution might appear to be.

This, however, is merely an aside—the important point is not only that constitutive systems have emerged as a political substitute for kingship in the modern history of Western countries, whether socialist or capitalist in ideological orientation, but that the same system has spread throughout the world to non-Western countries as well. And in the non-Western world, as in the Western, constitutive systems have replaced monarchic institutions, but with this important difference: more monarchies have survived as constitutional monarchies, proportionately, in Western countries than in the non-Western ones (the Arabian peninsula aside).

One reason for this, of course, is that constitutive systems, which have never worked very well in the Western world—they survive because we cannot really think of anything better—work much worse in non-Western countries. However, they do not work badly because they are not well designed. Indeed, the constitution makers of the non-Western world were generally familiar with the experience of the West and were able to incorporate all the latest improvements in the charters through which they attempted to design and establish constitutive systems. It is perhaps because they do work so badly that the monarchs who remain have profoundly distrusted them and sought to displace them—as have the military juntas and personal dictatorships that have also seized power and discharged elective assemblies, only to try, in gingerly fashion, to reestablish them once control over the state bureaucracy had been assured.

This explanation may seem unnecessarily complicated, but I believe it is necessary in order to show that the framework which already exists in most non-Western countries for the imposition of control over state bureaucracies is a framework that was imported from the West. However, it was only recently developed in the West as a substitute for monarchic control, and hence it was not essentially different from the basic institutional transformations that have been experienced most recently by the non-Western countries themselves.

Conclusions

Ecological Reasons for Institutional Failures

On the basis of these considerations I have concluded that one of the fundamental reasons why public administration works so badly in many of the new and developing countries is neither because they have refused to adopt Western institutions nor because they have inappropriately borrowed them, but rather because underlying ecological factors have made it very difficult for these institutions to perform effectively. More specifically, the failure of constitutive systems to work well means that the balance of power has swung decisively in favor of public (military and civil) bureaucracies in most of the non-Western countries. In a few, disproportionate power has, instead, flowed into the constitutive system, leaving the bureaucracy starved of an effective voice in public decision making, and in a few more the chief executive wields power in a non-accountable fashion, surviving by continuously playing constitutive system and bureaucracy against each other. None of these arrangements is conducive to effective and efficient administration.

Even where decisive power is now exercised by public bureaucracies—and the characteristic sign of this condition is the domination of a government by a clique of military officers—public administration is affected very adversely because the dominant motivations in the top echelons of government must consequently become more political than administrative. As top bureaucrats feel compelled to pay more attention to staying in power than to achieving program objectives, the quality of public administration necessarily declines.

My conclusion is that, although much of the work of administrative reformers is devoted to efforts to change the structure and practices of public bureaucracies, this effort is largely doomed to failure regardless of whether they seek to emulate Western examples or strive to invent new "non-Western" and "indigenous" solutions to their problems. The most important means to improve administrative performance—apart from the economic and social constraints discussed above—is, surely, to improve the effectiveness of the operation of constitutive systems. No doubt there are "political" reasons for being concerned with the way that constitutive systems work, but there are also administrative reasons. So long as administrative reformers refuse to think seriously about the performance of constitutive systems, limiting their span of attention to bureaucratic structure and practices, they will continue to be ineffectual and frustrated in their efforts.

These, then, are some of the alternatives which need to be considered. It is not essentially whether development occurs by Western or non-Western patterns, or with socialist or capitalist ideologies, but rather whether or not the environmental conditions favorable to improved administrative performance by public bureaucracies can be brought into existence. These conditions will be affected by economic growth rates, and by the ability of constitutive systems to work effectively, more than by changes in the structure of public bureaucracies, no matter how subtle and complex these changes may be, or where they originate.

Alternatives: Mythical and Real

It is not my intention to argue that no choices are really open to countries of the Third World, that there are not significant differences between the paths which they can and, indeed, are following. Since my conception of development is based precisely on the possibility of achieving greater freedom of choice—either as a consequence or, indeed, as the essence of development itself—I would like to measure the degree of success achieved by any country in its developmental strivings by the extent to which it can, effectively, make significant choices.

However, all choices, even in the most developed countries, are made within the limits of severe and identifiable constraints. Part of the wisdom needed to make effective choices is a clear understanding of these constraints. Success is never achieved by charging, like Don Quixote, at windmills. On many aspects of administrative or bureaucratic development, the die has already been cast in an irreversible fashion. Patterns of bureaucratic structure which involve organization along lines that stress functional specialization, and the use of salaries as a principal basis for personal compensation, have become widely accepted premises, within which, of course, there is much room for differences, for example in the particular functions to be emphasized, or the level of salaries to be paid for different tasks and statuses.

One can assert that these fundamental characteristics of modern bureaucratic organization originated in the West, even though, historically, some of them were actually invented, much earlier, in non-Western countries, like China. A more important point to make is that, having spread throughout the world today, these forms of organization, like the automobile, have become the property of the societies that have adopted them, and have therefore become as "indigenous" as anything else adopted or invented in that country. Even though Chinaware came to the rest of the world from China, there was a time when someone in China must have discovered a process for making porcelain. We can imagine the resistance he may have felt from the makers of pottery who faced disaster and who might well have attacked the innovation as "un-Chinese" because for centuries the Chinese had lived without it.

The point is that once a new generation grows up accustomed to something which their parents or ancestors may not have known about, they treat it as their own, regardless of whether it was invented by a fellow-countryman or imported from abroad. It quickly becomes theirs, and they may love it or hate it, but they soon stop thinking of it as "foreign." My grandparents did not enjoy—or suffer from—television, nor did the ancestors of my Korean, Thai, or Egyptian friends. It may have taken a few more years to introduce TV to these countries than it did to the United States, but to the young people of any country, the "boob tube" has become as much a part of their lives, perhaps even more important a part, than anything—like kite flying—which they may have inherited from their distant ancestors.

There are no doubt important alternatives between which choices have to be made affecting forms of bureaucratic organization and practices affecting the dynamics of administrative performance, but these choices rarely, if ever, involve the need to distinguish between "Western" and "non-Western" structures or, at least so far as bureaucracy and administration is concerned, between "socialist" and "capitalist" forms. In order to understand what the meaningful and possible choices are, we need a far more intimate and detailed understanding of governmental structures and ecological constraints affecting administrative performance in each country of the world than is now available to us, and we need also a more powerful theoretical framework that will direct our attention to the crucial variables which are, indeed, subject to manipulation and therefore matters of choice, where true alternatives can be found.

One of the differences which is frequently said to distinguish between Western and Eastern modes of thought is the willingness of Westerners to formulate plans as though they could deliberately make choices that would affect their own future, whereas Easterners are said to be more fatalistic, more inclined to accept divine or supernatural forces or mere chance as the determinant of future events. If so—and I by no means accept this popular view—then we might find ourselves in a paradoxical position if we urged non-Westerners to consider alternative patterns of development. For then, as Westerners, we would find ourselves suggesting to non-Westerners that they ought, like Westerners, be giving more thought to some developmental alternatives because, if they did, they might then choose more non-Western institutions and practices than if they permitted Western foreigners to impose their ideas and technology upon them. If they behaved more like fatalistic non-Westerners, they would accept the Western institutions that have, in fact, already been foisted upon them.

My own view is that the degree of confidence in planning and ability to choose between alternatives varies directly, in both East and West, with class position. Since affluence has permitted the countries which first industrialized to have larger middle class populations, a naive confidence in planning and alternatives spread more rapidly in the West than in the non-Western world, but the belief in alternatives and choice has by now become as powerful in non-Western governments as it has in Western ones. The task which scholarship faces is to cultivate among intellectuals, in both East and West, a more realistic understanding of the alternatives which are in fact open to developing countries, and the constraints within which choices can be made. The underlying myths about administrative development which we find all too prevalent must be replaced by a more realistic conception of what is possible and how it can be achieved.

Part II
Technical Assistance and Training for
Administrative Development

10 Toward New International Economic Development and Resource Transfer

Jan Tinbergen

Background

In order to reduce the danger of future major conflicts, the world has to step up its efforts to reduce poverty. By far the largest effort is being made and will be made by the developing countries themselves. They will not succeed, however, if they are not joined by the more prosperous countries, whose resources are so immensely larger.

Both the Pearson report and the proposals for a United Nations Second Development Decade (1971–1980) advocate that the financial flow from developed countries to developing countries be brought to 1 percent of their GNP very soon. Moreover, freer imports from developed countries are recommended. All this is in the long-term interest of the developed countries also. The success of the new development strategy will depend vitally on the contributions to be made by the United States; Europe will also be expected to do more than in the past.

We can now acknowledge that among the least of its consequences, the United Nations Development Decade of the 1960s provided stimulation to thinking and action in many aspects of the development process and in many national and international centers. The decade saw some sharp breaks in the stagnation and inertia characteristic of earlier decades. The productive capacity of some developing countries increased significantly and their ability to undertake additional tasks of expansion and advance was most marked. These gains, unfortunately, were not shared evenly and many defects still have to be overcome. On average, the developing countries fared far less well than the developed countries.

The purpose of this paper is to present some of the thinking for the way ahead in the 1970s. I hope to point to some of the areas of responsibility which both developed and developing countries must undertake if the decade of the 1970s is to be meaningful progress for all mankind. Many of my observations are included in the recently published Proposals for the Second United Nations Development Decade made by the Committee for Development Planning on which I served as chairman.[1]

Based on a speech given at the Whittemore School of Business and Economics, University of New Hampshire, May, 1970, in conjunction with a conference on Administrative and Management Problems in Developing Countries.

151

Economic Performance of the 1960s and New Objectives

During 1960 to 1967, the developing countries achieved an annual rate of increase of about 4.6 percent in total domestic product, but only about 2 percent in per capita gross domestic produce. In Africa the per capita rate was around 1.5 percent, for Asia 2.2 percent, and for Latin America 1.8 percent. In certain countries the average rate of increase in both total and per capita gross domestic product in this period declined compared to the rate achieved in the 1950s.

For the same period, the developed countries increased their total gross domestic product by 5.1 percent per annum, while their per capita gross domestic product rose by 3.8 percent. The centrally planned economies in general increased their annual total net material product by 6.7 percent and per capita product by 5.4 percent. The developed countries made progress in scientific and technological achievements which reinforced and extended their trade, cooperation, and influence.

These few statistics point to the fact that for many of the developing countries, economic performance during the decade of the 1960s has been quite inadequate and that the basic preconditions in the economic and social spheres for accelerating progress are still elusive. For their part, the developed countries made only minor contributions toward achieving the objectives of the first United Nations Development Decade. Improvements are to be noted, of course, in international development finance both as to institutions and policies. Nevertheless, this improvement has not been commensurate with the spectacular progress in the developed countries. This is seen in the fact that the net flow of financial resources to developing countries, which refer to disbursements to developing countries and to the multilaterial financial and technical assistance agencies, net of amortization, declined as a percentage of the Gross National Product of the developed economies. From .79 percent in 1960, it fell to .70 percent in 1968, and further reductions in appropriations for 1969 indicate a continuation of the decline. The terms of financing available are now more difficult and sources of soft lending have tended to evaporate.

Export earnings of developing countries rose by 6 percent per annum on the average during 1960 to 1968 which was considerably higher than for the 1950s. Exports of developed countries, however, have expanded at an even greater rate with the consequence that exports from developing countries which represented 31 percent of world exports in 1950, fell to 21 percent in 1960 and to 18 percent in 1968. Much of the export rise for the developing countries has been in petroleum.

These trade and aid features of the development decade of the 1960s underlie the urgency of more vigorous efforts in achieving world development objectives in the 1970s. Both developed and developing countries need more vigorous efforts to further the objectives of development. The past trends of growth in developing countries cannot be allowed to continue. International policies require serious modification to avoid more serious difficulties in the future. Progress in the wealthiest sections of the world make it mandatory to assist in the acceleration of development of the poorest nations. World tensions will only be aggravated if these gaps are not bridged.

Accelerated development must be the basic objective of international development strategy in the 1970s. For the developing countries, development does not mean simply an increase in productive capacity, it means fundamental transformations in the social and economic structure. Suffering from economic dualism, the developing countries face sharp contrasts between the modern technological sectors and the backward underdeveloped sectors. Inequalities and rigidities in social systems such as land tenure, administrative bureaucracies and hierarchies, inadequate educational opportunities, external pressures, and traditional customs widen the social and economic disparities.

Realistic indicators of development must embrace more than increases in output or income. The process of development has to be seen as consisting of fundamental structural changes brought about by appropriate planned social transformation. As much attention has to be given to social planning as has been customarily given to economic planning.

Basic objectives of development must focus on the following:

1. *accelerating the growth process.* The 1970s must be marked by growth of gross product per head, and the fruits of development should be available to the poverty stricken masses in greater abundance than before. These aggregative indicators are the easiest to produce and represent, in some broad way, quantitative impressions of underlying transformations. The Committee for Development Planning feels that for the 1970s it is possible to achieve an annual rate of expansion in the total gross product of 6 percent to 7 percent and a growth in per capita gross product of 3.5 to 4.5 percent. The lower rates of growth should be the minimum attained during the first half of the decade.

2. *containing the rates of population expansion.* The objective of an accelerated growth in product is based upon an assumption of 2.5 percent average annual increase in population during the seventies. Rates of increase are predicted to be higher than 2.5 percent so that serious measures have to be taken to reduce the average birth rates at a pace equal to the declining average mortality rate. The implementation of population policy with this purpose requires extensive measures including a wide range of services for family planning and other influences on reproductive patterns.

3. *increasing agricultural and industrial production.* Agricultural output can be increased by 4 percent per year on the average in the developing countries. This growth in supplies is matched by the likely growth in domestic demand for agricultural goods. The increase in output will be needed to feed growing populations, to improve food consumption, and to insure growing supplies of raw materials for industry. Furthermore, buffer stocks are needed to insulate the economies from external pressures on domestic prices and the balance of payments. The realization of these objectives in agriculture are made more feasible by the wider results of the green revolution. Even so, such agricultural breakthroughs call for expansion in supply and a more sophisticated use of complementary inputs such as irrigation and fertilizers. Manufacturing output to the developing countries will have .to be raised to

8 percent during the first half of the decade in order to achieve an annual increase of 6 percent in the gross product. A greater rise will be needed in the second half if development is to be further accelerated. Industry and construction in particular must serve as the major agents of the modernization process. The benefits of import substitution in a wide-range of consumer industries which should be extended, although for many countries there are greater needs in building, intermediate and capital goods industries. These stages of output will require greater economic cooperation among the developing countries. Developing countries will eventually need to seek a growing export trade in manufactures requiring a liberalization of trade policies in importing partners and more systematic industrial planning.

Glaring inequalities in the distribution of wealth which prevail in developing countries have to be eliminated. Mass poverty, social injustice, inequalities between regions and between groups can be eliminated by new employment opportunities, greater supplies of food, and more nourishing food, arrangements for better education and health facilities, and an easier application of these services for the benefit of the lower stratas of society.

The continuance of high degrees of concentration of economic power in both the traditional and modern sectors of developing countries impair the pursuit of social justice and efficiency. Rapid growth and a reduction in wealth and income inequality can be more complementary than competitive in the development process. Small-scale operations can frequently be made as efficient as large-scale operations, although prevailing land tenure systems usually weaken these possibilities. The preemption of significant areas of industry, commerce, and finance by large scale businesses stifle competition and eliminate the growth of enterprises on a broader social and economic base.

The only solution to incredible amounts of unemployment and under-employment is to take urgent steps aimed at expanding employment opportunities. The objective of an employment policy should be set in quantitative terms, and for this purpose labor force statistics will be urgently required in most countries.

Education is widely acknowledged as a powerful instrument for economic growth. The pressure for increased education grows rapidly with economic development, but investment in education is expensive and yields are made only over long periods of time. Short-run increases in productivity, therefore, which are introduced by education and training measures, are more important than the long-run educational programs. A high priority should be accorded to adult education, agricultural education, and to consumer education. UNESCO has recommended that by 1980 developing countries should aim at 100 percent enrollment of the relevant age group in primary schools. The educational aims for other groups should be as follows:

Region	Second-level Education	Third-level Education
Africa	23%	1.5%
Asia	36%	5.0%
Latin America	46%	6.4%

The standards of health require improvement in order for the other objectives of the 1970s to be realized. The infrastructure of health institutions and personnel for preventing and curing disease and for promoting health generally must be based on a well-organized system of education and training of the health team. The implemetation of the objectives established by WHO would require capital investment of $7 billion and recurrent expenditure of almost $9.75 billion from national and international agencies.

Along with raising health standards, an improvement in housing and community facilities is fundamental in raising productivity. The establishment of new townships away from the large centers of population is needed to stem the evils of urban agglomeration. Planned industrial development should be associated with viable new housing schemes. The considerable financial means required for improving low-cost housing can be provided partly through taxation of luxury housing and by levies on land speculation. Even so, international financial support will be needed to supply the long-term capital funds necessary.

Joint Tasks of Development

An extension of research capacity in technology is required for further industrialization in many developing countries. Much assistance has been provided in the past from the international community, but for the future, developing countries themselves should count on larger resources being devoted for these purposes. The percentage of GNP given to research and development should be increased from the present level of .2 percent to about .5 percent of the end of the 1970s. Particular attention should be given to the promotion of agricultural research and technology.

Accelerated development is not the concern of the developing countries alone; advanced countries can be expected to maintain economic expansion and to contribute to a reduction of the prevailing economic disparities. Measures to mutually reinforce individual efforts should include increases in the export earnings of developing countries, expansion of genuine financial assistance, and increased availability of expertise and the results of modern science and technology.

There have always been doubt as to the demarcation point between the developed and the developing economies. This matter is of importance in the measures to provide preferential treatment to the developing countries in areas of trade and assistance. There exists in practice an intermediate group of countries which should neither be accorded preferences nor undertake obligations toward developing countries. International examinations are also needed for defining an optimal international division of labor, so that production choices and trading structures can be improved in the developing countries.

In the area of international trade, measures must be designed to increase the capacity of developing countries to import, by at least 1 percent per annum greater than the desirable rate of growth of gross product. With the target rate of growth of 6 percent of the gross product in the first half of the 1970s, the capacity to import should increase by a minimum of 7 percent per year. Still greater increases in import capacity have to be provided for in the second half of the decade. External debt servicing requirements also demand enlarged export expansion. This is particularly so in the cases where external debts have become a barrier to further borrowing. Furthermore, it should be appreciated that export expansion can substitute for aid flows from abroad. An adequate supply of exportables in the developing countries is the first essential in achieving expanded international trade. Incentives have to be provided to see that the expanded supplies can be transferred to foreign markets, at the most appropriate time.

Developed countries which control the markets for exports have a great responsibility in the aim of expanded world trade. A further liberalization of imports for goods from developing countries should be undertaken by each developed country as a follow-up to the Kennedy round of tariff reductions. Impediments such as protective custom duties, revenue duties, and fiscal charges, quantitative restrictions and certain administrative practices discriminating against goods from developing countries should be progressively removed. These measures imply a shift in the economic structures of the developed countries. The strength and flexibility of the competitive markets in these countries should enable such shifts to be made. It should be possible to eliminate impediments to imports from developing countries during the second United Nations Development Decade.

A limited and gradual reduction in the production of high cost agricultural products in the developed market economies should be undertaken without delay. The heavy protection for the production of sugar beet, for example, works greatly to the detriment of developing countries. Existing forms of special protection for manufacturers which discriminate against imports from developing countries should be gradually eliminated by the middle of the 1970s. Likewise, tariffs on manufactures on raw materials produced largely in developing countries should be progressively reduced. The preferences proposed by UNCTAD is an appropriate step aimed at a reduction in trade impediments. The centrally planned economies also could greatly improve the conditions under which imports flow from the developing countries.

Market conditions are highly unstable for numerous primary commodities. Commodity arrangements to regulate markets is a necessary measure aimed at improving the import capacity of developing countries through rational organization. The potential balance of payments gap of the developing countries can only be closed if there is a substantial improvement in exports of primary products.

Fluctuating foreign exchange earnings of exporting countries should be dealt with through international measures which improve market organization aimed at stable price levels, adequate remuneration for producers, and achieving consumer equity. The number of international commodity agreements aimed at providing solutions to unstable markets in income has remained rather small. Agreements already in existence should be extended in line with suggestions by UNCTAD. Agreements on cocoa and tea should be concluded as early as possible and the scope of the sugar agreement should be enlarged through the participation of the European Economic Community and the U.S.A.

The financing of buffer stocks through support of the IMF and the World Bank Group should facilitate the establishment of effective commodity agreements. The special difficulties encountered by producers of natural goods facing competition from synthetic materials can be reduced by eliminating tariffs and non-tariff barriers to the import of the natural goods. These barriers frequently induce an artificial stimulation to the production of synthetics. Exports potentials can also be enlarged through diversification programs which seek to augment and stabilize locally produced food supplies and to promote processed exports of primary commodities. In these efforts the emphasis should be given to those commodities where growth world rates are rapid.

The Scope of Assistance and Government Policy

Obstacles to accelerated economic and social progress can be overcome through a more effective application of international financial and technical cooperation. Much of the existing technical assistance originates in bilateral arrangements, which face certain disadvantages in the recipient countries. The mobilization of international resources, therefore, appears more vital than ever before.

The UN Committee for Development Planning, particularly with respect to multilateral aid, is focused on:

1. Special contributions by multi-national corporations operating in developing countries;
2. special taxes on consumption on a selected list of commodities;
3. voluntary contributions by companies, public organizations, and individuals.

These endeavors would more closely involve the common man in the development in the world community. The proposal for a world solidarity contribution would be based upon the consumption of those goods indicative of high levels of consumption, as for example, cars, aircraft, pleasure boats, television sets, refrigerators, and so forth. Assessments collected by the national tax authorities would be made at a low uniform rate such as .5 percent on the purchase price of the commodity. The funds would then be available for financing international development. The implications of these proposals require more complete study.

Increases in the flow of financial resources will be indispensable in the second development decade. Developed countries have already accepted in principle the obligation to provide increasing amounts for resource transfer. These transfers should be based upon equitable considerations, such as the level and growth of per capita income of the aid-giving country. Financial resources can be provided as grants and interest free public grants without tying arrangements.

External resource needs are critical for accelerated economic growth. UNCTAD has recommended that advanced countries should aim at providing financial resource transfers at a minimum net amount of one cent of GNP at market prices. The United Nations Development Planning Committee recommended that the advanced countries should set 1972 as the target year for achieving the aid volume. It also recommended that the aid target be given a higher priority in marginal expenditures by developed countries over defense, space research, or highways. Within the 1 percent aid target set for 1972, developed countries should provide a minimum of .75 percent of GNP through net official financial resource transfers. These transfers include official cash grants and grants in kind, excluding those for defense purposes, sales of commodities against local currencies, exclusive of donor company use, net long-term government lending, and capital and bond subscriptions to multilateral aid agencies.

Financial transfers to developing countries have been restricted in recent years by some advanced countries on account of unfavorable balance of payments conditions. Frequently there is a close connection between financial transfers made and commodities produced in the aid-giving countries. Corrections to adverse balance of payments should not concentrate on the aid contributions to the developing countries. The UN committee is of the view that no restrictions to aid should be made on account of balance of payments reasons. The overall improvement in the liquidity position of the developed countries has been made possible through the Special Drawing Rights provision of the I.M.F. and balance of payments adjustments have consequently been made more flexible.

The target for the transfer of financial resources is set as a minimum; no limits are set for private capital flows. There is particular significance attached to the recommendation that the public sector component of net transfer of financial resources should be set as a minimum equal to .75 percent of GNP. This adds precision to the definition of resource transfers by concentrating on those disbursements aiming directly at the promotion of economic development and welfare of developing countries.

It is acknowledged that the 1 percent target may not be applicable to the centrally planned economies. On the basis of per capita income some of these economies are more appropriately classified with the developing countries. Since the 1 percent aid target has included commercial transactions in private capital, it is not applicable for those countries where such transactions are not completely relevant. Nevertheless, the centrally planned economies have greater control over the mobilization and use of their resources than have the market economies and they tend to prefer making more substantial contributions in trade than in financial cooperation. The centrally planned economies could make greater contributions through an expansion of economic, scientific, and technical cooperation. This cooperation depends upon the scale of credits that they can offer to developing countries.

The terms for the new financial resources should be tailored closely to the needs and capabilities of the individual recipient countries. Coordinated action is required for necessary rescheduling of debts of the developing countries. Occasioned by possible export difficulties from time to time, such rescheduling is made more difficult through a hardening of the terms of lending taking place in recent years. The UN committee recommends that the developed countries should undertake to provide immediately at least 70 percent of their total official development assistance as grants, which are concentrated mainly in poorer countries and those with special difficulty. The grant component of official commitments should be progressively raised to 80 percent by 1975. As much as possible of the transfers should be in convertible currencies for untied purposes.

Developing countries require assured external support for a reasonably long period. Aid-giving countries should match their financial aid operations to the needs of medium term planning. National funds in the developed countries should be created which facilitate consistent flows of aid on a program and revolving basis. Short-term balance of payments financing is frequently inappropriate to deal with disruptions of export incomes of the developing countries. Supplementary finance of this kind requires cooperation among international agencies. An expanding proportion of financial transfers to developing countries should be channeled through multilateral institutions which should be adaptive and flexible to developing country needs.

The creation of the Special Drawing Rights improves international liquidity which should be regarded as an extension of the capacity of the developed countries to implement and expand aid programs. A positive link should be established between this form of international liquidity and development assistance because the new reserves involve no surrender of real resources from the developed countries. The Committee for Development Planning supports the UNCTAD recommendation that the developed countries declare that part of the increased reserves should accrue to the developing countries. One method for implementing this proposal would be to permit a direct contribution by developed countries of some proportion of their allocations of SDRs to the International Development Association and to the regional development banks. Another method would be to contribute national currencies to IDA in some proportion of the annual allocations of SDRs to developed countries.

Foreign private capital can be directed to activities which meet the economic and social objectives of the development plans of the developing countries. Developing countries should adopt measures for inducing and making effective use of foreign private capital. Systems of investment insurance against limitations on the transfer of earnings and against expropriations promotes the flow of foreign private capital.

Political considerations in the allocation of financial transfers makes for inequitable distributions among the developing countries. Economic and social development can be accelerated on a world level if external assistance is allocated on the basis of equity and efficiency. Not all aspects of equity and efficiency can be precisely formulated but aid-giving countries and organizations need to supplement one another's assistance in order to make more appropriate distributions.

Instruments and Institutions for Utilizing Assistance

The major criteria basic to allocating financial assistance are:

1. the needs of developing countries;
2. the development efforts as represented by establishment of social, economic, and institutional reforms systematically implemented in the developing countries;
3. the productive use of external assistance such that there is optimal marginal contribution to development from the external assistance;
4. the direction of resource flows to areas where greatest potential lie so that the international community's capacity is enhanced.

Because humans are the subject of all development strategy, the greater their number the greater the need for development. On the basis of equity, the lower the per capita income, the greater the assistance per head of population. Other considerations, such as balance of payments trends, size of country, the nature of the development, the costs of infrastructure per capita should also be considered in the allocation of aid. Because the responsibility for development lies primarily with developing countries, external assistance should match efforts made by these countries in mobilizing domestic resources. Attention should be given to indicators of the ability to use assistance effectively.

There are many difficulties in defining criteria for allocating external assistance. The test of performance using savings ratios may not always indicate the effort involved. Success in this area may be more due to balance of payments circumstances than to the basic effort extended. The test of performance using a tax ratio may tend to overlook the efforts used in expending the revenues generated. Export performance, training effort, new technical personnel, farm productivity, and new institutional establishment are other possible tests of performance on which aid allocations might be based.

Complex technical assistance cooperation schemes have been provided in the developing countries. Such schemes help channel much needed skills from areas of relative abundance to areas of relative scarcity. Greater flows of technical assistance, especially through multilateral agencies, will be required for the Second Development Decade.

National plans of development indicate the priorities and directions for the use of technical assistance in aiding the solution of critical economic and social problems. Effective cooperation between bilateral and multilateral agencies is needed. The experience gained by international technical assistance experts needs to be made known on a wider basis. There is much to be gained from a closer relationship between technical assistance and financial aid programs. Also coordination and more regular consultation among bilateral and multilateral agencies for technical assistance should be fostered. Economies of regional programs and regional efforts in technical assistance should not be overlooked. Developing countries which have already experienced some development success can provide much needed guidance to the less advanced economies.

Scientific research and technology appropriate to modernization in the developing countries should be greatly strengthened. The special technical problems of the developing countries need greater attention by the world's scientific community. Progress in the use of solar energy ground water development, water purification, and desalination would be of world-wide benefit. Many of these efforts can only be undertaken through regional research programs, assisted by international agencies.

Great potentialities exist for improved regional economic cooperation among developing countries themselves. Countries which are relatively small in economic size possess greater needs for economic cooperation. The creation of unified multinational markets in many of the small countries would foster faster expansion and provide for wider economic diversification. Productive efficiency would be enhanced through greater specialization and a more appropriate economic scale of operations.

Trade opportunities among developing countries could be exploited to a greater extent with a greater diversity among the economies. There is ample opportunity to expand trade for mutual benefit. Opportunities exist for trade in foodstuffs, raw materials and industrial commodities. The barriers to intra-trade and cooperative production should be abolished and joint-ventures established to exploit market potential.

Summary and Conclusions

Throughout the period of the second United Nations Development Decade arrangements must be made to appraise the progress made towards achieving the objectives. Appraisals should focus on the extent to which plans and policies are implemented, targets and other objectives obtained, and commitments fulfilled. Individual developing countries will need to know the state of their progress and the success of their policies. Technical advice and a proper dissemination of information must be provided through the international community. Greater exchanges of information are needed between the aid-providing and the aid-receiving countries. Knowledge of informational and operational linkages between neighboring countries and comparisons of problems handled by countries within regions are key parts of a system of appraisal. Adequate statistical information is essential for the assessments. Support has to be provided for improving the statistical services in developing countries. More appropriate indices of economic and social progress have to be fashioned and consistency in the use of concepts and nomenclature must be promoted.

Acceleration of the economic and social progress of the developing countries during the 1970s is crucial for the world community. Progress should be marked by increases in production as well as in employment, educational opportunities, improved distribution of income, and an enhancement of the social life of great masses of people.

The major recommendations made by the UN Committee for Development Planning to governments and international organizations, in order to obtain the objective of accelerated economic and social development, are as follows:

1. the socioeconomic structure and institutions of developing countries should be reformed so that outmoded privileges, injustices, and inefficiencies are eliminated and replaced by more viable elements of the modernization process;
2. maximum effort must be extended in mobilizing the internal resources of the developing countries;
3. developed market economies should expand the flow of financial resources to developing countries so as to reach by 1972, 1 percent of their own GNP of which three-fourths should be in the form of public funds; the composition of aid should aim to reach a grant component of 80 percent by 1975;
4. within five to ten years, international trade in products with unstable markets should be regulated by commodity agreements or other measures so as to assure greater stability and institute long-term price equilibrium;
5. the policies of protection in developed countries discriminating against the exports of developing countries, particularly semimanufacturers and manufacturers should be abolished;
6. technical assistance in the application of science and technology to resolve the problems of developing countries should be intensified;
7. centrally planned economies should create conditions for increasing imports from developing countries and expand financial assistance at rates commensurate with the efforts that the developed market economies are being required to undertake;
8. developing countries should expand trade and other avenue of economic and technological cooperation by more of their own efforts.

Vigorous efforts are required by both the developed and developing countries to fulfill these goals. Without such efforts greater disruptions on the world scene are inevitable. Careful research shows a greater frequency of internal conflict in low income countries than in high income countries. Increasing internal tensions generate external conflicts which rapidly escalate into international involvements on a vast scale. The concomitant problems of poverty and threats to international peace constitute the most important challenge of the 1970s.

Notes

1. United Nations, *Towards Accelerated Development,* Report of the Committee for Development Planning, E. 70.II. A. 2.

11 New Perspectives for Aid and Technical Assistance

Gustav F. Papanek

In this review of the prospects for foreign aid and its potential scope, the aims are, first to contrast the 1950s and 1960s with the likely situation in the 1970s in respect to development as a whole and then, to draw some conclusions concerning organizational needs, technical assistance, and the transfer of technology and resources.

Lessons from the Aid Experience of the Last Two Decades

One of the startling lessons of the past fifteen years is that the pre-capitalist problems that we were concerned about in the late 1950s and early 1960s turned out to be a great deal more manageable than we thought they would be. Social, psychological, and cultural obstacles to economic development, assumed to be serious in traditional societies and supposedly very resistant to change, turned out to be less substantial. We should not have been surprised to have found that economic incentives work almost as well in underdeveloped as in developed countries.

A second lesson learned was with respect to the importance of socio-political problems, which are really quite similar to the problems facing the developed countries. These include problems of regional differences, of ethnic and class conflict, problems of nationalism, ethnocentrism, and the problem of unemployment.

A third lesson is with respect to the inefficiency and the very poor equity which results from the kind of government intervention engaged in by a number of less developed countries. In this regard, India has been in the lead, displaying a pattern of government which Galbraith has called "post office socialism," and which has proved to be a relatively ineffective way of achieving growth and equity.

On the other hand, we have also learned some lessons about the danger of controlled capitalism. By this I mean the attempt by government to use the market to achieve the aims of society, with government setting the stage, and influencing the directions in which market forces move. We have found that this too creates serious problems, not only in economic terms, which are difficult enough to handle, but also in political terms. A controlled market system produces a great deal of political power for the business and industrial groups in the society, who are often able to use that influence to negate the controls which government has imposed in the social interest.

163

The major strategies adopted by the less developed countries—widespread detailed government intervention or reliance on the market in a framework of government influenced prices—have proved defective, or at very least problematical. There is now an honest search for new approaches and strategies.

The fourth lesson is that foreign aid does not always grow with world development. There continues to be a lack of realization of how serious the present decline in aid has been, because comparisons have always been in terms of monetary transfers and have not taken into account the decline in the value of real resources as a result of inflation and the effects of aid-tying restrictions.

The fifth point we have learned is the importance of foreign exchange. In the Pearson Report, there is one conclusion which is reasonably startling and clear cut: the only relationship they could find between growth and some other factor was between growth and the ability to import. This emphasizes the importance of access to foreign exchange. With a decline in aid, the only way it is possible for less developed countries to get increasing access to foreign exchange is by increasing their exports or by receiving larger amounts of foreign private investment. There is a subsidiary lesson that has been learned in respect to exports: the potentials in this field are much greater than most people thought in the 1950s and 1960s. Countries that take the right steps and adopt the right policies do manage to expand their exports very rapidly, although this does require increasingly sophisticated policies and management. On the private investment side, the growth of the multinational corporation which is willing to invest anywhere in the world where there is a profit, has accompanied the increasing needs of the developing countries for foreign private investment.

Sixth, in the 1950s and 1960s there has been an education explosion. Even countries whose growth has been feeble and whose per capita income has barely increased have had a vast increase in the numbers in schools. As a result, many countries have developed a new political constituency— the university and high school students. At the same time, this educational explosion has meant greater technical competence at all levels. If one compares the number of engineers, teachers, doctors, economists, and so on, available to the less developed countries now, to the situation in 1955, say, one is impressed by the massive change.

Finally, one of the results of the increase in the number of indigenous experts has been the greater possibilities of using foreigners in sensitive positions. In the past, when a foreigner was brought into a position involving high-level government policy and political implications, the minister concerned was in the very difficult position of evaluating the advice and work of the foreigner. In most cases there was no one between him and the foreign expert. This is no longer true. In many countries—some parts of Africa are an exception—the foreign expert now works as part of the Fifth International, that of technocrats. He has a competent indigenous technocrat as his counterpart, who serves as a buffer and filter between him and the political leadership.

Changing Patterns of Technical Assistance

The effect of these developments on technological transfer and assistance do not include, I believe, any sharp decline in the usefulness of foreigners in the less developed countries. However, I foresee some change in their composition and in their roles. First of all, the education explosion, the increased importance of nationalism and ethnocentrism, and the change in the perception of sociopolitical problems which face the less developed countries should result in a decline in the number of foreigners who will be working in the less developed countries, but an increase in the level of their competence. Fewer, but better, people will be needed. Their relationship to counterparts in the less developed countries is likely to be increasingly collegial and less that of teacher and student compared to the 1950s and 1960s.

Second, as a result of the decline in aid and the increased importance of sophisticated policies to expand exports and to deal with the multinational corporation, the focus of foreigners work is going to shift. Both in their own country and as technical assistance agents, the foreigners will need to concentrate more on the now crucial aspects of the relationship between the developed and the less developed countries. In the late 1950s, and early 1960s, sometimes the most useful function of foreigners in a variety of fields was to help less developed countries get more foreign aid. In many countries there were few activities that either foreigner or the competent local professionals could engage in that were as productive, or whose cost benefit ratio was as great, as attempts to increase the aid flow. Foreigners had a particularly important role, since they could sometimes talk more easily to compatriots on the other side of the table. They know what kind of presentations were needed, what kind of documents, what kind of arguments, to persuade the aid-givers. That function has declined, in some countries almost to the vanishing point. In any case, officials in less developed countries are now often better than foreigners in fulfilling that function.

On the other hand, the problems of dealing with exports and with foreign multinational corporations have greatly increased. These are not easy problems. In dealing with foreign investors the legal, economic, and business competence of a Bethlehem Steel, a Phillips, a Mitsubishi, or of the great international oil companies, are often unfairly matched against a poorly trained bureaucrat from a developing country, with no experience in business economics or accounting. Foreign advisers can now make a major contribution in helping less developed countries deal with large foreign investors.

Even so, I foresee a decline in the number of foreigners involved in supporting developing countries. There should be an increase in the number at the forefront of knowledge. Foreigners will need to be much better than in the past. There will no longer be a need for many whose task is the simple transfer of some elementary tools and some relatively easy techniques. As a result there will be a shift in career patterns, because people with the kind of experience and knowledge required are now generally not available for lengthy periods. More advisors will need to follow the type of career which enables them to move in and out, spending part of their time in less developed countries and part at home, in order to remain at the forefront of knowledge and have something to transmit.

These changes will require adjustments in the aid-donor agencies and in the agencies that provide technical assistance to the less developed countries. A gigantic organization, like the United Nations, which has in the past dealt in large numbers often with a relatively low order of skills, is going to have the most difficult adjustment to make. The technical assistance programs of major bilateral aid-donors that have some of the same characteristics will have a somewhat less difficult, but still major adjustment, to make. The programs which in the past have stressed quality rather than quantity will have the easiest adjustment.

This forecast of trends is far from unique. The Canadian International Development Agency claims that its aim now is not to be the smallest of the bilateral aid-donors; their aim is rather to be the largest of the small, high quality organizations of which the Ford or Rockefeller foundations are characteristic. Even some people at the U.S. AID have said that their major aim is not to be a large-scale bilateral aid agency as AID was in the past, but to be more like a foundation. Despite this recognition of different circumstances, it will be difficult for the large aid organizations to adjust quickly to the different needs of the less developed countries, in the 1970s.

12 Administrative Aspects of Education for Developing Countries

Jan F. Glastra van Loon
Kenneth J. Rothwell

Outstanding Tasks in Educational Change

A major change has taken place in our thinking about education for developing countries. Originally there were two streams of thought: one was based on a simple belief that people in the emerging economies were backward in education and therefore should attend European or American institutions in order to obtain the education that advanced people were privileged to have; and the other approach was that since there was a lack of knowledge, skills, and know-how, specialized institutions should be created so that skills and particularly administrative skills could be transferred in a more rapid fashion than if provided in regular schools and universities. Both views were naive, and have now been considerably modified in most European countries. This is because it was realized that the problems were much more complicated than the current level and style of the social sciences were capable of coping with. Moreover, the rate of change of the basic elements in such programs as management and administrative studies has been so great that even in the space of a few years retraining becomes an important part of the educational operation.[1]

There seems to be a tendency to perceive our task in the institutions of higher education and development studies as one of *de-Westernizing* the type of educational opportunities we present. We even like to go so far as to contribute to the de-Westernization of education in the developing countries. Some experiences are quite disconcerting: frequently it is found that so many of the participants who have had training in their own country have obtained a completely false view of the situation in their own country or have obtained all kinds of educational preconceptions or skills which are inapplicable in their own societies. So, we first have to de-educate them before we can hope to achieve anything or to make them more fit to cope with these problems in their own country.

The second task we face is in abandoning the notion of just transferring skills. We feel that the foremost task should be to "learn to learn," and to be aware that every problem has to be analyzed in its own context or terms. It is not a case of mechanically applying lessons picked up at any institution in the west. "Learning to learn," and its concomitant, "Teaching to teach," are basic to this approach.

A further task is to examine the nature of education in a development context. Most agree that it is no longer tenable that education necessarily makes for economic growth, or that there is an endless flow of opportunities for participants in educational programs of the conventional type.[2] In many of the developing countries the growth of higher education has moved entirely out of any meaningful relationship to the needs of the countries concerned. Quite apart from an over-production of university graduates, there is widespread unfitness of many primary school leavers for such employment as there is. In much of the educational structure in developing countries, the export of the European and American models has made it more difficult for the developing world to identify its own needs and to arrive at its own solutions.

A major administrative concern of educational development is the place accorded education in the governmental structure of the country and in the value patterns of society. Educational and training systems can be public or private, religious or secular, and planned or unplanned. The system is greatly affected by the part played in decision making by the people and their representatives, by administrators and by teachers.[3] The enormous expansion of organized education, mostly public, in both developed and developing economies, reflects the assumption of functions by educational and training institutions in the socialization and nationalization of occupational selection and training and social welfare activities. Many of these functions were formerly matters for the family or local community. Organizational expansion in both public and private spheres implied that training was a growing function of management, and that an expansion of training created new complex administrative undertakings.

Problems of Education and Training in Developing Countries

Despite considerable differences in the concepts of education and training, both terms connote a cultural context and both involve some job orientation as well as some life orientation. For developing countries it is desirable that a clear indication of broad educational needs be provided although this can usually be done only in a comparative approach in which lags and gaps are noted between some "ideal" Western educational structure and a particular pattern that can be estimated for a developing country. The two major approaches to educational planning are from the social demand approach behind which political pressures are mounted to serve such notions that every child has an inalienable right to be educated, and the other from a manpower planning approach which treats education as a factor of production related to development targets. Either approach adds perplexing dimensions to the educational problem. A confused educational approach does not provide precise guides for formulating educational programs to assist the development process.

The educational picture of the developing countries is well known. Observations of the Pearson Commission,[4] however, help to show some of the problems ahead.

It is broadly acknowledged that there has been spectacular growth in educational effort in the developing economies. In principle, free and universal education has been accepted as a basic human right and for most new nations primary school education is acknowledged as a constitutional right. To a large extent, social prestige and assumed economic value of education have overridden initial reluctance of parents in rural communities to forego the earnings from child labor.

Between 1950 and 1965 enrollment in schools and universities in developing countries almost tripled. With enormous growths in primary education, pressures have gradually built up for expanded facilities for secondary education. The share of education in national budget has increased proportionately to enrollment, being now in the vicinity of 16 percent on the average. Taking private and government expenditures together, it is calculated that developing countries are devoting, with considerable struggle, about 5 percent of their national income to education, compared with about 7 percent for developed countries.[5]

As a consequence of higher education and special training programs in developing countries there is today a substantial body of competent administrators, scientists, and engineers in Asia, Latin America, North Africa, and the Middle East, and a growing body of teachers in all the developing countries. Concern with education has provided a more alert populace and immeasurable influences on the organization of society. However, questions of quality and direction plague educational systems in many of the developing countries.

Major problems of education in developing countries include:[6]

1. high drop-out rates—as much as 70 percent in primary schools;
2. an orientation of secondary schools to purely academic study—vocational training represents less than 10 percent of total secondary enrollment;
3. only about 10 percent of the graduates from academic courses actually enter university;
4. few of the graduates from vocational schools become active in fields for which they have been trained;
5. university programs are heavily weighed towards law and political science or traditional fields of engineering;
6. educational facilities are inadequate, libraries are antiquated and teachers are poorly trained;
7. educational systems are not generally designed to produce immediate skills or proficiencies that match the needs of industry, agriculture, or government in the developing countries.

Rather than always producing solutions to growth and development, then, the educational systems frequently produce maladjustments and structural unemployment. Irrelevant education breeds discontent and frustration and generates an ominous burden for the entire social structure.

Because higher education is heavily subsidized mainly for a few individuals from upper income levels, arguments have been advanced that there would be greater use of educatable resources with a greater equality of opportunity if education were based on full-cost pricing combined with a system of low interest loans based on sounder systems for identifying the most competent.[7]

Transferability Problems in the Social Sciences

We would argue against those who hold that the Western social sciences have already obtained the tools with which one can tackle the problems of development. Briefly, the argument rests on the nature of rational decision-making.[8] Rationality, which for Hegel was the self-conscious reflective activity of mind pointing out reality and giving power over nature and history, can only have a meaning in connection with a particular decision-making procedure. There are all kinds of decision-making procedures: some are pencil and paper decision-making procedures, others involve conference rooms, chairmen, and standing orders, while others involve autocratic leaders in technocratic situations. The wider the context, of course, the greater we are involved in the complexity of real-life situations: specialized roles for diverse social activities are performed according to the standards of rationality of a particular social discipline.

The social scientist should always take into account the patterns of diffusion of knowledge and the modes of its application. It is not always possible to know the extent to which social sciences create the conditions of their confirmation and refutation. Demands for a particular pattern of training in a developing country, therefore, should be examined for its origins. In many cases the origins can be traced to some social science requirement emerging from transferred knowledge which is possibly culturally irrelevant, rather than emerging from social needs which are more likely relevant from a national developmental point of view. The comprehensiveness and generality of the social sciences are socially and culturally restricted in ways in which the range of applicability of *the physical sciences* is not.[9]

To a remarkable degree, the division of the social sciences and the occupational role systems of industrialized societies are highly congruent with one another. It is not clear whether this congruence and interdependence indicates an adequacy of knowledge acquired by the social sciences or is an effect of the normative application of views held and transferred by social scientists.[10]

Lawyers, sociologists, economists, political scientists, social psychologists, and experts in business management and public administration are trained to analyze and interpret social phenomena in terms of particular social disciplines and apply their concepts and techniques in organizations that have been structured in accordance with their precepts. Increasingly, social action in industrial societies is influenced by the teaching and training of social sciences. The cultural limitations to which the cognitive validity of social theories is subject makes transferability awkward if not truly invalid for the developing societies.

As noted by others, we are increasingly aware of the importance of political problems in developing countries, and we are more aware of institutional change as an important element in developing countries. Greater understanding of political and institutional change is needed. From the point of view of the educationalist, we should pay more attention to what could be called medium-level social science which lacks the elegance of the more abstract type of reasoning.[11] More importantly, this level of social science lacks the precision of much of the more quantitative type of decision-making.

It seems clear that the educational systems at the moment run the risk of creating political problems in developing countries with which they will have to cope in the future, unless their aims, demands, structures and outputs change. Insofar as there are educational systems, they have usually been created during periods prior to our awareness of developing problems as they are known now. During the colonial period, it was simply the transplantation of a Western educational system either at a primary, secondary, or university level.

Apart from the paraphernalia of prestige and decorum, these systems are not even applicable anymore in our own society. Nevertheless, the institutions have been transplanted, and they are the best available in many developing countries, although one should not overlook indigenous educational systems which cannot be labeled Western. They are still surrounding the institutions with an aura which we no longer attach to them. It is incumbent that we assist in breaking down these artifacts and antiquarian attitudes especially to assist in supplying more prestige to an intellectual concern for the problems of political and social situations that exist in the developing countries.

The most acute problems in the developing countries require new, original thinking, which is as challenging basically as that of the furthermost frontiers of the most advanced social sciences. Social sciences should attract greater attention from the most highly qualified people in the next decade. Most important, we should have more talented, devoted people attracted to the social sciences willing to apply themselves to the less prestigious aspects of the development of science.

Patterns of Change for Training in Developed Countries

We are increasingly aware that we should not try to educate in our own societies as many people from developing countries as we have in the past, but rather we should try to transfer the educational process itself to the developing country. Therefore, we should reduce the numbers of people who come to developed countries to be educated and raise the level of the people selected to be educated, or trained.

An examination of the use of educational resources in the United States showed that two-thirds of African students studying at U.S. universities could equally well be educated at African universities and that over 50 percent majored in courses not directly related to nation building. The question was posed, however, of whether or not U.S. universities should take African manpower needs into account or whether African governments should shape their own training programs more effectively.[12] Considerations of optimal use of resources suggest that training in advanced countries should be for the higher levels, with smaller numbers and for shorter periods. This would counter major defects of training courses in the West: the alienation that takes place when a man is away from his own country for too long with conditions more comfortable than his own country, and secondly, the adverse flow of science-based personnel which can occur.[13] If people are trained at a young age and are away from their own country for a long period of time, the chances are greater that they will prefer to find jobs in an industrialized society rather than their own. On the other hand, if training is given to a man who has already had a degree in his own country, who already has held a job and who comes for a relatively brief period on leave from that job, the chances are much greater that he will return to this job. Moreover the chances are greater that he will learn things more useful for nation building in his own country.

The workshop type of education, where you bring together people who have had similar experience, such as in a particular branch of administration, both in developing countries and industrialized countries, is preferable to formal instruction by lecturing. There are great advantages if each can learn from the other. One of the most beneficial effects of bringing participants together from various countries is that they begin to see their own problems in the mirror held up by someone from another area. Perhaps the most powerful tool of an educational situation is to make someone look at his own problems more objectively.

Approaches of these kinds create strange problems for the educational institution because by utilizing this kind of education the institution becomes less attractive to the academician of the traditional type. What you want is no longer a man who will try to develop his speciality inside a well-established discipline in that frontier where the highest prestige in academia is gained, but a man who will forego the prestige of Western academia. He should have capacities to do as good a job, but possess motivations to place him in a new instructional mold.

One example of changes in training approaches is provided by the particular concerns of the Institute of Social Studies in the Hague. During the last nineteen years, the interpretation of the Institute's tasks has undergone significant changes.[14] Formerly, emphasis was given to the transfer of applied knowledge in the social sciences; nowadays, this emphasis is placed more on the development of analytical tools with which to achieve a better understanding of development problems. As a result of this shift in emphasis, there is a continuous undertaking to work towards the outer limits of social scientific theory as has thus far been developed in the Western industrialized countries.

Institutions primarily concerned with training programs for the developing countries must necessarily cooperate with other organizations and individuals, and strenuous efforts are required to improve and extend our theoretical knowledge of the development process. This is done partly by including both Western and non-Western scientists on the teaching and research staff, and partly by the constant exchange of ideas between lecturers and participants. Because most participants in the institute are normally postgraduates who have already had some years of practical experience, the courses of instruction usually take on the character of in-service training, in which the exchange of experience and insights among participants play an important role. This clearinghouse function must be given more significance in the future by all institutions for development training. Courses must increasingly aim at attracting people with still higher qualifications which in turn will have favorable consequences for the educational program. Individuals, as visiting and exchange lecturers from developing countries, should take an increasing share in the activities of the institutions in the West concerned with development training.

Since these institutions need to operate on the borders of scientific knowledge in the study of developmental problems, research should form an essential part of their task. Such research while normally action-oriented should also have its purely scientific aspects. A useful development in the international sphere is the establishment of so-called *contact points* through which research is carried out in cooperation with and under the co-responsibility of an institute of higher education in a developing country. Moreover, staff members gain in their practical acquaintance with the development process through consulting posts in the socioeconomic sphere. International organizations such as the U.N., O.E.C.D., and F.A.O., as well as certain governments, can regularly utilize staff members for carrying out field objectives.

It follows, therefore, that although the central task of institutes of development training is the transfer of knowledge to participants from developing countries, this is not the total sum of its activities.

Long-range planning of the educational program of an institute for development training must take account of three major activities:

1. determination of future training needs of developing countries,
2. developments in the social sciences, particularly the new insights gained into developmental problems, and
3. restructuring of the program to fit changing needs and new insights.

It is clear that the new understanding of development problems partly determines our estimation of the future training needs of developing countries; the several activities cannot be sharply separated, although it is administratively helpful to distinguish between them.

In the future, manpower training should be conducted as much as possible in the developing countries. However, this does not automatically imply that the sort of training offered by organizations like the Institute of Social Studies can or should be given over to these countries within the foreseeable future. The possibility and desirability of holding training courses in the developing countries is greatest for elementary, secondary, and undergraduate education as well as for practical technical training.

The situation is different, however, for international post-graduate training. The need for such training, although changing, is continuously growing. This is due primarily to the fact that considerable scientific knowledge is available in the developed countries which will not be available in the developing countries to a sufficient degree for some decades. In the West, this knowledge continues to develop at a rate which cannot be maintained by western-trained educators in developing countries. A continued transfer of knowledge entails that more and more people from developing countries must be given postgraduate training in Europe. This is the objective of teaching the teachers. Insights into the possible applicability of social techniques are developed partly by renewing and gaining new knowledge of techniques in the Western context, and partly by better understanding of the problems of developing countries and of the ways in which the application of Western methods and procedures is furthered or hindered in such countries.

University education in developing countries is almost always handicapped by being modeled on the Western pattern and showing scant interest in national problems and circumstances. An outstanding change in courses given by an institute of development training would be to translate formal knowledge into terms of the development situation. The university in the developing country has yet to mark out its distinctive role as an agent of development.[15]

At present, the type of training offered by organizations such as the Institute of Social Studies cannot be given efficiently in the developing countries. This is due partly to a lack of competent staff available in the developing countries and partly to the absence of facilities. At a recent conference of the Institute for Economic Development and Planning of the U.N. Commission for Africa in Dakar, most African universities saw the critical need for teaching teachers largely in institutions in the developed countries. In addition, regional educational institutions have insufficient viability as a result of political tensions between the countries and the instability in many of them.

The universities and other educational institutions in developing countries will continue to lag behind Western institutions for some time to come. This lag is not only a question of equipment but also of contacts with colleagues, both national and international. Institutions concerned with development training can perform a unique function by providing a basis for developing contacts and providing a clearing house for pedagogy useful in development training. Universities in developing countries need assistance in casting themselves in a more development oriented role. The U.S. A.I.D. has suggested the formation of "Development Universities" which while experimental are also revolutionary and have the aims of:

1. providing a direct, immediate, and urgent commitment to development in all its aspects,
2. weaving together all the strands of study and research on development,

3. equipping young people to act on development problems in the special settings of their own environments,
4. emphasizing the moral content of education and the values associated with service to society, rather than personal affluence and prestige.[16]

Quite apart from the degree to which a country can provide basic education, the need continues to exist for international institutes, wherein participants are given the opportunity to meet with colleagues from different countries and different professions, having dialogues on a whole range of development problems. In this way, each one gains better insight into his own problems as mirrored in those of others. The geographic distance also gives a better chance to see problems in a broader frame of reference. Institutions must establish a world-wide reputation as organizations which, on a global basis, strive for synthesis via an extensive interchange of people, knowledge, experience, culture, and disciplines.

At the conference organized by the Agricultural Development Council on "The Problem of U.S. Graduate Training for Students from the Less-Developed Countries" at Johns Hopkins University in April 1969, it was noted that despite all efforts to develop graduate training in many of the less-developed countries, it seemed very likely that the numbers coming to the United States for graduate work will remain high for many years. This continuing flow of participants from developing countries suggests the need to promote still stronger institutes for development training in the decades ahead.

The obvious demands and opportunities for greater education and training in the developing economies to be met in a short space of time place increasing pressures on the managers of the educational systems in all countries. The new tools of administrative studies which are increasingly introduced into courses in development studies will therefore have to be applied more effectively to the educational institutions themselves.[17] There will be formidable obstacles to the politics and planning in education for social reform and economic growth, but one outstanding product of these challenges to education will be the need for administrative reform in educational institutions.

Aspects of Training Programs

Specific objectives of programs for institutes of development training should include the following features:

1. *Training of Trainers*

The training of trainers can be done in different ways and can obviously include the adaptation of course programs. Course programs and teaching materials should be made available as much as possible in written form so that the participant may return with them to his home country and reproduce the course in an adapted form.

Because the execution of such a programing project is a time-consuming task, part of the staff should be freed of extensive teaching assignments. Outside experts should preferably be involved in order that the best possible results may be achieved. Such an investment will not only help to attain objectives but will also improve the quality of the courses. A related longer-range activity is the publication of textbooks, manuals, and readers especially designed for developing countries and their problems.

2. *Follow-up*

The follow-up of courses is an expensive proposition and is not feasible for all alumni simultaneously and with equal intensity. Concentration on particular geographical areas is sometimes necessary. Continuing contacts can be provided through journals and publications and other exchange media between the institution and individual alumni. Pamphlets and monographs dealing with exploratory topics related to earlier course material will provide continuing stimulus between the institution and the alumni.

An activity more directly related to follow-up would be the organization of short seminars and other work groups designed for alumni and other specialists and held either in the developed country or in various developing areas. The extent to which special regional seminars on topics related to earlier course work can be held in developing countries in cooperation with and designed for alumni should be investigated.

Another follow-up activity worthy of attention is the stimulation and support of research carried out by alumni in their own countries. In this connection it might be desirable for the institution of development training to work with other universities to extend the range of research capabilities.

3. *Seminars for Senior Officials*

The educational programs of training institutes in developed countries are principally intended for mid-career people, mostly government or university-employed. However, it is becoming increasingly necessary to involve senior officials in this training process. This is because, in the first place, such people represent important sources of information regarding the needs, problems, and experiences of developing countries, and such knowledge is of vital importance for the institution. In the second place, the exchange of views, experiences, and problems among such officials, in surroundings that are removed from the political sphere and the pressure of daily work, can provide an inestimable contribution to the developmental process.

This can have both direct and indirect effects. The direct effects include comparisons between development objectives of senior officials, the opportunity to analyse and systematize experiences and insights with the aid of scientific techniques, introductions to new methods, and ways of thinking which help to increase efficiency at the top level of the administrative structure in developing countries.

The indirect effects are also significant. Better leadership and supervision will help improve the achievements of others. Research recently carried out by van Hoek showed that the brain-drain is aggravated by differences in training levels between supervisors and subordinates to the disadvantage of the former.[18] Supervisors who are unfamiliar with modern techniques frequently hesitate to appoint or retain younger people to whom such methods are not strange. These are then frequently forced to seek work in more developed countries.

An important part of the program of an institute concerned with development training should be seminars and congresses attended by senior officials and experts, and held in cooperation with international organizations and other scientific institutes, whether at home or in developing countries.

4. *Cooperation with Scientific Institutions
in Developing Countries*

Cooperative research should be actively supported for the base reason that the complete understanding of the development process and significant new advances introduced by research in a diverse array of fields of study in a large number of countries is beyond the normal capability of one educational institution. Cooperation is needed between institutions in both developed and developing countries. Also cooperation is required between the various disciplines of academic study. Comparative analysis and multi-disciplinary approaches are needed to provide worthwhile solutions to the enormous number of problems that arise in the development field. Universities and national and international agencies need regular channels for exchanging data on the development process.

In the developing countries particular cooperation can be provided through research and teaching on the undergraduate level, as well as in the training of counterparts who will continue the research activities after termination of the specific project. In this way, the educational program of the institution in the developed country is partly transferred to a developing country. The reverse must also take place, however, and to an increasing degree; namely, lecturers from developing countries must participate in the teaching programs of the institution in the developed country. The two-way traffic in the educational process at between participants and lecturers, should be extended and augmented. Realization and consideration of the consequences of such a move will enable us to avoid any pernicious paternalism and superciliousness in the educational program.

Conclusions

The nature of the issues presented here as tasks facing educational institutions in the developed countries which are most involved in training for development, signifies that this work should be internationally oriented and must be further developed and strengthened in the future. A scientific institution with a tradition of international cooperation and an appreciation of cultural influences of various origins has a particularly favorable chance to develop into an international center of cooperation in the study of developmental problems. The organizational form must be geared to particular training needs and exercised over a broad range of the social sciences in order to be beneficial for a study of development problems. Flexibility and versatility of scientific input is essential for the objectives of an institute concerned with development training.

Educational policy concerned with development should be directed towards making education an integral part of the development effort.[19] This objective for developing countries themselves requires tremendous efforts in changing existing curricula and teaching methods. Teacher-training programs must be expanded and improved to meet new educational structures. The size of the task demands imaginative application of educational technology in a short space of time. New educational techniques such as educational television, programed learning and team teaching has to be mobilized for far reaching and flexible operations. There is a special need for post-secondary technological or professional institutions to offer training which is closely related to the needs of the labor market. Overall, the educational objectives and activities must be closely geared to the environmental design of development and its emerging pattern.

The principal task of educational institutions in the developed world which are committed to the advance of the slowly emerging economies in the rest of the world must be to make the optimal use of favorable administrative circumstances, and to be constantly alert to keener devices for more effective use of world educational resources. Even so the manager of educational development should be alert to the problems that Samuel Huntington brings to our attention: that educational development which is too rapid, like unbalanced economic development, runs ahead and consequently weakens political development by awakening or creating social groups which cannot readily be accommodated in the polity.[20] The training of future managers and administrators has numerous dimensions, ranging from instruction in the safeguarding of national social values to the advocacy of rapid change; but training itself has its administrative dimensions also and the development perspective must be well served by sound conceptualizing, training, organization, and planning.

Notes

1. A well-documented statement of the evolution of training concepts is provided in United Nations, *Handbook of Training in the Public Service,* New York Sales No. 66. II. H. I.
2. See E. G. Wedell, "Adult Education and Development," *Journal of Administration Overseas* 10, 2 (April 1971), 81.

3. See George Baron, Dan H. Cooper, and William G. Walker (eds.) *Educational Administration: International Perspectives* (Chicago: Rand McNally and Co., 1969), pp. 99, 100.

4. See Lester B. Pearson, *Partners in Development: Report of the Commission on International Development* (London: Pall Mall Press, 1969).

5. Ibid., p. 42.

6. L. B. Pearson, op. cit., pp. 67, 68; cf. U.S., AID. *Priority Problems in Education and Human Resources Development in the Seventies,* November 1970.

7. See Daniel C. Rogers, "Financing Education in Less Developed Countries," *Comparative Education Review* 15, 1 (February 1971): 20–28.

8. See also Jan F. Glastra van Loon, "Social Science and Social Change," *Development and Change* 1, 1 (1969): 35, 49.

9. Ibid., p. 40.

10. The dividing lines between the social sciences can be seen to correspond to sets of variables which are nearly independent in the rich countries. Such sets of variables are not so neatly separated in the developing countries, as is shown in Michael Lipton, "Interdisciplinary Studies in Less Developed Countries," *The Journal of Development Studies* 7, 1 (October 1970): 5.

11. Note the criticisms of scientific trends given in Thomas S. Kuhn, *The Structure of Scientific Revolutions* (Chicago: Pheonix Books, 1967).

12. Jane W. Jacqz, *African Students in American Universities* (New York: Africa-American Institute, 1967).

13. F. J. van Hoek, *The Migration of High Level Manpower from Developing to Developed Countries* (The Hague: Mouton, 1970).

14. See Institute of Social Studies, *Annual Reports,* 1969 and 1971.

15. See Kenneth J. Rothwell (ed.) *Higher Education and Accelerated Change* (Durham, N.H.: New England Center for Continuing Education, 1971).

16. U.S., A.I.D., op. cit., pp. 20, 21.

17. See Richard M. Durstine, "Technical Trends in Educational Management, Opportunities and Hazards," *Comparative Education Review* 14, 3 (October 1970): 327–34.

18. Van Hoek, op. cit., p. 25.

19. Lester B. Pearson, op. cit., p. 68.

20. Samuel P. Huntington, *Political Order in Changing Societies* (New Haven: Yale University Press, 1968).

13

An Interpretation of Management Skills: Some Problems of International Transferability

David J. Ashton

Dimensions of the Challenge

Serious outside efforts to help speed the development of the world's less developed areas are relatively new, particularly if one discounts the profit-motivated investments of present or former colonial powers in their overseas territories. It was not until the end of the 1940s when post-World War II reconstruction efforts had made sufficient headway that a proposal such as President Truman's Point 4 became feasible and that the International Bank for Reconstruction and Development was able to give adequate emphasis to the two functional aspects suggested in its title.

Since their start in the early 1950s, Development Assistance Programs have gone through several stages. At the outset, as Hoffmann notes:

there was certainly a widespread belief that simply by informing a large number of people in the less developed countries about known industrial administration . . . . and other techniques generally applied in North America and Western Europe one could expect that these techniques would rather rapidly be adopted and applied. . .[1]

After acknowledging the naivité of these early views, Hoffmann goes on to state:

What is really needed most in private (and for that matter in public) enterprises in the less developed countries is continuing assistance with management and in the training of management personnel. If there is one thing that we have learned in the past fifteen years, it is that it is comparatively easy to build something . . . . It is much more difficult . . . . to operate and maintain the enterprise . . . . And it is more difficult yet to convey from one culture to another the capacity to manage an affair.[2]

Hoffmann concluded at the time he was writing (late 1963) that the assistance programs then in effect, except for some low-level technical programs of the International Labour Organisation, had failed to provide any significant managerial assistance.

Juxtaposed to many such statements of need and frustration are the equally numerous statements of faith and obligation, such as that from

This paper draws heavily upon a paper given at the "Education for International Business" Conference, Lausanne, Switzerland, July 1966, and also on related presentations in Cambridge, Mass. (1968) and Turin, Italy (1969).

181

former U.N. Ambassador Charles H. Malik of Lebanon, who has written: "The West commands a unique wealth of experience and knowledge in all the aspects of management and organization, a wealth from which all non-Western countries, Communist and non-Communist alike, Asian or African, can enormously profit."[3]

The obligation of the Western World to share this capability, and to find effective ways of doing so, is central to the whole question of transferability of management skills. Our function is not primarily to exhort, for many substantial and dedicated organizations are already in the field. Yet, we continue to be confronted by a sense of growing frustration and confusion. While there are numerous advisors and researchers working in developing countries and trying out weird theories or using obtuse theoretical terms in discussions with people in these countries there are, on the other side, slow stifling approaches to business matters, so that it takes years to process a small loan, enterprises are largely joint private-government concerns with nepotism and political appointments common and in general there is considerable over-staffing with incompetents. The question to be raised is why some of the world's ablest administrators and teachers have so often been ineffective in their efforts to understand the managerial realities of other parts of the world.

Terminological Confusion—Organizational Roles and Tasks

Part of the problem of comprehending management needs lies in the relative newness of the fundamental relevant areas of academic discipline. Although organized economics is less than two centuries old, and, as a recognized formal discipline is no more than a century old, sociology, psychology and cultural anthropology are primarily disciplines of the twentieth century.

Most of the serious thinking about management as a distinct discipline is the product of the last fifty years; the first formal meetings of college teachers concerning management curricula and course content being held in 1924. As an interesting sidelight, those professors arrived at only one unanimous agreement; namely, that a basic management course should be a required part of all collegiate business curricula. As to what the course content should be, this is still under debate nearly half a century later, which may account for many of the problems in transmitting these managerial skills to the less developed areas.[4]

Most of the terminological underbrush must be cleared away before our discussions can be meaningful. Two principal difficulties are apparent: first, to differentiate management from the other types of authoritative responsibility which must be exercized in an organization; second, to clarify the outstanding functions of management. Here, a useful stratagem is to specify activities or functions with which management is often confused but which, in my judgment, are not a part of the managerial process. Clearly, management is *not* ownership or entrepreneurship, that is to say, it is not concerned with the task of supplying equity or basic risk capital for business enterprise and taking the lion's share of the profits or losses. Management is *not* playing the capitalist's role; that is, the supplying of creditor capital. Management is *not* the rentier role, that is, the supplying of property to the enterprise. Management is *not* promotion, that is, the seeking out of new business opportunities and assembling the resources needed for their initiation. Management is *not* technological invention, that is, the creation of new scientific processes or devices. Thus, although some might wish to argue the point, we proceed on the assumption that the manager, qua manager, is not an entrepreneur, owner, capitalist, rentier, promoter, or inventor. The things which he does and which qualify him as a manager are not among the activities just listed, although each of these precedent roles requires good management to be effective, and persons whose duties are primarily managerial may be adept at, or accustomed to performing, any or all of these roles in relation to their organizational duties.

The fact, too, that all of these roles may be performed by the same person, in addition to managing, in the small or family enterprise, has contributed much to the history of terminological confusion. Indeed, the historical predominance of smaller enterprises has been a major reason why management was for so long indistinguishably imbedded in the variety of tasks which must be performed in any social organization if it is to be an effective operating entity. Until enterprises grew to a size sufficiently great to justify individual specialization, it was all too easy to confuse managerial tasks with other, and equally vital, work which managers often perform in addition to their managerial duties.

This matter of critical size is also helpful in explaining why some of our earliest insights into the managerial process were derived from the church and the military, for these were among the few social activities performed on a scale sufficiently large to provide an occasional opportunity for a person to specialize in managing. Moreover, because they were not engaged in producing and marketing a product, at least in the conventional sense, there was less reason for the managerial function to become entangled in these functional areas.

Terminological Confusion—Organizational Functions and Managerial Spheres

The second major terminological morass, requiring an additional stint of definitional extrication concerns organizational functions. Our design is to separate management from the functional activities which characterize commercial and manufacturing enterprises and, *mutatis mutandis,* all social organizations. In the conventional terminology of business administration, these fuctions are usually entitled production, marketing, accounting, finance, personnel, and research and development (R&D). Each of these functional areas requires managing, but none of them by itself *is* managing, but rather an organizational activity which is dependent upon good management, among other things, for its effective performance.[5]

The Three Managerial Spheres

Another way to emphasize the distinction is to note that an effective manager must be properly equipped with knowledge, attitudes, and skills in three interdependent spheres of activity.

1. He must have a thorough knowledge of the function or process which his organization performs; e.g., oil refining, fruit canning, insurance underwriting, or university admissions.
2. He must be aware of and able to cope with both the macro- and microenvironmental factors related to his work.
3. He must be competent in performing the basic roles of the manager.

Functional capability, environmental capability, and managerial capability, these are the requisites for effective executive performance, and it has been the inability to divorce these at the conceptual level which has contributed heavily to the confusion and difficulties associated with the need and the ability to transfer management skills to the less developed areas.

Management Vs. Functional Skills. The author has found in numerous instances that an alleged need for management skills has really been a need for engineers, market researchers, accountants, or quality control technicians. This is not to denigrate these activities in any way, but it must be noted that capability in any of them does not in itself imply managerial competence. The problem here is the tendency of some to raise the terminological umbrella of "Business Management" over such a wide area as to make the terms virtually meaningless. Similarly, it includes the problem of aggressive, duplicative research by new Ph.D.s in overworked areas of study in underdeveloped regions. In many instances, what the developing country needs, at least in towns and villages, is low-level technical or functional assistance of the type customarily taught below the university level in the developed countries. If management assistance is needed, it is more likely to be at the foreman level rather than the general manager level, and the relatively abstract approach of the academician is rarely relevant except perhaps in the Ministry of Planning and Development.

Management and the Social Environment. It may seem unreasonably subtle, but there is a real difference between stating, on the one hand, that American management principles are not applicable in Ruritaria and, on the other hand, that the business environment in Ruritaria includes so many counterproductive social factors such as extreme nepotism, disregard for law and authority, and executive secrecy that it is not possible at this time and at this stage of development to perform managerial functions in an objective and efficient manner.

Rather than negating the universality of management procedures, a statement such as the second above confirms it, in fact, and is in my opinion far closer to the truth than the first statement. The planner or manager who is trying to generate a greater economic and social product for his nation or enterprise succeeds to the extent that he is objective, impersonal, and rational. Indeed, we may postulate that there is but one road to an increased productivity sufficient to satisfy basic human needs, and that this is through rationally organized and managed machine-powered production. At any given point in time, however, a particular society or nation may be unable to achieve this because of poverty or ignorance, or it may be prevented from achieving it by social or political oppression, whether imposed by foreign conquerors, traditional oligarchs, or radical demagogues. Once we appreciate this fact, it becomes more reasonable to accept as valid a statement that "management is management wherever practiced, a universal profession whose principles can be applied in every organized form of human society . . ."[6] while at the same time recognizing that the external environment may be so hostile to the objective practice of management as to preclude its application. This is analogous to the old truism that: What is economically logical must wait upon what is politically possible.

Another example is to be found in the Soviet Union where, traditionally, the objective practice of management has been prevented by the Leninist dogma that purity of political purpose is more important than objective economic achievement. This should not in any way call into question the validity of the underlying economic concepts, although some within and without the USSR have occasionally pretended that there was some distinct body of knowledge called "socialist economics." The conflict between practice and purpose indicated rather that Russia's leaders felt that rapid economic growth would have to be foregone if it meant a lessening of political control. The efforts of Professor Yevsei G. Liberman and a new band of relatively non-political technicians and industrial planners and business executives who agitate for radical changes in the approach to planning have been seemingly pushed aside. Now most of the tentative and (for the USSR) daring experiments of the 1960s in managerial decentralization and marketing have given way to resurgent orthodoxy. In China, apolitical managerial rationality seems to arise mostly in the military and, to date, has usually gotten its advocates political purgatory or worse, although China's recent political re-emergence may hold out some hope.

We repeat for emphasis, then, that a modern economy and the relatively rational managerial practices which its enterprises must employ are fragile social constructs, dependent upon a benevolent sociopolitical environment for effective performance. They do not develop in any pattern of Marxian historical inevitability, but must be nurtured by appropriate cultural, social, and politico-legal institutions. Environmental shortcomings, however, do not mean the inapplicability of managerial universals, any more than the failure of waterlilies to grow in the desert contradicts the laws of plant biology.

The Managerial Essence—A Residual Concept

Some may feel that by excluding business functions and environmental factors, we have stripped the managerial process of its substance. This is not the case at all. We have already noted that an effective manager must be able to perform capably in these areas; i.e., that he must have substantial (although not necessarily a fully detailed technical) competence in the function which his organization is designed to perform, and that he must be able to cope with external environment. But we are taking some pains to emphasize that neither of these two aspects of executive performance is management or managing, per se. Management is the sum total of those organizational tasks in which executives direct their subordinates toward the achievement of organizational objectives. The component parts of the management process, generic to all organizations, are planning, organizing, staffing, directing, and controlling. The central question of our discussion, therefore is "To what extent can American and Western European capabilities in planning, organizing, staffing, directing and controlling be transferred effectively, to other countries, and at what cost?"[7]

At this point, we should take note of the groundbreaking work of Professors Richman and Farmer.[8] A major point of their contribution is the creation of a macro-economic model which encompasses the business environment, the functions of business enterprise, and the management process. Not only have they created taxonomic listings of functions and variables but they have also built matrices to make some first approximations of the interrelationships between the management process and those environmental factors (they use the term "restraints") which affect the manager's ability to perform effectively. Those who have had glimmerings of these interrelationships as a total system are greatly in their debt, and undoubtedly the questions raised, and the interrelationships suggested by their work will provide academicians and thoughtful practitioners with food for thought and research projects for many years to come.

The Richman-Farmer model is far too complex and, as yet, too little researched to provide a definitive answer to our earlier question about the possibilities and costs of the transfer of managerial skills. At present it might be said we know a fair amount about the obstacles to transfer, a little bit about the possibilities of transfer, and we have virtually no framework for computing either the money cost, real cost, or opportunity cost of effecting such a skill transfer.[9]

As we work our way through the conceptual underbrush in search of whatever it is which makes managers able to get things done in organizations, seeking the so-called "pure disciplinary underpinnings" of these procedural amalgams which are planning, organizing, and so on, we must acknowledge an obvious indebtedness to systems concepts and organizational homeostasis. These make us ever aware of the role of the social and cultural environment in conditioning reflexes and responses in such a way as to facilitate, or thwart, the manager's professional objectives. We know that high productivity depends upon technology, to be sure, but recent developmental frustrations make clear that it also depends upon a whole list of personal characteristics.

Productivity, whether managerial or menial, depends upon a Western-conditioned understanding of cause and effect, logic and rationality; upon energy, ambition, and a belief in the possibility of progress, and upon many other things too numerous to specify here. One cannot say where we shall be a generation from now, but the present generation of poor people, whether black, white, or in between; whether in North America or in Asia; whether under socialism, capitalism or feudalism, has been sent a message loud and clear. This message which has been repeated time and time again in many forms might read:

The price to be paid for affluence is the development of standards of personal reliability, conformity and motivation comparable to those of middle class America. In addition, you must move purposefully toward a comparable social setting, one marked by mass education, a reasonably responsive and unoppressive government, and a meritocratic social structure.

This lesson was also explicit in the 1968 invasion of Czechoslovakia by the Soviet Union, for a chief, although seldom mentioned, casualty of the re-imposition of Stalinism on Eastern Europe was managerial rationality. The increasingly apparent inability of central planners to forecast and allow for the almost infinite variations and special situations which characterize an affluent economy has been one of the compelling arguments in favor of decentralized decision making, and the removal of the ideological commissars from the councils of management at the enterprise level. Such reversions to Stalinist orthodoxy had their Far Eastern counterparts in Chairman Mao's assignment, during the Cultural Revolution, of responsibility for universities and communications media to worker-soldier-peasant teams, accompanied by denunciations of the deviationist technicians and professional academics. These latter were denounced as slavish toadies to Western bourgeois rules of cause and effect, when they should have been relying on the purity of Maoist thought to guarantee a fruitful solution of any so-called technical problem.

It seems paradoxical that there should be such unanimity between those to whom materialism is a religion, and those whose religions deny the ultimate reality of matter, in this concurrence that material laws of cause and effect are not governing in the affairs of men. If nothing else, it shows us that the central issues in comparative management are of concern far beyond the realm of enterprise management, and encompass religion and political philosophy as well.

Organization and Management—Basic Ambiguities

Management "is" because organizations "are." This is because all management except self-control occurs within an organizational setting. The inherent ambiguity is contained in the customary failure to differentiate between (1) an organization comprehended as a social entity, and (2) organization as the managerial process whereby such entities are created, which might be better stated simply as organizing.

The Organization as a Social System.   Scholars such as Person, Whyte, Selznick, and Bakke have provided us with a good foundation of understanding about organizations. Moreover there has been a broad consensus on the understanding of the basic nature of organizations. All managers at some time must be concerned both with maintaining the ongoing functional integrity of an existing organization and with creating new organizational entities. In either case, it is useful, if not vital, for managers to understand that all organzations, large and small, are composed of certain basic ingredient processes and relationships. All of these must be maintained and renewed if the organization is to remain in that "evolving state of dynamic equilibrium"[10] which makes possible continued progress toward the organization's functional missions.

The concept of the organization as a system of interdependent social networks helps the manager to see the total dimensions of his task while providing him with a check list, proper attention to which will enable him to maintain the integrity of his organization in a self-conscious and deliberate way rather than as a blind reaction to external forces. It has been noted that the commanders of naval vessels find their managerial tasks simplified, not only because of their access to military discipline to carry out their directives, but even more because the limited dimensions of the vessel and the ability to comprehend all of the facets of its operation in isolation from society in general are conducive to comprehending the vessel as a social macrocosm. These ingredient parts and their interrelationships are highly significant but cannot be examined in this paper. Suffice it to say, however, that this concept constitutes a managerial generality which is not culture-bound, is reasonably specific, and is transmittable in its present form.

Technical Skills and Processes

The planning and control operations are increasingly employing sophisticated methods such as linear programming, and correspondingly complex hardware such as computers, to facilitate the problem solving associated with their performance. We have a fair amount of evidence that the ability to use these tools, both intellectual and mechanical, can be taught and transferred very effectively to persons of appropriate intelligence and prior schooling. Mathematical capability seems to be a function of the general level of outlay on higher education, and while it is no easy job to come up with the necessary funds to bridge the educational gap, this area at least is relatively free of cultural obstacles.

Technique Vs. Transformation. In discussions with managers, educators, and bureaucrats in the developing countries, one almost invariably encounters a statement such as the following: "We have the greatest respect for Western managerial and technical know-how. We shall absorb and apply those techniques which we now lack, but we shall retain our own culture and values." Such a statement seems, at first glance, to be a prudent combination of modern technical awareness and traditional national pride which might be a sound basis for economic and social modernization. Yet more and more serious students of these modernization processes, led by Gunnar Myrdal, believe such views to be impractically naive. They insist that a cultural "Westernization" or even "Americanization" (à la Servan-Schreiber) must precede the social and economic restructuring which, in turn, holds the key to the much desired economic and social progress.

If this is so, the inescapable conclusion is that those societies and cultures which consciously reject Western values are opting for continuing poverty and sociopolitical futility (e.g., Arabs vs. Israel) no matter how avidly they embrace computer technology and PERT. Most certainly, this is a conclusion the implications of which far transcend any technical concern with defining management practices.

Achievement, Change, and Rationality

Negative popular and official attitudes toward personal achievement, social change and rational problem solving (scientific method) are among the environmental constraints which mitigate most strongly against managerial effectiveness. The U.S. or European manager is used to operating in an environment where at least some of his subordinates and associates can be expected to work nights and weekends, without prodding or bonuses, to meet a particular work deadline. Such attitudes are rare in some societies, and their absence may mean lower enterprise productivity than the manager is accustomed to.

Similarly, many of the world's poorer societies have managed to avoid mass starvation only because they have organized themselves with great care, and then imposed drastic social sanctions upon those who deviate from the organizational norms. Such persons may well be highly resistant to all forms of social change.

People living in poor societies, where the prospect of individual improvement through one's own efforts has traditionally been remote, often escape from reality through superstition and a belief in magic as the only solution to pressing problems. Such persons often need repeated indoctrination and close supervision effectively to implement even such basic chains of cause and effect as, "If the machine is not oiled on schedule, it will break down."

Such judgments as these do not, in my opinion, necessarily mean that management is culture-bound, and non-transferable from modern societies to less developed societies. Such attitudes *do* mean, of course, that to the extent that they persist, these countries and their enterprises will suffer from low productivity. We have said before that the manager, to be competent in his position, must be possessed of managerial, technical, and environmental capabilities. The competent manager, therefore, will certainly not factor into his budgets for an enterprise in a developing tropical nation the same labor productivity estimates which would be relevant in Detroit or Dusseldorf. He will realize, also, from his social environmental awareness that his plans must allow for more direct supervision than might be needed back home. Similarly, his president and Board of Directors will not fault him as a manager if labor productivity is lower. After all, wages are probably significantly lower as well.

Counterstrategies and Tactics

Although the future may prove otherwise, it now appears to scholars and practitioners alike that there is no path to development generally, or to management competence in particular, except through the emulation of the behavioral patterns of what William Gorman calls, "The North West First World."[11] Thus, to the Third World aspirants to development, the North-westerner must respond somewhat as follows:

We're not entirely certain just how we successfully set off on the road to affluence, but we think that the keys to success include national and international economic integration, fossil-energy-based *mechanized* production, and achievement-oriented ethic, mass education, private (but not *free*) enterprise in *most* economic activities, and a legal system which safeguards commercial interchange and private property acquisition.

The real issue, not yet settled, is whether there exists "a presiding science . . . . (which has) arisen from reflection on, and analysis of, experience in the North West . . ."[12] A final question is whether a change from the traditional to the Northwestern can be significantly advanced in a group of employees during one manager's overseas duty tour, say three to four years, or whether such changes require the passage of generations. Examples are abundant showing counterproductive behavior based on traditional mores. As for organized and well-accepted countermeasures, there is as yet no consensus, nor do many individuals have noteworthy success stories to tell.

Perhaps, even more basically, we need to study the traditional society more carefully to see which aspects of its behavioral patterns are *incompatible* with a modern economy, and which are merely *irrelevant*. If the peasant, who once said his morning prayer to his bullock, wishes to perform the same ceremony before his new tractor, no harm is done. If, however, he refuses to change from his traditional flowing and loose fitting costume to one which will not jeopardize the machinery and his own safety, this means trouble. All-inclusive statements which imply that cultural transformation must be complete in order to achieve modernization have given rise to defensive allegations that modern management "is essentially an Anglo-Saxon phenomenon, not applicable or transferable to Latin America," or other culturally diverse societies. It may well be that the degree of transformation, while substantial, is less than we suspect, and that cultural homogenization is not the inevitable consequence of modernization.

We conclude with the reminder that there seems to be building up in the "Northwest" some revulsion against the conscious stimulation of modernization and development, even as development planners seem more and more to despair of eradicating even the most crushing poverty from many of their countries, let alone achieving a comfortable affluence. Dissident groups in the "Third World" rise in protest against attacks on their value systems, feeling that modernization is too destructive of family structures, social solidarity, and their rhythms of work and play. The avant garde of the Northwest also proclaims the bankruptcy of development and its attendant theology, materialism. With their exhortations to "freak out" from a constricting rationalism, these apostate priests are saying that the quest for development is, after all, a delusion, and that the poor people won't really be happy once they "arrive."

Finally, an M.I.T. management conference schedules a debate entitled:

RESOLVED: That economic growth may be effectively halted in the forseeable future by ecological presssures.

Caught in the middle of this greater debate, the executive must get out the work and justify his substantial salary, while keeping himself and his entireprise socially and politically acceptable. This dilemma is one example of the basic conflicts which emerge with economic change and the revaluing of social goals. Far more complex are the conflicts created in the international transfer of management skills, yet this is a flow which must accelerate in the decades ahead.

Notes

1. M. Hoffman, "Development Needs the Businessman," *Lloyds Bank Review*, No. 68, April 1963, p. 32.

2. Ibid, p. 39.

3. Charles H. Malik, "Ideals for Export," *Harvard Business Review*, Jan.–Feb. 1964, p. 56.

4. J. F. Mee, "Changing Trends in the Body of Knowledge Pertaining to Management," Proceedings of the American Association of Collegiate School of Business (St. Louis:AACSB, 1965), p. 51.

5. This point is very clearly made in E. W. Bakke, "Concept of the Social Organization," in M. Haire (ed), *Modern Organization Theory* (New York: John Wiley & Sons, Inc., 1959), pp. 16–75.

6. Austin W. Tobin, Executive Director, Port of New York Authority, cited by H. F. Merrill, *Management News* (January 1963):4.

7. Paraphrased from B. M. Richman, "Significance of Cultural Variables," *Academy of Management Journal* (Dec. 1965):294.

8. R. N. Farmer, and B. M. Richman, *Comparative Management and Economic Progress* (Homewood, Illinois: Richard D. Irwin, Inc., 1965).

9. Note however Richard D. Robinson, "Measuring the Impact of a Business Investment on a Developing Society," in Karl E. Ettinger (ed.) *International Handbook of Management* (New York: McGraw-Hill,1965).

10. Bakke, op. cit., p. 59.

11. See N. H. Jacoby, *The Progress of Peoples* (Santa Barbara: Center for Democratic Institutions, 1969), p. 35 seq. Gorman's points are raised in a recorded discussion of Jacoby's paper, a discussion which included, among others, Harry Ashmore, Denis Goulet, and Stanley Sheinbaum, chaired by Robert M. Hutchins.

12. Ibid.

14

Training for the Transition from Entrepreneur to Manager: A Case Study

Allan R. Cohen

This paper focuses on some opportunities for, and methods and difficulties in training entrepreneurs who wish to acquire managerial skills. It is assumed that the skills and techniques necessary for successfully introducing an innovation are not the same as those needed to manage a large enterprise on a day-to-day basis. Different managerial styles are appropriate for different organizational tasks and phases. In looking at an entrepreneur who wanted to become a manager, we can shed light on the requirements of differences between the two roles, even if few entrepreneurs can personally make the transition. In August 1969, I worked in India with a man, Mr. Laxmi (a disguised name), who is in some ways a classical entrepreneur. It might be instructive to describe my consultation with him and his company, to see if this examination helps solve issues raised in trying to provide useful entrepreneurial training.

Growth and Planning for Laxmi's Company

Work in the Laxmi company had been started by my colleague, Rolfe Eastman, who was working as a small-industry consultant with the Peace Corps. He had tried to work for a time with a young man who was not responsive or enthusiastic. The man explained to Eastman that his brother, Mr. Laxmi, was really the progressive businessman and suggested talking to him.

Eastman started out by examining several financial problems Mr. Laxmi was facing. Laxmi's company makes small diesel engines, 3.5 and 6 horsepower, which are used by farmers for pumping water to irrigate their fields. The company was growing 70 percent a year, selling engines as fast as they could be made, yet the more they sold the less money they had. The books were showing profits, but in the small businessman's classic dilemma, Mr. Laxmi found that the more he sold the less cash he had available.

In the process of doing the cashflow analysis, a technique of which Laxmi had never heard, Eastman showed that the problem was the rapid growth

Gratitude to Henk van Roosmalen is expressed for thoughtful comments on an earlier version of this paper.

of sales. That led them into talking about growth and what that meant in terms of Laxmi's goals. In order to talk about growth they needed to project into the future. Most small businessmen do not do this very well, since they are always busy fighting brush fires and dealing with what happened yesterday.

While discussing projections they estimated the rate at which Laxmi could reasonably expect to grow. They took the assumption that the current 70 percent was too high, but that with Mr. Laxmi's energy, ability, and ambitions, a 50 percent growth rate within the next five to seven years was not unreasonable. Laxmi suddenly realized that from the current roughly $1 million in sales his firm could soon become a very large company. A 50 percent growth rate over seven years multiplies rapidly, and in fact would make him larger than Kirloskar, the present largest company in that industry. In order to accomplish such growth, Laxmi acknowledged that he would have to learn a great deal, although he was not certain what learning was needed.

Eventually, as a consequence of new work on financial planning, Laxmi and Eastman undertook a pilot project which has the potential to completely change a basic marketing practice in India. In one state they are experimentally employing their own salesmen, developing considerable autonomy for the state sales manager, who is responsible for selling engines purchased from the company at a set price. Creation of company salesmen is an attempt to gain control of marketing practices currently in the hands of distributors who carry other products. Normally, establishing and maintaining a sales force would be a very expensive proposition, but together they invented a clever way to finance it, luring funds from "investors" who previously hoarded money, by offering a guaranteed return for keeping in stock a minimum number of engines. These are two very innovative entrepreneurial activities which appear to be significant and likely to lead to successful development.

Mr. Laxmi, The Entrepreneur, and the Organizational Problem

Mr. Laxmi is a very energetic, imaginative person. His earliest childhood memory is of an imported English engine running in a field, and from that day, he decided that he wanted to learn to make engines. He acted like a model entrepreneur: a highly self-confident man in areas where he has expertise, he took several jobs by saying to people, "just pay me 40 rupees a month until I prove myself." When once he was offered 200 rupees, he considered himself as worth more, so he refused any pay at all. Within two months he was earning 1200 rupees a month. But he was never satisfied working for anyone else. He needed a high degree of autonomy.

He began his own company with one rented machine. In the next year, 1962, it was up to four machines. Since then the number has grown at a very rapid rate. Mr. Laxmi is motivated—so far as one can accept conscious statements of motivation—by an intense desire to be known as the man who built a great company. He apparently is not motivated by money or power for their own sake; he doesn't want to build a company in order to dominate it. He lives frugally, unlike many with his wealth, and he seems to have little need to order others around or be waited on. But he has an absolutely overwhelming determination to be widely known as the man who was responsible for building a great company which produces considerable social value. He would like to be the leading name in Indian farm equipment, employ many people at high wages, and create a working environment that really lets them grow and develop.

Mr. Laxmi had managed to get the company to where it was, but now it was achieving a size where he could no longer control things by himself. Up to this time he had been the chief designer, chief production manager, the whole marketing department, and the man who made all the financial arrangements. He was really doing virtually everything, and, because he is so energetic and bright, he had been doing creditably. Yet he knew that there was too much happening to keep things in control, and that in order to grow into a large, significant company he must learn how to be a manager of others rather than the energetic doer.

Identification of the Organizational Problem; The Entry of an Organizational Consultant

When I came to India for the company I did not know what was really expected. The management need was not clear at all. Upon arrival, I was asked to write a job manual describing each executive's functions so that Mr. Laxmi would know who was supposed to be doing what. The organizational structure was so unclear to Mr. Laxmi that he grasped at job descriptions as a way to clarify responsibilities. He wanted me to find out what people did, write that down, and then he would have what he thought he needed. I argued that anyone in the company could write a better manual than I, since they were the ones doing the jobs and knew what they were doing. I asked why he needed me to do it. As we talked, we began the process of defining what the problem really was. Basically, it was that Mr. Laxmi did not know what to do with his time as a manager. He was spending as much time on trivial problems as on such big problems as arranging a bank loan necessary to stay in business. He also was not sure what other people ought to be doing. He had no real conceptual model of how an organization might work apart from what he could personally supervise.

Frequently, I find that the way people treat their consultant is a microcosm of their problem. He began by requesting me to spend time on an activity which had relatively low priority, because of his uncertainty on how to use my time. Only when we discussed the task and what it was meant to lead to, did he begin to become clear about the basic organizational problems which needed attention.

My first approach was to undertake a problem-census. We held an offsite conference for several days with the top fourteen people in the company. To prepare for this, all the executives were interviewed as to what problems they saw in the company in relation to their own or others' jobs. They developed a list of 167 separate problems; it seemed miraculous that a company could run with so many problems! They ranged from ". . . no one knows when a machine is going to be bought, or why it is being bought," to ". . . how should Laxmi spend his time?" All of these problems were grouped into three or four major categories. Three teams were formed and during the days away each team worked on possible solutions. Then, near the end of the conference, each team reported on its work to date.

It was at this time that a most significant event occurred. The first team began to make its report. One of the younger executives had barely begun reporting for his group when Laxmi said: "That's ridiculous, you don't really think you are going to solve the problem that way." There was a sudden dead silence. The young fellow withdrew, became very defensive and had great difficulty in continuing. Considerable tension had been generated. My wife, also a consultant to the project and working with the team reporting, finally said, "You know, when we worked on that problem I wasn't particularly committed to what we came up with. But right now, I'll defend this team and its proposals to the end of the earth."

Laxmi's brother-in-law was also on that team. Asked in the meeting about his reaction to Laxmi's comments, the brother finally said, after a long pause: "I really felt bad; that was a poor thing to do." In the year since he had left his high civil service job and had begun to work for Laxmi, this was the first time he had ever said anything so directly negative to Laxmi, his brother-in-law and boss.

Laxmi responded to the situation in an extraordinary way: rather than becoming defensive he was genuinely moved and showed it. With tears in his eyes, he said: "I absolutely didn't realize the effect I was having. I can't apologize enough." This was a major turning point, because though we had been talking about Laxmi's difficulty in getting others to take initiative, (and it was one of the 167 problems on the list), Laxmi had not really emotionally experienced the way in which his own quickness and critical abilities contributed to the problem by reinforcing the general cultural fear of authority figures. In the past, whenever an idea was presented to him, he would instantaneously analyze the innumerable things wrong with it. Also, because he was so loaded with details and decisions, he seldom initiated anything except in occasional "brainstorms" which overwhelmed others with their complexities. We had been suggesting to him that he encourage others to come to him with ideas so that instead of being cast in the role of boss, squelching others' ideas, or tossing up ideas for others to shoot down, he could be in the role of helper, developing the ideas and proposals of others.

These suggestions meant that Laxmi would have to be a lot more open about what he wanted from subordinates. In the past, he would silently observe each employee's performance. Then he judged its worth and the person's merit, but the person never knew on what the judgment was based. Because the employee never knew what Laxmi was expecting of him, demanding of him, he would become very cautious and take no initiative. After the confrontation at the conference, Laxmi's behavior changed considerably. He began to think about and put into practice ways of getting other people to creatively use their imaginations, entrepreneurial and management abilities, and their own innovative approaches. He began to explore how he might let them know, generally in advance, the kind of performance he expected. He considered what kinds of criteria he could use for evaluation so that he could then set others to work to use their imaginations. He tried to get himself into a more helping role.

Sorting Out the Roles and Functions in the Company

From the conference there began to be a growing awareness of role confusion in the company. People were not sure what they were supposed to be doing as part of their jobs, since their duties had never been defined or even talked about. One consequence of the lack of clarity was that no team effort existed. Actually, there was no organizational form, such as management committees, which encouraged team work. There was no way for collaboration, in organizational terms, to occur, since there were no regular group meetings.

John Thomas and Ishwar Dayal[1] have developed an intervention tool called role-analysis-technique: Each executive defines how he sees his role, what the duties are, and the way in which that role connects to other executive roles. Together they talk through what each person will do. We used this technique as the first agenda item of a newly formed executive committee. Until then it had never occurred to them to meet as a group of executives. Previously, people had come one at a time to Laxmi for decisions. An executive committee of the top seven executives was formed and began weekly meetings, starting with mutual role analysis. As a consequence, everyone had a clearer idea of what others were supposed to be doing and how it interconnected.

It was also decided that a production coordination company was needed. Production problems constituted approximately 100 of the 167 identified problems. Almost nothing had been done to insure that production scheduling correlated with the actual work flow, the numbers of workers employed, or the output required. Consequently, another form of organizational change took place: A commitment was made that the production coordinating committee would meet once a week with opportunities for daily meetings among certain members.

The discussion on roles led us into considering what the top seven executives were actually doing. It turned out that the administrative officer, Laxmi's brother-in-law, was in a position that he did not really like, which was not taking advantage of his interests and skills, and was not satisfying

Laxmi. This had gone on for a year, since in India, as in many developing countries, it is very hard for family members to talk straight to one another; relationships affect what is allowed to be said. After discussing the problem openly, the brother-in-law was moved to the position of sales manager, which was a much better job for him, capitalizing on his agricultural background and personal abilities. The chief accountant was then able to become the financial manager, because the administrative officer position above him was eliminated. He had known much about modern management accounting, but he had learned it all by reading, never had the chance to apply it, and did not feel the confidence to implement such a new practice in the company until he was clearly in charge. Laxmi also began to include him in negotiations with bankers in order to build his confidence.

Another aspect we worked on was to help Laxmi identify the various roles he was playing at different times. Because the organization was so loose, he was in effect acting as chairman of the board, president of the company, sales manager, finance manager, and general manager, but it had not been clear at all that he was responsible for all those jobs. As we began to define what functions needed to be done in the role analysis mentioned earlier, we were able to help Laxmi recognize and make explicit when he was temporarily acting as sales manager or production manager. More and more we were trying to help define just where Laxmi's responsibilities began and where they ended. Until that time, he had not been able to visualize other's responsibilities and separate them from his own.

Problem-solving and Tolerance for Ambiguity: Manager or Entrepreneur?

Another of Laxmi's problems seems closely linked to the differences between skills needed for entrepreneurship and those desirable for managing. Laxmi had a very low tolerance for ambiguity. He became very tense when he encountered an unresolved problem and, as a consequence, he would either make rapid, intuitive decisions on matters about which he felt confident, or, if he did not feel confident, he would become paralyzed and not make any decision at all until he could totally master the subject matter by voracious reading. This resulted in an at-first surprising mixture of confidence and lack of confidence which surfaced in an interesting way. He had been using another consulting firm as an industry information source; though he paid them for more than five years, he had never been satisfied with their performance. He had never understood why he was not satisfied, nor had he stated this dissatisfaction to them. It seemed to me that though the consultant had particular marketing expertise which should have been useful, he was not able to help Laxmi define what problems should be attacked. Since Laxmi's chief problem centered on his confusion about how to utilize his own time, the consultant could never come to a firm agreement about what services to perform, though he had written innumerable vague exhortations and proposals. Laxmi invited us to meet with him and the consultant. When at our encouragement Laxmi expressed concern about future sales, the consultant proposed a comprehensive sales plan. Though his firm had good marketing information, was connected with a successful competitor, and had already done the requisite market research, Laxmi uncharacteristically refused to make a commitment on the spot. We adjourned for a strategy meeting, at which Laxmi approved of the concept but admitted he did not feel confident about how to use a consultant. He had to think it through until he felt he understood completely that issue. Once he did, it was very easy for him to approve the plan. As it turned out, that decision considerably changed the relationship with the consultant. He finally began to work concretely on a problem that Laxmi had defined in a way that let him use his expertise.

We discussed what it meant to get into a problem where one could not see the solution and what it meant to live with a high degree of ambiguity. The ability to do so is very different from the skills needed for entrepreneurship. In order to get an innovative enterprise establishd an entrepreneur somehow has to believe that he can overcome any of the difficulties he will face. I think that is one of the overriding requisites of entrepreneurship: self-confidence in one's problem-solving ability. In order to believe that he can turn his idea into an organization, an entrepreneur has to be sure that he is going to solve his problems, even if later it turns out that he is wrong. But a *manager* very often does not know how things are going to come out. One of the qualities that a manager needs is the willingness to live with unresolved problems, along with the willingness to live with the uncertainty of somebody else dealing with a problem instead of himself.

It is interesting to note the relationship of this point to McClelland's findings on entrepreneurial risk-taking; he discovered that entrepreneurs tend to have high need for achievement, which is associated with *moderate* risk-taking and desire for immediate feedback on performance.[2] In this context, a relatively low tolerance for ambiguity makes sense; high ambiguity increases the risk of failure and prolongs the likely interval between problem-solving effort and feedback. Conversely, we might expect that a problem with very low ambiguity would be insufficiently challenging and therefore avoided. A good manager, however, must attempt to routinize and make entirely unambiguous all problems which can be handled that way, which calls for different personality characteristics.

The Application of Openness and Confrontation—Managerial Tools— to Family Relationships

It was mentioned earlier that Laxmi was preoccupied with being known for building the company. He was afraid that his own brother and an older executive did not give him enough credit for his contributions when they met outsiders. Laxmi was convinced he had evidence that his brother and the executive were publicly undermining him and not giving him credit for all his hard work. Although he and his brother had been business partners for more than ten years and lived in the same house, they never talked genuinely to each other. Laxmi had built up a theory of brotherly disloyalty which he believed as absolute reality, but which he had never directly conveyed to his brother.

Eventually we conducted several intense sessions between the two brothers. While the younger brother had probably not complimented Laxmi to others, it was apparently because he felt so inadequate compared to Laxmi, rather than that he did not recognize Laxmi's achievements. The way he coped with those inadequacy feelings was by bragging and showing off, especially with relatives. Laxmi had taken that literally. It never occurred to him that because his brother felt inadequate he might overcompensate by inflating his own contribution. After considerable confrontation, Laxmi admitted that his convictions might be based on fantasy, but still preferred a complete business separation. They were already each managing separate companies connected only by finances. For years, Laxmi had wanted to be totally separate from his brother, but hadn't known how to say no. That decision was finally made in a much less recriminative way than had been brewing; at least they were able to talk it out and part on amicable mutual terms.

Issues Raised by this Case

(1) It is worthy to note the way in which modern management techniques interpenetrate with behavioral changes. The Laxmi project started with cash flow analysis, which led into projection of growth, then to setting a policy on growth, which led to looking at what kind of organization would be needed in order to achieve that growth, then to bringing in some foreign consultants, resulting in a new organizational style, which ultimately led to new kinds of organizational relationships. These matters are rarely dealt with in the literature because each link is usually treated separately. People who know techniques like managerial accounting, financial analysis, and operations research often work as if they were in quite separate fields, but implementation of these techniques—which are based on numerous assumptions about behavior and managerial style—require behavioral changes, too. The techniques cannot be imported without affecting organizational relationships.[3]

(2) Another issue raised in the Laxmi case is the problem of reversing the source of initiative in an organization. It requires moving the top man, with his energy, drive, and ambition, out of the role of constantly initiating for all others. That necessitates his going through some serious changes. As Laxmi began to change, he suddenly said, incredulously, that he never knew he had people in his company with so much talent. Part of the satisfaction of getting the initiative to come from below was seeing that the talent was there. An illustration of this occurred with a newly-hired produc-

tion manager. When the man arrived, Laxmi did something he would never have done before: He stated the results expected and advised the manager to hire an outside consultant if needed. Although the manager tried to achieve the results alone, in three months he decided for himself to adopt Laxmi's suggestion in order to meet his goals. This represented a learning experience for both Laxmi and the manager.

(3) An issue of significance is the need to raise the tolerance for ambiguity, a crucial new skill which an entrepreneur needs to learn if he is to become an effective manager. It must be learned in a way that does not reduce the drive for knowledge. Laxmi had an insatiable thirst for learning; when he needed to know something, he had to know it all, through reading and discussion. That results in part from not being able to stand ambiguity. Yet one must be able to live with unresolved issues as a manager while others are going through their struggles to learn.

(4) Another important issue was that in order for Laxmi to become a manager and not just the entrepreneur he had been, he had to make explicit choices about his life style. Until we talked about it, he did not see that he could choose not to try to learn those new managerial skills. For example, he could have hired a professional manager and stayed as the chief designer in the company—something at which he would be extraordinarily good. He had unusual innovative engineering ability. The choice was posed to him as sharply as possible. "You are having to learn things from scratch which are not necessarily natural to you, such as marketing and production control, just as you had to learn managerial finance. Do you really want to do that?" To Laxmi these tasks unquestionably had to be mastered because he was driven by his need to be known as the man who built the company, but another entrepreneur might choose to stick with what he is good at.

It is important that ways be found to entrepreneurs to see explicitly what choices they have so that they do not work on the wrong issues.

(5) The case stresses and demonstrates the need for real openness. Laxmi could not become a manager and could not get other people to be committed until he was willing to make clear his expectations, his demands, and the criteria by which he evaluated people. Before that, many distortions intervened in work relationships because there were many things which people could not or would not say to one another. As noted earlier, the influence of family position in patterns of discourse are strong in India as in other developing countries.[4] Laxmi as the boss and elder brother felt those reciprocal inhibitions going back down the hierarchy. As a consequence, he would build up strong feelings about people, but would not inform them, thus denying them the feedback that could possible improve their performance. The more they did not improve the stronger the feeling came, leading to very tense and unsatisfying relationships as well as unsatisfactory performance.

Openness is important, because without it, others are denied the data needed to grow. It also helps keep the top man from abusing his position of high influence. The entrepreneur, the manager, the owner, should not abdicate influence by remaining silent, nor dominate others by constant criticism; he must be open about what he is asking for so that he exerts influence in a way which develops others.

(6) Another important issue deals with the clarification of roles. In many developing countries, one's outside role behavior carries over very strongly into one's role in the organization. Therefore, a high status person in one social system has to be treated similarly in all situations. As a consequence, behavior is not always consistent with one's formal function in the organization. Entrepreneurs wanting to manage need to learn how to make formal distinctions, how to say "This is your territory, and this is mine." Another need which seems to be very common, since entrepreneurs often start out in family businesses, is to clarify family expectations as well as company needs. Clarification and explicitness help in making choices when there are conflicting demands. If a company is to grow, the decision must be made as to whether or not the organization's needs are going to take precedence over the family's.

(7) A further issue is connected to a finding in McClelland's earlier work. The person with high need for achievement has been found to have, in general, little dependence on others. Thus, when using outside experts, the entrepreneur is likely to automatically have extra resistance to any consultants he hires. On the other hand, he also genuinely wants help because he has problems he wants to solve. Thus, like any client, he can slide from one pole of resistance to another—from dependence to over-dependence. Since his personality and aspirations are likely to exaggerate these swings, learning how to use outside experts and how to help define a problem in a way that lets them use their expertise seems to be another crucial training need for entrepreneurs.

(8) Finally, the most important issue has to do with the problem of transfer of knowledge. Can a developing country avoid the mistakes of the West while adapting what is useful? To pose the question more concretely, we must briefly describe a model of organizational phases, developed on the basis of earlier research in India.[5] We can categorize organizations by three overall managerial styles:

a. the paternalistic or personalistic,
b. the bureaucratic or mechanistic, and
c. the organic.

To be effective, an organization's managerial style ought to be related to the complexity of the organization's tasks, the rate of change in markets and technology, and, to some extent, organizational size. The personalistic or paternalistic management style characterizes most entrepreneurs when they enter management. Despite a tendency to dominate decision making arbitrarily, they have great concern for the people who work for them and a very personalized identification with what happens to the company and each individual in it. When a company grows, however, and has more and more complex activities, it eventually becomes too much for one person to handle. No matter how smart, he cannot personally be in touch with everyone and know everything. Therefore, he has to find ways of getting other people to take responsibilities. The classic way has been through bureaucracy—formal rules, separate and discrete jobs, hierarchy, circumscribed authority through a chain of command, and information passing up and down the chain consistent with the Weberian model of bureaucracy. In a stable environment, bureaucracy can be effective.

An "organic" organization is a recent alternative concept for dealing with complexity. In it, decisions are made at the lowest possible level by those who know the most about the particular issue, rather than by hierarchical position. People are assigned to particular projects or tasks according to their expertise, and work together until they finish that project. Then they break up into new project groups. Consequently, leadership goes with skill rather than with formal position in the organization.

The organic organization is postulated to be most effective for dealing with a rapidly changing environment.[6] If we can presume, as does Victor Thompson, that the environment in developing countries is and will continue to rapidly change,[7] then the key question becomes, can developing countries learn to skip the bureaucratic stage when appropriate? Bureaucracy is in some ways very different, if the organization has a fairly stable technology and markets. But, on the other hand, the human costs and also the organizational costs of bureaucracy are very high. The personalization and organizational rigidity of bureaucratic Western society have been painful prices to pay for "progress." Part of the attraction of the bureaucratic mode in countries like India, however, where management has in general been personalistic and arbitrary, is the promise of impersonal, impartial management. Even though that may not be so effective, employees and managers can believe that there is not going to be favoritism and particularism; by adopting broad rules and impersonal job categories, working life will be much improved. Companies which have tried to move rapidly to bureaucracy often run into problems, though, because employees often feel abandoned and uncared for. Thus even where bureaucracy might be appropriate, it is difficult and costly to adopt it.

On the basis of the Laxmi case as an extension of my earlier research in India, I think that the bureaucratic phase can be omitted in many individual cases. It certainly would take considerable training, consulting, and willingness to allow those in the organization to be involved in the changeover from the old style to the new. Replicability needs testing, but at least in some cases the bureaucratic organizational style can be skipped—along with the depersonalization and dehumanization that goes with it. One hopes that there are many other examples of human resource development, comparable to the case of Mr. Laxmi, to be found in developing economies.

Notes

1. John Thomas and Ishwar Dayal, "Operation KPE: Developing a New Organization," *Journal of Applied Behavioral Science*, 4, 1968.

2. David C. McClelland, *The Achieving Society* (New York: D. Van Nostrand Co., 1961).

3. Note, for example, the conclusions of John Terninko on the failure of Operations Research applications in "Applications of Operations Research: Current Trends," (Ph.D. diss., Case Institute of Technology, 1968).

4. See Allan R. Cohen, *Tradition, Change and Conflict in Indian Family Business* (The Hague: Institute of Social Studies, in press).

5. Cohen, op. cit. Also see Allan R. Cohen, "Human Dimensions of Administrative Reform," *Development and Change* 2,2 (1970–71): 65–82.

6. Warren G. Bennis, *Changing Organizations* (New York: McGraw-Hill, 1966).

7. Victor A. Thompson, "Administrative Objectives for Development Administration," *Administrative Science Quarterly* 9,1 (June 1964).

15 Public Administration in the 1970s

Chi-Yuen Wu

It would be presumptuous for anyone to attempt at this time to forecast what eventually would be the public administration of countries of the world at the end of the decade. Public administration functions in a particular environmental setting. Public administration of a country depends on the political, social, economic, cultural, as well as the physical and technological environment in which it operates. Any attempt to discuss what would happen to public administration in the next ten years will encounter two difficulties: One concerns the rapidly changing and increasingly turbulent environment, characterized by its complexity and uncertainty. Another difficulty concerns the divergencies of public administration in different national environments and therefore the danger of over-simplification in making generalizations.

In discussing at the beginning of 1971 possible developments in public administration in the Second United Nations Development Decade, we are facing the same difficulties as one did in 1961 trying to foresee the many significant developments in public administration during the First United Nations Development Decade. At the beginning of the 1960s, to cite just one example, not many were able to anticipate the extent to which the role of management in public administration would expand or to realize fully the potential contribution and implication of a wide variety of modern management techniques for increasing the administrative capabilities of governments.

Bearing in mind the diversity of public administration systems and situations as well as the rapid, dynamic, and often unpredictable environmental changes, one can still identify certain broad trends in public administration in the 1970s.[1] Many of these trends were evident in the 1960s, at least in embryo, but are expected to be impactful in the new decade. At the same time, it may happen that "the age of discontinuity" will also bring forth new trends which cannot be foreseen. My purpose here is to deal with the former. In this paper, I shall try to do two things: One is to discuss the main trends directly pertinent to public administration in the 1970s. (These

Reprinted with permission from *International Review of Administrative Sciences*, (Vol. XXXVII, No. 3, 1971, pp. 161–75), and with the consent of the author.

Based on a paper presented to the 1971 National Conference on Public Administration of the American Society of Public Administration, at Denver, U.S.A. on April 19, 1971. The views expressed in this article are the author's and do not necessarily represent those of the United Nations.

are grouped here in ten broad clusters.) The other is to give a brief indication of the major contents of the United Nations public administration programme, as formulated in the light of the anticipated trends in the Second United Nations Development Decade.

Size and Complexity

Concerning public administration in the 1970s, it should, *first of all*, be pointed out that it will continue to grow in size and in importance. Government activities will expand because certain important undertakings and issues can be handled only by government or with governmental support. In the more developed countries, these may include major programs and issues relating to outer space, deep-sea exploration, atomic energy, supersonic aircraft, resources conservation, education (except what can still be handled by private sources), comprehensive environment control, use of financial, monetary and other means to influence economic trends, social welfare and many others. In the developing countries, the government plays a leading role in the whole area of economic and social development, with varying degrees of individual participation, depending on the political and economic system and situation of the country. In a large number of low-income countries, capital for economic development and funds for social development are, to a considerable extent, dependent on the government which either provides the financial resources directly or encourages the flow of funds from external or internal sources through various facilitative measures, including laws and regulations, guarantees and other means. Qualified manpower, another decisive factor in economic and social development, is educated or trained mainly in the public sector. Technology, either through research and development or through transfer from other countries, increasingly involves the support of the government. In the developing countries, the government is expected to take new initiatives and to increase its role of entrepreneurship and risk-taking in economic undertakings. Public enterprises will continue to increase in number, in size and in importance (as an instrument of economic development). Even in those economic and social areas which the government does not handle directly, there will be increasing need for new governmental regulation and control. Most important of all, it is the government which has an overall view of the economic and social development of a country and which is responsible for development planning.

The public administration in the 1970s must be geared to the requirements of the expanding functions of the government. The number of public employees (including those in the public enterprises) at the end of the decade will no doubt show significant increase both in absolute terms and in relation to the population. This will happen in spite of the expectation that improvement in effectiveness and efficiency would reduce the number of public employees required to perform the same function and that financial and personnel cuts would occur in one place or another from time to time. In any case the percentage of the gross national product attributable to the public sector is expected to continue to increase in the course of the decade.

Second, government activities will increase in complexity.[a] They are becoming much more specialized, requiring highly technical personnel to handle them. They are influenced by an extraordinary degree of interdependency among individuals and groups. They often involve more than one discipline and cut across traditional functions, requiring interdisciplinary and multifunctional approaches. They also involve different levels of government, including central, regional, and local administration, and often cut across traditional geographical or political boundaries. Public administration in the 1970s must be able to respond to the complexity of government activities.

This leads to the *third* point, i.e., the great need for planning, coordination, and control. In addition to the factors mentioned above, planning also becomes important to assure total analysis of all aspects and effects and to avoid the unanticipated consequences of partial development measures. Only governments are in a position to take an overall view of the economic and social development of the country and to plan comprehensively and effectively. Planning has been widely accepted as a useful tool for developing public policies. However, the emphasis has been on economic planning. What will be needed in the coming years is the broadening of the concept of planning to include non-economic dimensions which are essential both for the practicability of plans and for making the results of development relevant to national, social, and human development. Viewed in this context, development planning will have to become truly interdisciplinary in nature and the responsibility of all development administrators. To make planning a more meaningful tool of policy, greater attention should also be given to translation of plans into programs and actions. This would require better integration among planning, policy making, and budgeting. Increasing attention should be paid to the administrative aspects of planning and plan implementation. Development plans should become more implementable, containing both administrative plans and plans for implementation.[b]

Coordination is another result of the complexity and interdependent nature of public administration problems, which include many multifunctional problems, problems involving different levels of government, and problems cutting across existing political boundaries within a country. Economic development, social welfare, family planning, human environment, urbanization, regional (sub-national) development, and many others all involve interrelated and interwoven problems and therefore require a great deal of coordination. By coordination in public administration is meant the administrative measures taken to bring various parts or units in an administrative system into proper relation. The purpose of coordination is to ensure unity

[a] Complexity is used here to denote both a high degree of knowledge required to produce the output of a system and a high degree of division of labor.
[b] The United Nations Public Administration Division is completing a comparative study of administrative aspects of planning and plan implementation.

of action within complex organizations or systems, to establish the consistency of the decisions of more than one unit, to avoid contradictions, conflicts and unnecessary duplication of efforts, and thus to facilitate the administration to achieve specific objectives. There are many ways of achieving coordination. It may be effected through better communication and exchange of information, through formal or informal discussions, through joint coordinating machinery, through subordination of related units to a higher authority, or through central planning and control. Coordination is particularly important in the administration of economic and social development.[2]

Inherent in the concept of planning is the idea of control, either through direct intervention or through regulatory mechanisms of one kind or another. Control is required to make sure that (1) measures for plan implementation are actually carried out; (2) the expected results are achieved; (3) the adjustments necessitated by rapidly changing environments are made in plan targets, strategies and operations; and (4) information is available for evaluation of results.[3] Traditional budgetary controls may not suffice for this purpose and there is already a ferment in control theories. The science of cybernetics has contributed ideas of feedback and homeostatis which will become increasingly relevant to public administration and use of management information systems for development.[4] New policies, organizational arrangements and procedures will also be needed to influence the activities of individuals and organizations to assure consistency in actions for achieving planned goals.

Politics and Administration

Fourth, public administration will have to be increasingly sensitive to the political environment. Basically, public administration always functions within a political context. Theoretically, it is possible to treat the administrative and the political tasks as two distinct and distinguishable functions.[5] It is the political machinery which sets national objectives and priorities, decides upon important policies, adopts development plans, allocates resources, and provides public administration with the necessary guidance for action. It is the responsibility of public administration to execute the policies and plans decided by the political leaders, to get things done in accordance with the political directives. Under the theory of the supremacy of the political process, the public administrator or the civil servant is considered as politically neutral.[c] He maintains continuity in government and serves as a link between an outgoing and an incoming government. In the post-war period, the existence of a politically neutral but durable civil

---

[c] The emergence of a politically neutral civil service in a number of countries has been related to the growth of representative government and linked to efforts to "cleanse" the political system and/or attempts to establish a career system on a merit basis for the civil service.

service in a number of countries did perform the function of maintaining continuity in spite of the many changes in political leadership.

In recent years the tendency is away from the sharp distinction between politics and administration. Administration has become increasingly involved in politics in the sense of policy making. Such a tendency is expected to continue in the coming years. Among the reasons responsible for this are the increasing complexity and the increasingly technical character of many government functions, with the following consequences: (1) In order to make political decisions on complicated and technical matters, the political leaders have to rely heavily on the civil servants to provide them with knowledgeable advice. The way in which the civil servants define the problems for policy decision, collect and analyze essential facts and data, as well as formulate policy alternatives or options will go far in influencing political decisions. (2) In a complicated situation, policy making and policy execution are interrelated and affect each other. Policies often have to be modified and revised in the course of execution, taking into account the experience gained. Various operational decisions taken during implementation often have significant policy implications. (3) Policies are often subject to various interpretations. In such cases, the administrators responsible for the implementation of a policy can use their own discretion in its interpretation. In view of the crucial role of the administrators in all these three aspects, those responsible for political decisions or those having the authority for final decision and legitimation of policies will naturally insist that the administrators should be acceptable to them from the political point of view. The administrators, especially those at the senior level, must not be opposed to the objectives upon which the policies are based. "If he is to function effectively," as the report of an interregional seminar points out, "a politically neutral senior administrator must be committed to the national goals of his society and be sensitive to its political processes."[6]

Concern has frequently been expressed that the public administrators in many countries are often crucially involved in influencing political development. Strong criticism has been raised that the "political" role of the civil serivce in developing countries is extremely prominent as compared to the "norm" in the political systems in North America or Western Europe. Not only the scope and content of many development projects and programs frequently originate from the civil servants, but often the initiative of some important policies also comes from the administrative staff. As long as government operations continue to increase in complexity and include more and more technical and professionalized activities, as is expected in the coming years, the administrative arm of the government will assume greater and greater discretionary power and will be more and more open to the criticism that it plays too prominently a "political" role.

Students of political science and public administration hold widely divergent views on how to deal with this important trend. Referring to situations in developing countries[7] some scholars, usually having in mind a preconceived "norm" (based on the experience of North America and

Western Europe) concerning the relationship between public administration and politics and a particular theory of political development, feel strongly that it would be a mistake to do anything to strengthen the bureaucracy in developing countries, which they regard as "dangerously powerful," and that any attempt to increase its administrative capacity would result in the retardation of political development and would contribute to political maladjustment. Referring to situations in developed countries, some students of public administration, especially those belonging to the younger generation in the United States, who are frustrated about certain deficiencies in the society and about what they consider to be an unmoving, inflexible bureaucracy, responsible in a significant way for the failure of the society to achieve certain social and political goals, turn against the concept of a "politically neutral" public service, against the "inhuman" approach of modern management, against the system maintenance role of the public administration, and feel strongly about the necessity of political involvement of the public administrators, especially in the search for objectives consistent with "human values" and with the well-being of the people. They call their movement "New Public Administration," which is similar to "New Economics" and new movements in other fields. While it is not clear that this is really "new,"[8] one may share the underlying assumption that the public administrators must be committed to the national goals and be sensitive to the political processes. As public administration is not, and in its nature cannot, be self-legitimizing, it cannot really be successful without the support of the political leaders who alone have the legitimizing authority.[9] There is no reason, however, to draw from this conclusion that one should not even attempt to strengthen the administrative capability of a government until the administrative system should conform with certain political and social values.[10] Nor need one accept the extreme view that there is no non-political role for the public administration arm of a government.

Quantitative Analysis

The *fifth* point concerns one of the non-political aspects, i.e., the increasing importance of the management role and the rational and quantitative (economics-based) approach in the public administration of the 1970s.[d] The need of public administration in the 1970s calls for a managerial orientation. The public administrators will be increasingly expected to bring the benefit of modern science and technology to bear on the management of

---

[d] I deliberately emphasize the non-political nature of management science and management technology, but (as indicated in previous paragraphs) I am fully aware of the possible encroachment of management upon politics. The analysis of problems relating to cost, benefit, effectiveness, efficiency, etc., of a given objective or policy could often lead to involvement in "policy politics" (dealing with which policy to adopt). For the contention that the thrust of certain modern management techniques makes it an integral part of system politics, see Aaron Wildavsky, "The Political Economy of Efficiency," *Public Administration Review* 26, 4 (December 1966).

public affairs and to develop new managerial concepts and systems. They must be familiar with the potentialities and also the limitations of management technology, including the more modern and more sophisticated techniques. They must be capable of applying as appropriate such technology in their administrative tasks. There is no doubt in my mind that management technology, including the use of computer in government, will become increasingly important in the coming years.

In the 1960s, there were, from the standpoint of public administration, two serious defects in the development strategies of many developing countries: (1) Not sufficient attention was paid to administration and management. As a result, development plans failed to include plans for developing the administrative and management capability to implement the plans. (2) Those responsible for development often failed to understand that modern technology includes not only technology in the narrow or purely technical sense, but also management technology. In fact the latter is a partner of the former. Thus, the first industrial revolution (which involves mechanization) gave rise to such management technology as rationalization or "scientific management." The second industrial revolution (which involves automation) has given rise to operations research and a agement. As a result, development plans failed to include plans for developing countries must be able to adopt, to develop, and to improve appropriate management technology in order to be successful in accelerating economic and social development.

The low level of administrative capability in many developing countries creates a disequilibrium system in planned development since the administrative load continuously outpaces administrative and management capability. The strategy should not be the scaling down of planned targets to the level of existing management capability, but rather the continuous upgrading of that capability, as part of the development plan, especially through the adoption of scientific methods and the use of modern management technology (including rational and quantitative technology). This is what I would expect to happen in the 1970s, if the Second United Nations Development Decade is to succeed in its objectives and to achieve its targets.[11]

To use rational and quantitative management technology in public administration is not a simple task. Basically, rationality is the servant of objectives or goals. An optimal solution can be produced through a rational method only if the objectives are clear. Where objectives are clear and quantifiable, the use of economic-oriented rational and quantitative techniques will be much more effective. This is especially true of public enterprises, where the use of rational management techniques for the improvement of performance[12] will no doubt become increasingly important in the 1970s. For many non-economic areas, clarity of objectives is often difficult to achieve in public affairs. In some cases, the method of minimizing costs rather than that of maximizing benefits is often adopted. In some others, different methods and techniques will have to be used or developed.

The Behavioral Sciences, Management
Sciences, and Human Welfare

Sixth, one of the basic tasks of management is to mobilize support for organizational objectives and to provide an environment which would release creative human energies and potential in the pursuit of those goals. To achieve this, increasing attention has been turned, and is expected to turn in the coming years, by public administration to behavioral sciences for the solution of problems concerning human motivation and human relations.[13] Under this trend, the motivational horizons of administration and management are extended beyond the economic to the political, the sociological, and the psychological. Techniques based on behavioral sciences such as participation, informal organization, democratic leadership, and many others are used to achieve greater individual satisfaction from work, to integrate the interests of the individuals and those of the organization to which they belong, to bring about mutual satisfaction of organizational goals and individual needs, to release the motivational forces and creative potential of public personnel, to have better communication, to resolve conflicts, and generally to improve performance through improvement of organizational and managerial behavior. It is important to motivate the individuals not only as individuals, but also as members of an organization. In order to function well, an organization requires commitment from its members and its members look for opportunity for participation and development in the organization's life. In recent years, increasing efforts have been made to marshall the capabilities of individuals for meeting organizational objectives and to improve organizational climates for better performance. Such efforts, comprehended within the term Organization Development (OD), constitute one of the significant contributions of behavioral sciences in administration and management.

While behavioral science technology has been growing in substance and in influence, its progress has been mainly based on the experience of highly developed countries. The relevance and validity of such technology has been conditioned by the implicit assumption about the sociocultural environment in which it emerged. It should be borne in mind that in another environment the ecological factors could greatly limit both its acceptability and its validity. To extend such techniques to the settings of the developing countries, environmental or ecological conditions need to be examined in order to work out approaches, methods and techniques that are relevant and suitable.

Rational management technology (which is sometimes called "management science") and behavioral science technology may be based on different assumptions. Strictly speaking, they are not always compatible. The objective of the rational and quantitative management technology is to maximize output and/or to minimize cost and that of behavioral science technology is to release creative and motivational capacities and to strengthen interpersonal relations. But both have the common objective of improving administrative effectiveness and/or efficiency and improving individual, group and organizational performance. On the assumption that these two kinds of management technologies can be made compatible, as I believe that they will eventually be, I am inclined to agree with the view that the behavioral science technology "is not an alternative to management science, or a softener of its impact," but rather the "adjunct of management science."[14] Thus the public administrator of the 1970s will be one requiring cognitive and analytical skills in dealing both with the technical systems and with the human systems. He is expected to integrate in an institutional system that which is technical and that which is human.

Progress in management technology both technical and human, however, often result in a style of administration that is more oriented to efficiency and effectiveness, than one to human values and human well-being. Governments in some countries already face a great challenge to prevent the domination of man by an inhuman mechanism based on a set of sophisticated management tools. From this point of view behavioral science technology can have an even more critical impact than computer technology and other rational technology.

Thus the *seventh* point is that in the 1970s, both in the developed and in the developing countries, the demand will significantly increase for the government to focus on human well-being as a central concern of public administration. (This is closely related to the fourth point, in so far as human well-being is defined by the political process and forms part of the political objectives.) This trend will bring into prominence the need to evolve formal channels of citizen participation in decision making, for decisions focused on human well-being ought to possess the characteristic of utmost acceptability. It is expected that the 1970s will witness increased involvement of all concerned in the decision of political and administrative policies and will become a decade of involvement. If this analysis is correct, the classical models of organization would have to be supplemented or adapted to these new dimensions.

Change

Eighth, change will characterize the public administration in the 1970s. While no society is really stable or permanent, the magnitude and tempo of changes in the 1970s are expected to be broad, far-reaching, rapid, and often turbulent. Perhaps, one can even say that change will be the only constant fact of life in the decade.[e] Among the factors which have brought

---

[e] In view of the frequency and rapidity of changes our society has been called "temporary" or "transitional" by some authors. These terms have the advantage of highlighting the unprecedented rate of change taking place in our society. But I am not sure whether it would really be correct to characterize any society as temporary or transitional. When the time comes to write the history of the 1960s and/or the 1970s, it will be evident that this period will have its distinct features. The difference is not that between a permanent society and a transitional society; the difference is rather that between a period when the transition from one society to another would take a long time and one when the transition is very rapid and short.

about political, economic, and social changes in the 1960s, and which will generate further significant changes in the 1970s, we may mention the spectacular advances in science and technology and the consequential knowledge explosion; the expanding efforts to conquer space and distance and to make use of resources hitherto unused, unexploited or unknown; population increase, industrial growth, and agricultural revolution; increasing interdependence of countries and at the same time growing nationalism; rising expectation of people concerning improvements in their economic, social, and political status; changes in the concepts of human values, human well-being, and human rights; as well as upheavals caused by natural and human factors.

The administrative implications are many. The public administrators will have to cope with changing circumstances, to face new problems, and to perform new tasks. The administrative machinery must become flexible and be able to respond quickly and effectively to changing environment, as rigid and inflexible systems will not be able to deal with changing situations. There should develop personnel and organizational capabilities to provide useful forecasts for both the controllable and the uncontrollable variables and to devise methods to anticipate environmental changes.[f] To the extent possible, needed changes should be made, not too little nor too late, and be directed to serve constructive purposes. This would involve the readiness of the administrators to take risks. It also adds new temporal dimension to public administration (requiring action to be taken speedily and timely), which is assuming a new significance in a rapidly changing world. In other words, public administration will become more a change agent than a system maintainer.[15] The public administration of the 1970s will have to be more change-oriented and development-oriented.

Increasing Role of Administrative Reform and Management Improvement

Ninth, partly due to the changing environment and partly due to the need to improve the administrative machinery for better performance, administrative reform and management improvement are expected to play an increasing role in the coming years. In this connection, a few words on the endless controversy between the macro approach and the micro approach may be appropriate. Those in favor of the latter would cite the many failures of attempts at comprehensive administrative reform, would advance the view that the prerequisites to comprehensive reform simply did not exist in sufficient strength to permit such reform to succeed in most developing

---

[f] As Yehezkel Dror points out, interest in the future is nothing new in government. What is new are three interrelated developments: (a) increasing necessity to take the future into consideration; (b) increasing possibility to take the future better into consideration (due to better knowledge on how to foresee the future, instead of relying on a variety of religious, mystic, intuitive and random devices); and (c) increasing demand to meet needs of the future. ("Futures in Government," *Futures*, September 1968).

countries, and come to the conclusion that partial reforms would likely be applicable in all conditions and could serve as models for, and induce, further reforms. Those in favor of the macro or comprehensive approach, on the other hand, would emphasize the complexity and interdependence of various administrative factors, would highlight the need for a comprehensive reform program to meet the overall development requirement and to provide common principles and frameworks within which partial and piecemeal reform measures could be adopted, and would point out that piecemeal approach could inadvertently introduce inconsistencies and even contradictions and conflicts in an administrative system. There are elements of truth in both approaches. Even a strong advocate of the partial approach recognizes that given the right political and social environment, comprehensive reform would be useful, and in cases where the comprehensive approach should prove not feasible, partial improvements could lay a basis for future global reform.[16] In any case, when one tries to improve a single organization, he should remember that no organization with an important role in the development process can be self-sufficient and that some other organizations form part of its environment which may provide certain constraints on its reform effort.[g] On the other hand, it is important for the advocates of comprehensive reform to recognize that all comprehensive plans and programs comprise individual projects and that the basic unit of public administration is individual organization. In certain circumstances, it is often necessary and desirable to concentrate scarce resources in particular projects or particular organizations to the neglect of others. The success in a number of important projects in key sectors or the building of "islands of excellence" may have both demonstration and multiplier effects on the country as a whole. The important point to be remembered is the need to evaluate particular projects or particular reforms in relation to their system-wide consequences.

Taking all factors into consideration we are inclined to give greater emphasis on the macro or comprehensive approach, because of the complexity and interdependent nature of the problems faced by the public administration, but much will depend on the environment of the country at a given time. In the 1970s we expect that administrative reform and management improvement at all levels will become increasingly important, but we also expect that those engaged in comprehensive reform will give special attention to performance and development of individual organizations and the personnel therein and that those engaged in micro management improvement work will take fully the overall picture into consideration and will base their action on certain common principles and frameworks, so as to avoid inconsistencies, contradictions, conflicts and other possible serious effects.

---

[g] A purely micro or project approach often leads to serious results. For example, success in individual industrial projects in the past was often accompanied by some worst aspects of urbanization, environment pollution, and many other unfavorable effects.

Personnel Training and Management

The *tenth* point, one of the most important, concerns personnel administration and training. The overall effectiveness of any public administration system essentially depends on the quality of the public employees, especially those at the senior grade. Therefore two basic tasks for the public administration of any country are (a) to establish and maintain a personnel system which will attract, retain, reward and motivate competent, dedicated, and responsive public employees, and (b) to train, develop and up-date them through training and career development. These will become increasingly important during the 1970s, because of the growth in size and in complexity of public administration.

Public administration in the 1970s will be increasingly diversified. New forms of organization, new functions, new techniques, new processes will require new types of skills. More scientific and technical personnel will have to be inducted in public services. As a result, the structure and composition of the civil service will grow more complex. New methods and criteria for the selection, recruitment, performance evaluations, grading, promotions, pay, and career development will have to be devised in order to answer the needs of an increased variety of categories of staff employed in the public sector. This situation will make new claim on the capacity of central personnel agencies, which will have to be so organized as to be able to accommodate important new dimensions of personnel policy.

The personnel function, however, should be not only in relation to the overall efficiency of the administrative system, but also in the light of the government's responsibility for making effective use of national manpower resources, of high-level skills especially. In most developing countries this special responsibility clearly flows both from the relative size of the public service (as a proportion of the total labor force) and from the repercussions of civil service policies on many spheres of economic and social life. The government should, therefore, exert a constructive influence on the national labor market, to encourage the production of skills, which are required to meet the changing needs of government and country and to circumscribe the wastage of such skills. To achieve this objective, a global, long-range view of problems of personnel is required. At the same time, the public personnel system must also be such as to enable all public employees to make their maximum contribution.[17]

These ten points do not exhaust the list of important trends in public administration in the 1970s. There are other trends.[h] New bases may emerge for organizing economic and administrative activities, especially in such fields as regional development, community development and decentralization. The growing concern with human privacy in the face of greater governmental needs for information gives rise to difficult questions of access to information and the more fundamental question of individual versus collective needs. These questions may come to dominate public administration

---

[h] Some of these may be considered as part of the overall trends mentioned above, while others may represent independent points.

in the 1970s and lead to development of new arrangements and safeguards for collection and use of information. The legal systems, of which public administration is an integral part, are developing new orientations and the concept of development law is already making its impact felt in public affairs. These and other developments may add still new dimensions to public administration in the 1970s.

In short, "public administration must be recreated, renewed, and re-vitalized to produce the changes and achievements required in the trans-formation of societies . . . The challenge and the task of the 1970s is to devise and install administrative systems that can actually accelerate development and better enable developing countries to make effective use of their resources."[18]

The United Nations Program in Public Administration

The United Nations program in public administration may be explained briefly in the light of various points mentioned above.[19] The basic aim of the program is to promote effective public administration in order to ac-celerate economic and social development. The unit in the United Nations responsible for this program is the Public Administration Division (PAD) in the Department of Economic and Social Affairs. The projected program in the 1970s is based on past experience and on the planning exercizes which were undertaken to elaborate proposed objectives and programs in public administration in the Second United Nations Development Decade.[20]

The PAD program falls into two broad categories: one takes the form of specific technical cooperation projects with developing countries; and the other comprises activities of a general kind, the benefits of which are equally available to all countries. The latter includes action-oriented re-search and comparative studies, seminars and expert working groups, as well as dissemination of information, including results of research and seminars. (The former will be called in this paper "country programs" and the latter, together with other work necessary for rendering substantive support to the country programs, "the PAD Headquarters program.") The actual content of the country programs in technical cooperation will be determined by the requests received from the developing countries.

A cardinal principle of technical cooperation is that it is given only at the request of the governments concerned. This is based on the principle of non-interference in the internal affairs of the recipient countries. The country programs are supported by the PAD Headquarters program, which has been designed both to assist the developing countries generally to im-prove the capability of PAD to backstop the country programs.[i] These gen-

---

[i] As public administration is a "developing" discipline or rather a cluster of disci-plines, much research, comparative studies, and exchange of experience and views through international seminars and meetings are needed. According to an evaluation by the Second Meeting of Experts: (a) research is "indispensable for fostering ad-

eral characters of the program are expected to continue in the 1970s with an increasing emphasis on flexibility, experimentation, and impact.[j]

The developing countries show great diversities in development of their administrative systems and in the need for outside assistance. Many countries are in the process of building and developing their basic public administrative infrastructure, while others have more sophisticated administrative systems. There are also wide differences among developing countries concerning their size as well as their political, economic and social systems. Their needs in the field of public administration are different from each other. In order to respond to the varying needs of developing countries and to the challenge of the 1970s, the United Nations has (a) to maintain a wide-spectrum program in public administration and to increase its substantive scope as necessary; (b) to take fully into account the environmental factors as well as changing administrative problems;[k] and (c) to be specially sensitive to the political environment.

Administrative Modernization and Social and Economic Development

A significant development in the United Nations public administration program of the 1970s is the recognition of the importance of public administration in economic and social development. When the United Nations declared the 1960s as the first United Nations Development Decade, the role of public administration in development was not clearly spelled out. It was not until the convening of the First Meeting of Experts on the United Nations Public Administration Programme in January 1967 that public administration really became an integral part of the economic and social development work of the Organization. When the Second United Nations Development

---

ministrative reform, for training, and for many other activities"; (b) "The Division had demonstrated the effectiveness of interregional seminars in major emerging administrative problems"; and (c) these activities "had advanced knowledge in important areas of administration for development as well as enhancing the competence of the officials who participated" (document ST/TAO/M/57, pages 19 and 21).

[j] The total technical cooperation program in public administration for which the Public Administration Division has substantive responsibility, in terms of U.S. dollars, reached one million in 1953, one and half million in 1960, and two million in 1962, two and half million in 1964, three million in 1967, and stood at three and half million in 1969 and 1970. In 1969 and 1970, the number of experts assisting developing countries exceeded two hundred. In both years (also in 1971), for substantive support of country projects and for research and seminars, the Public Administration Division has fifteen professional posts in its regular manning table, plus six consultants and special technical advisers for Special Fund projects, totaling twenty-one. It also has four interregional advisers to render short-term assistance to developing countries. The program is expected to increase in 1971 and in subsequent years.

[k] The solution of administrative problems should not be based on any preconceived ideas or prescriptions, but should depend on the actual situation which varies from country to country. Technical cooperation must take the environment factors fully into consideration.

Decade began in January 1971, there was a clear and definite recognition of the role of public administration. The General Assembly in resolution 2561 (XXIV) emphasized the importance of public administration to development and invited the Secretary-General to develop a coordinated program for international activities in this field in the 1970s. When the General Assembly adopted late in 1970 the international development strategy for the Second Development Decade in its resolution 2626 (XXV), it asked the developing countries to "pay special attention to the orientation and organization of their public administration at all levels for both the effective formulation and implementation of their development plans." The Second Meeting of Experts, which met in January 1971, called for bold action to increase the administrative capability for development and for an "administrative revolution" in support of revolutionary changes in the economic and social fields. The recommendations of the Second Meeting of Experts were approved by the Economic and Social Council in its resolution 1567 (L) on May 6, 1971.

The United Nations public administration program will emphasize both the complexity factor and the change factor. In rendering advisory services to developing countries, public administration experts sent by the United Nations are requested to take these factors fully into consideration and to bear in mind the importance of public administration as a change agent in the development process. The PAD Headquarters program for the coming years includes a research project on "administration for change." It will analyze the administrative implications of change and arrangements for anticipating and developing measures to deal with them. The program will continue to include work relating to the technical and specialized departments of the government, including the employment and development of scientists and technical personnel required.

The PAD Headquarters program will include certain general items as methodological study for developing quantitative or qualitative indicators of administrative capability for development, preparation of a comprehensive handbook on development administration, and if resources should become available, also the preparation of periodic reports on progress in public administration on a world-wide basis. Although the program does not include any specific project regarding the need of the public administrators to be sensitive to human values and human well-being, these will underline every project in the program, especially in connection with "control" (especially judicial review and other measures to protect the rights of citizens against administrative action), with participation and involvement (especially in decision-making processes), and with management technology (to ensure that it would be oriented not only to effectiveness but also to human well-being).

The program will give considerable attention to planning, coordination, and control. Increasingly, technical cooperation projects in public administration will be closely integrated with the development planning process in the countries. Governments are realizing the importance of preparing administrative plans as part of the development planning process to determine the public administration inputs essential for the implementation of plans. The United Nations public administration program is expected to help the requesting countries in the formulation of such administrative plans. Technical cooperation will then be determined in the light of the requirements for implementing such plans. In the PAD Headquarters program, a comparative study in this field is being prepared and an interregional seminar is being planned for 1972.[21]

Multi-Functional and Interdisciplinary Projects

The future PAD Headquarters program will give considerable emphasis on multi-functional and interdisciplinary projects having important coordination components, such as family planning, environment control, urbanization, and many others. The interdisciplinary approach to development problems will increase as realization grows that these cannot be perceived or resolved in terms of individual disciplines. There are other substantive offices as well as specialized agencies in the United Nations family or organizations which are concerned with different aspects and sectors of development. Public administration is a common element in all such cases, for example, agricultural administration, education administration, health administration, labor administration. Over and above the question of sectoral administration is the quality and capability of public administration systems in general, as expressed in institutions and processes of government-wide import. Overall administrative capability in fact assumes much more importance with the advent of development planning. For this reason, it is only logical that the United Nations must increasingly work with offices and agencies concerned with different sectors and projects not only to make a contribution concerning common administrative elements but also to suggest system-wide changes which may be necessary to assure effective results. For the same reason, it is important to increase collaboration with other disciplines and specialists to develop the necessary capabilities to solve development problems. Relationship and coordination among different levels of government is also expected to be increasingly important in the 1970s PAD program. The program will stress four priority areas crucial to improving the administrative capacity of local government and regional (sub-national) development. (1) There will be continued emphasis on the development and strengthening of central agencies for local government improvement.[22] It is expected that technical assistance will continue to be given to Ministries or other central agencies concerned with local government and regional (sub-national) administration such as are currently being provided to Jamaica, Niger, Uganda, Tanzania, Venezuela, and others. (2) There will be continued interest on the development of effective systems of decentralization and central-local relations. (3) There will be stress on administration for regional (sub-national) development. (4) There will also be stress on the distinctive problems in urban administration that most developing countries are confronted with in ever increasing intensity.[23]

Technical cooperation work under the general heading of "control" is expected in increase in the coming years, especially as part of major administrative reform projects and projects relating to plan implementation. The PAD Headquarters program in the coming years will include research and studies on methods of control of plan implementation as well as systems for monitoring the progress during the 1970s of achievements in different development plans, programs and projects. The program will also include studies on accountability, on regulatory administration, on judicial review of administrative action and other measures to protect the people from administrative action at all levels of the government.

A large number of countries have reached the stage where their primary need is information on comparable experience elsewhere. There has been considerable demand for the establishment of a public administration information center which can serve the needs of countries by organizing information and making it available to them as required. This is a major project with many technical, substantive and financial aspects. It has not been possible in the past to implement it because of lack of resources. If resources should continue to be unavailable to do it on a global basis, this could be done at a regional level.

In fact one of the major developments of the United Nations public administration program in the 1970s will be the establishment of a number of key regional centers to perform four interrelated functions (training, research, advisory services, and information services). First, an Asian Centre for Development Administration (ACDA) will be established with UNDP assistance in the middle of 1971 with the support of ECAFE and the United Nations. The African Training and Research Centre in Administration for Development (CAFRAD) will become a Special Fund project to be executed by the United Nations in close collaboration with UNESCO. In Africa, there will also be a training institute of the East Africa Community (which is expected to become an important sub-regional training center). In Latin America, discussion is being undertaken to strengthen regional cooperation in public administration. There is in Central America the Central American Institute of Public Administration (ICAP), a regional institution which has received United Nations cooperation for some time. There is also a possibility for some development in the Middle East. Such institutions are expected to play an important role by focusing on the particular problems of the countries in their regions and also by becoming links in the process of disseminating and adapting global experience to regional needs, to undertake comparative studies and research at the regional level, and to feedback field experience to the Headquarters.

Some of the technical cooperation projects are likely to become experimental in nature, to be undertaken in cooperation with the requesting governments willing to enter into such arrangements. The objective would be to develop administrative practices and methods specially suitable for certain groups of countries. Experience gained in such programs will then be made available for application in other similar countries.

Multipliers

To use the limited resources available for maximum impact, it is important to allocate these to highly selective activities which promise to yield optimum results and to generate multiplier effects. For this purpose, the emphasis in the program is expected to shift further toward institution-building for administrative development, including central agencies dealing with personnel, O & M and management improvement, public enterprises, local governments, as well as administrative reform and training. The purpose is to assist governments in the establishment and strengthening of key agencies and institutions which can become the focal points for administrative improvement in their countries. While assistance for solving problems on *ad hoc* basis is essential in many instances and must be continued, it does not yield the same kind of results. Availability of key national institutions for administrative improvement, on the other hand, means that the dependence of government on outside assistance will decrease and we do expect such institutions to play a significant role in the 1970s. The concept of institution-building has many facets and the program operations should be modified to provide for them. This will mean, for example, that the size, duration, and working methods of country projects will undergo certain changes. Projects of larger size and longer duration, with greater impact and using more sophisticated techniques, are expected to increase.

Among the institutions which the United Nations helps to build, the most important are institutes or schools of public administration for the training of public personnel.[1] In the United Nations program of public administration, the major emphasis from the very beginning has been on the training of the public service,[24] especially institution-building in the training field. This is expected to continue in the 1970s. In recent years, there has been significant changes. While training has remained the most important item, it has been linked with administrative reform and management improvements. More institutes assisted by the United Nations have expanded their functions to include research and advisory services. As to the levels of training, the program has been extended from the entrance and middle levels to the senior level. Greater emphasis has been placed on the improvement of training materials and training aids, the use of more effective training techniques and on the training of trainers.[25] These trends are expected to continue in the 1970s. The PAD Headquarters program of research and

[1] Among the countries with which the United Nations has cooperated, or is cooperating, in establishing national institutions for training public servants we may mention Brazil, Burundi, Colombia, Ethiopia, Ghana, Iran, Libya, Niger, Peru, Somalia, Sudan, Turkey, United Arab Republic, and Uruguay. More limited training activities have also taken place in many other developing countries.

seminars has showed similar trends with considerable emphasis in the present and future programs on the development of senior administrators,[26] training of trainers, improvement of training techniques, preparation of certain training materials, and evaluation of training programs and appraisal of performance of training institutions.

Closely related to training is that of personnel administration. This will continue to be a core element in the program. The Division will continue to provide a wide range of advisory services on national personnel policies and to accord importance to areas which received concentrated attention during the past decade. These areas include (a) the structure, organization, location and functions of central personnel agencies; (b) the employment, role and development of scientists and technical personnel in the public service; and (c) the employment and development of senior administrators. Concurrently, the Division's future program includes a number of new projects as tasks of high priority: (a) career development policies and programs for securing a rational and efficient utilization of manpower resources in the public service; (b) strategies for improving the competitiveness of the public service with the private sector and also with external sources (brain drain); (c) new, more refined techniques and methods of staff selection, recruitment, job classification and performance evaluation; (d) methods of forecasting manpower and training needs in the public service.

Major Administrative Reform

Another major component in the program is in the area of major administrative reform and management improvements. The country programs now include assistance in major administrative reform in a number of countries, including Algeria, Bolivia, Ceylon, Dominican Republic, Iran, Panama, and Venezuela. The administrative reform programs show certain marked trends. The request for assistance from the countries is on the increase. More emphasis is placed on clear definition of the objectives of an administrative reform project at the beginning so that their nature and scope can be determined realistically. Increasingly, administrative reform projects are approached on an interdisciplinary basis and linked with specific requirements of national development plans and programs.

The related program in management improvement has been growing and expanding in scope. There are such projects in over forty countries. The shift has been from classical organization and methods (O & M) to management improvement. In addition to application of conventional techniques (e.g., organization analysis, work measurement, work simplification, purchasing and supply, records management, office layout and equipment, focus control, etc.), the program includes growing use of newer techniques such as systems analysis, operations research, information processing, and behavioral science techniques. The broader conception of O & M is becoming a powerful tool for general reviews and improvements of administrative structures and systems as well as for improvement of management itself.

The PAD Headquarters program of research and seminars has given considerable attention both to major administrative reform and various aspects of management in the public service. Two interregional seminars were held in 1970. The Seminar on the Administration of Management Improvement Services (held in Denmark) considered the machinery and strategy by which governments can systematically adapt their structures to changing program requirements and update their administrative and management practices. The Seminar on the Use of Modern Management Techniques in Public Administration (held in the United States) identified the major approaches, techniques and concepts in modern management, areas of administration where they can be applied with maximum impact, and the prerequisites for their effective and judicious use. At present, plans are underway to hold an interregional seminar on national efforts for major administrative reforms in developing countries and another on use of computers in public administration, both to be held later in 1971. Future studies will be undertaken and seminars held on organizations and administration of central planning agencies, regulatory administration, and related subjects. In addition, comparative studies are undertaken on organization and management of public enterprises and on performance improvement of public enterprises. There is also a concrete plan for the establishment of an interregional center for the improvement of performance of public enterprises, especially from the viewpoint of the supervisory authorities.

A major effort will be made by the PAD in the 1970s to develop (through national institutions, through regional and interregional centers, and through research and experimentation) management technology relevant and suitable to the environments of individual developing countries. This will include both rational and quantitative technology and behavioral science technology. The degree of progress in this will greatly influence the administrative improvement projects.

The foregoing is essentially a very broad view of public administration in the seventies and of the United Nations program in public administration in the Second Development Decade. The commentary is illustrative rather than exhaustive. However, even this cursory glance should be sufficient to bring out the fact that public administration is on the threshold of a new era. Both the problems faced by, and the opportunities available to public administration are tremendous. To meet this challenge, bold and imaginative action will be needed by national governments to improve their administrative capabilities for economic and social development. The international organizations can help in significant ways but the momentum must come from the countries themselves. They must foresee and provide for necessary administrative arrangements and processes which may well turn out to be the cutting edge in national efforts for economic and social development.

Notes

1. Reference may be made to a recent report by the Secretary-General of the United Nations on "Proposed Objectives and Programmes in Public Administration in the Second United Nations Development Decade," which is being published with the Report of the Second Meeting of Experts on the United Nations Public Administration Programme, under the title *Public Administration in the Second United Nations Development Decade* (United Nations document ST/TAO/M/57, New York, 1971).

2. See the report of the XIVth International Congress of Administrative Sciences (Dublin, September 1968) on "Administrative Problems of Co-ordination in Economic and Social Development," prepared by André G. Delion (General Rapporteur).

3. See for example, "Control of Operational Plans, Programmes and Projects," *Administrative Aspects of Planning* (United Nations document E.69.II.G.2, New York, 1969), pp. 405–431.

4. For explanation of these concepts, see Norbert Weiner, *Cybernetics or Control and Communication in the Animal and the Machine* (Cambridge, Massachusetts, Second edition, 1961). See also Stafford Beer, *Management Science: The Business Uses of Operations Research* (Garden City, 1968) and *Systems Technology Applied to Social and Community Problems,* Report prepared for the use of the Committee on Labour and Public Welfare, 91st U.S.A. Congress, First Session (Washington, D.C., 1969).

5. See Fred W. Riggs, "Professionalism, Political Science, and the Scope of Public Administration." Dwight Waldo, on the other hand, considers "that a separation of politics and administration is impossible." This thought is found in many of his writings, including his article on "Scope of the Theory of Public Administration." Both articles are found in James C. Charlesworth (ed.) *Theory and Practice of Public Administration: Scope, Objectives and Methods* (Philadelphia, 1968).

6. United Nations Public Administration Division, *Report of the Inter-regional Seminar on the Development of Senior Administrators in the Public Services of Developing Countries* (ST/TAO/M/45), p. 5. It should be emphasized that the commitment is to national development objectives and generally supported social preferences, and not necessarily to the political policies of the party in power. It should also be mentioned that the national goals in certain countries may lack clarity and/or consensus.

7. For a review of different views on this subject, as applied to the developing countries, see Ferrel Heady, *Bureaucracies in Developing Countries: Internal Roles and External Assistance* (Occasional Papers of the Comparative Administrative Group, American Society for Public Administration, Bloomington, Indiana, July 1966).

8. As Herbert Kaufman points out, the administrative history of govern-

ment machinery in the United States can be construed as a succession of shifts of emphasis and reliance on (a) the representative mechanisms (Congress, etc.), (b) the political leaders in the executive branch (the president, his Cabinet, etc.), and (c) a politically neutral, competent civil service. See his "Emerging Conflicts in the Doctrines of Public Administration," *American Political Science Review*, No. 4 (December 1956) and "Administrative Decentralization and Political Power," *Public Administration Review*, 9, 1 (January 1969). There are similar shifts of emphasis and de-emphasis of the civil service in the administrative history of other countries. In general the civil servants would occupy a more important position in a period when they are committed to the national goals.

9. See Carl J. Friedrich, "Bureaucracy Faces Anarchy," *Canadian Public Administration* 13, 3 (Fall 1970), p. 231. "Legitimacy" is used here in a narrow sense, referring to the political process. If one defines "legitimacy" broadly as the degree to which behavior is socially approved, then certain administrative behaviors can be "self-legitimizing." In the latter case, it can generally be said that "organizations which have a high degree of legitimacy are more likely to have a high degree of effectiveness than organizations which have a low degree of legitimacy." James L. Price, *Organizational Effectiveness* (Homewood, Illinois, 1968), p. 49.

10. As such an erroneous conclusion was drawn in connection with discussions on technical assistance to developing countries in the field of public administration (Heady, ibid.), it would be important to raise the basic question of what should be the political model or system of values. The imposition of any political model or system of values (even one called "democratic") by foreigners to a developing country would involve unacceptable political interference in its internal affairs. In this connection, attention may be drawn to a completely different, though not entirely unrelated, view of Gunnar Myrdal that it would be important if the developed countries used their influence to press the under-developed countries "in the direction of establishing more social discipline," but the strengthening of social discipline in a country "must be accomplished by that country itself." See his *Challenge of World Poverty* (New York, 1970), chapter 7.

11. See United Nations Public Administration Division: *Report of the Interregional Seminar on the Use of Modern Management Techniques in the Public Administration of Developing Countries* (ST/TAO/M/52). Both here or with reference to rational technology or behavioral science technology, the term "technology" is used as a collective noun, denoting a cluster of techniques.

12. The United Nations Public Administration Division has published a number of documents in this field. A major study on performance improvement of public enterprises will be issued this year. See also *Measures for Improving the Performance of Public Enterprises in Developing Countries* (ST/TAO/M/49).

13. See Nesta M. Gallas, "Managerial Applications of Behavioural Con-

cepts as Techniques in Public Administration," (1970), a paper included in United Nations document ST/TAO/M/52 mentioned above.

14. William G. Scott, "Organization Government: the Prospects for a Truly Participative System," *Public Administration Review* 29, 1 (January/ February 1969): 47. There are two meanings of the term "participation." One is participation as a technique (as part of the behavioral science technology). Another is participation as an involvement of the people in the decision-making process as part of the political process and in the effort to improve human well-being. The former belongs to the sixth point and the latter relates to the fourth and the seventh points. Both will be important in the 1970s.

15. Regarding the question of organization for change from a micro point of view, Richard A. Bobbe and Robert H. Schaeffer, in their *Mastering Change: Breakthrough Projects and Beyond* (AMA Management Bulletin No. 120, New York, 1968), made some contributions which could be useful for a manager or an administrator, public or private. Regarding the question of organization for change from a macro point of view, it forms part of the question of comprehensive administrative reform, which will be discussed in the next (ninth) point.

16. Albert Waterston, "Public Administration for What?," paper submitted to the First Meeting of Experts on the United Nations Programme in Public Administration (document ST/SG/AC.6/L.9), pp. 4–6, 11.

17. See United Nations Public Administration Division, *Handbook of Civil Service Laws and Practices* (ST/TAO/M/29, New York, 1966); C. Glenn Stahl, *Public Personnel Administration* (6th edition), New York, 1971; United Nations Public Administration Division, *The Central Organs of the Civil Service in the Developing Countries* (ST/TAO/M/41, New York, 1968); Chi-Yuen Wu, "Training in Public Administration for Development: Some Lessons of International Experience," *Journal of Administration Overseas* 10, 1 (January 1971); United Nations Public Administration Division, *Handbook of Training in the Public Service* (ST/TAO/M/28, New York, 1966).

18. Quoted from the Report of the Second Meeting of Experts on the United Nations Programme in Public Administration (document ST/TAO/M/57, page 4).

19. The program was initiated in 1948 and operation started in 1950. For historical development of the program, see the following two documents by the United Nations Public Administration Division: *United Nations Programme in Public Administration* (ST/TAO/M/38, New York, 1967), pp. 49–205 (covering 1950 to 1966) and *Public Administration in the Second United Nations Development Decade* (ST/TAO/M/57, New York, 1971), annex III (covering 1966 to 1970) and annex IV (covering 1971 to 1975). See also Chi-Yuen Wu, "Public Administration for National Development," *International Social Science Journal*, 21, 1 (1969).

20. The relevant documents include "Proposed Objectives and Programmes in Public Administration in the Second United Nations Development Decade," "Proposed Work Programme of the Public Administration Division: 1971–1975," and the report by the Second Meeting of Experts. These three reports are contained in document ST/TAO/M/57.

21. Reference may also be made to *Administration of National Development Planning* (ST/TAO/M/27) and *Administrative Aspects of Planning* (E.69.II.G2), papers of an ECLA Seminar.

22. Previous PAD studies under (1) and (2) include *Decentralization for National and Local Development* (ST/TAO/M/19, New York, 1962); *Study of Local Government Personnel Systems* (ST/TAO/M/33, New York, 1967); two reports being finalized for publication: *Credit Institutions for Local Authorities* and *Central Services to Local Authorities*. A study of major efforts in local government reform is currently in progress. Projects included in future plan include administrative aspects of integrated rural development, and of comprehensive urban planning.

23. See United Nations Public Administration Division, *Administrative Aspects of Urbanization* (ST/TAO/M/51).

24. See Chi-Yuen Wu, "Training in Public Administration for Development: Some Lessons of International Co-operation," *Journal of Administration Overseas* 10, 1 (January 1971).

25. See Chi-Yuen Wu, "The Use of Modern Training Techniques in Administration for Development: Some Lessons of International Experience," paper to be published as a chapter in a book on modern training techniques, edited by the United Nations Institute for Training and Research (UNITAR).

26. Attention may be drawn to the following two Public Administration Division documents: *Handbook of Training in the Public Service* (ST/TAO/M/28) and *The Development of Senior Administrators in Developing Countries* (ST/TAO/M/45), in two volumes.

16

A Training Strategy for Organizational Improvement: A Case Study—The Development Administrators Training Program

Vinton D. Fisher, Jr.

A Training Strategy for Development

If training is to be justified in the budget of any organization or government, it must be related to the goals, the top management's objectives and, finally, to specific job needs. There is an increasing awareness that in order to recognize the numerous problems of introducing and sustaining change in an organization, there must be more than a simple linking of individual training and effective action. The application of individual skills to a particular task calls for a wide range of skills from others as well as additional resources. It especially calls for encouragement, support, and a receptive organization. It has been pointed out that:

Taking an organizational approach means starting training off with a set of organizational questions. Instead of asking what X or Y needs to learn in order to carry out a new activity, the first training question needs to be addressed to all involved in the projected change. What do they, as interrelated workers, have to do differently, and what various things, therefore, do they have to learn anew and need training in? This question concerns those who collaborate directly on the job and also those who provide new services and organizational support. This very different assumption leads to *a systems approach to training*.[1]

This approach by Lynton and Pareek is useful as a model for such institutions as the Development Administrators Training Program. Basically the staff of DATP acts as *"training strategy" consultants*. This means that the Program aims at developing a total training strategy with an organization to meet its management and training needs. This action plan is a modified organizational development approach that could include:

1. analysis of various needs and objectives;
2. development of a training team, and, if appropriate, task-centered organizational patterns;
3. implementation of training and consultative services, and
4. a follow-up program to "back stop" the organization's training team upon whom most of the responsibility for implementation and training would be placed.

The author is indebted to other DATP staff members, especially Flemming Heegaard and James Wolf, for many hours of discussions which sharpened his ideas. Also, this paper includes selections from a talk given by the author at the "Symposium on Training in Africa for the 1970's" (University of Nairobi, Kenya, July 1971).

229

Though I prefer a more dialectical approach to management development, Table 16.1 on training concepts taken from Lynton and Pareek's work seems to portray the prevailing behavior found in most training institutions. In my opinion these approaches are not static and are not mutually inclusive; therefore, a synthesis between the two seems most likely to occur.

Table 16–1. Assumptions Underlying Two Concepts of Training

The Prevailing Concept	The New Concept
1. The acquisition of subject matter knowledge by a participant leads to action.	1. Motivations and skills lead to action. Skills are acquired through practice.
2. The participant learns what the trainer teaches. Learning is a simple function of the capacity of the participation to learn and the ability of the trainer to teach	2. Learning is a complex function of the motivation and capacity of the individual participant, the norms of the training group, the training methods, and the behavior of the trainers, and the general climate of the situation. The participant's motivation is influenced by the climate of his work organization.
3. Individual action leads to improvement on the job.	3. Improvement on the job is a complex function of individual learning, the norms of the working group, and the general climate of the organization. Individual learning, unused, leads to frustration.
4. Training is the responsibility of the training institution. It begins and ends with the course.	4. Training is the responsibility of three partners: the participant's organization, the participant, and the training institution. It has a preparatory, pre-training, and a subsequent post-training phase. All are of key importance in the success of training.

Source: R. P. Lynton and V. Pareek, *Training for Development* (Homewood, Illinois: Richard D. Irwin, Inc., 1967), pp. 8–9.

If Lynton and Pareek's assumptions are correct, and I believe that they are, then for a developing nation there is a high priority need to relate training to organizational objectives as suggested in "The New Concept" column of Table 16–1. This is because the allocations made—released participant time and travel, institute staff, library, buildings, and so on—are from a pool of scarcer resources than are found in so-called "developed" nations.

Since a "shotgun" approach to training is too costly—in money and human resources—a key government organization, staffed with senior administrators who are sympathetic enough to support this training approach, is a high priority item for a training institute to find. DATP's staff works closely with the organization's staff and top management to identify problems and to attack them *if* training seems a means to the desired end.

This training model is presently being utilized in programs for N.E. Brazil and in Nigeria (see "New Programs and Perceived Needs" section below).

Background and Program Rationale

The training strategy described and endorsed above has not always been employed by the DATP staff. In fact, in 1960, when the Institute of Public Service of the University of Connecticut was requested by the International Cooperation Administration (the predecessor of the Agency for International Development) to obtain work observation experiences for administrators from developing nations, the only educational function was to provide on-the-job training. However, within two years DATP built upon the base providing work experience and began to offer complete public service educational programs. Presently, DATP is exclusively concerned with the training of manpower for developing nations. This is accomplished through specially designed management development programs in the following areas:

electronic data-processing/systems analysis
financial management
local government/urban development
management analysis (organization and management)
personnel administration: the management of manpower resources
project analysis and management
training administration: training of trainers.

To date, approximately one thousand administrators from forty-eight nations have been enrolled in these programs. Sponsorship of the trainees has been from a number of sources. Most were sponsored by the Agency for International Development of the U.S. Department of State. However, organizations such as the United Nations, Ford Foundation, World Health Organization, as well as individual countries, are currently sponsoring trainees in increasing numbers.

The men and women enrolled in DATP's programs are usually mid-career or senior administrators from developing nations. Most have undergraduate degrees. They are usually married with families and have established positions. They are motivated toward change, not only in their individual organizations and countries, but in their personal lives as well. They are growth-oriented individuals who are chosen by their countries and sponsoring agencies to participate in a program which will allow them to approach the problems of their organizations and nations with new perspectives and necessary skills.

The programs listed above are usually six months in length and are non-degree and non-credit. In addition to the courses contained in each program, trainees receive practical experience through on-the-job training. There is an average of 250 hours in each program and the ratio of class work to practical experience is usually three-fourths class and one-fourth practical experience. On request, special programs can be arranged, as has been done for the governments of Nigeria, Thailand, and Brazil.

The *rationale* for the program is to be found in the development administration literature where the features of bureaucracies in developing nations are described with rather consistent agreement. The symptoms in the citation that follows can also be found in the writings of Abueva, Lee, Pye, Riggs, Siffin, Montgomery, Heady, and many other development-oriented students of public administration:

The disinclination of higher level administrators to delegate, with consequent delays, overload, rigidity, and authoritarian style; the equal disinclination of subordinates to take initiative and accept responsibility; patronizing and abusive attitudes toward the public; legalism and procedural formalism; the institutionalization of corruption; overstaffing—these recur as massive syndromes in developing countries with no clear variation among political systems and cultural traditions.[2]

A training program for development administrators should be specifically designed to analyse and hopefully, alleviate some of these problems.

Some Program Values and Educational Philosophy

The Role of the Development Administrator

During training it is necessary to distinguish between those qualities and skills that we would expect of development administrators, but that would not distinguish them from administrators generally; and those that are peculiarly related to development. For example, an individual might run a very "tight" department; his plans and budgets get worked out and submitted on time and they are reasonable; his staff performs in a technically competent manner; they get along with one another; and his department has good relations with other departments—he can compromise, he can give a little and take a little. If we measure him on criteria like these, he stands up well. But he may still not be a very good development administrator. By this we mean that his technical knowledge, his political savvy, his social skills, and his imagination are not systematically employed in the interest of *the main objective: development.* It can be supposed that, in an underdeveloped country, anybody who is honest, competent, and hardworking serves the ends of development to some extent. But that is not the same as having a good understanding of development requirements and a strong sense of development priorities, so that in planning, problem solving, negotiating, political in-fighting, compromising, he is continually oriented to *development* as the main criterion for choosing between alternatives, so far as he has any control over the situation.[a]

---

[a] The author wishes to express his appreciation to Dr. Albert K. Cohen, professor

One can classify the countries that most of these men come from as "transitional." Some authors have found it inappropriate to have training programs that reflect the mix of the value systems of traditional and modern societies. Riggs feels that there is a need for "an intermediate type of training, adapted to the needs of transitional societies, which might give considerable attention to ethical and social values requisite to policy making, without sacrificing the study of techniques and knowledge needed for policy implementation."[3]

According to Golembiewski, training should provide a greater self-awareness which may lead to new behavioral patterns. He feels that most public administration training has "not aided (administrators) in having a long hard look at who they are and where they are. Failure to take such a look implies perhaps the most basic lack of realism."[4]

Both Golembiewski's and Riggs' approaches are merged in the curriculum planning of DATP. There are essentially three areas that are emphasized by the learner/managers:

1. An awareness of being involved in a political/administrative system that is supposed to emphasize development, and this requires an increased capacity to understand organizational change and personal and work group motivations.
2. An increase in management skill and concept areas (e.g., decision making, communication, and planning), so that the returned managers can better perform in a work team for organizational improvement.
3. The perception of themselves as professionals with a problem-solving function to perform in their society, whether in governmental or parastatal bureaucracies.

In the literature on comparative or development administration, there seems to be a dichotomy of thought between those who have commented on the worth or need to train administrators from developing nations. One school of thought seems to feel that educating bureaucrats any further is only contributing to the malfunction of the political system because administrators will take over the political system and not allow it to function. The other school believes that bureaucracies are needed for government to function, and to purposefully avoid increasing the performance of bureaucracies is dysfunctional and/or unrealistic. Milton Esman states the dilemma:

Should training vary with the demands of the regime in which the administrators will be working? If so, what are the implications for curricula and teaching methods at schools of administration in developing countries? . . . Should foreign advisors, including U.S. universities, be prepared to adjust their teaching in development administration to the expected roles of their students? Or is this emphasis misdirected? Is bureaucracy necessarily a dependent function of political systems? . . . Can bureaucracy and administration discharge a creative function under some or all regimes?[5]

of sociology at the University of Connecticut, for his insight into the behavior required of a "development administrator."

Esman provides his own answer to these questions:

We ought to be much more concerned with increasing the capacity of the bureaucracy to perform, and this we see as a function of greatly enhanced professional capability and operational autonomy rather than further controls . . . Those who emphasis controls tend to distrust bureaucracy and therefore see the need to circumscribe it with controls. I regard it as a powerful, indispensable and generally beneficient agency of public service, especially under conditions of rapid change when social and economic progress depend in great measure on governmental performance. Therefore, I prefer a strategy which places higher priority on building its capabilities than containing its abuses.[6]

A Question of Neo-Colonialism

One problem we should confront is the question of Western neo-colonialism, uni-culturalism, and imperialism. What right have we to determine which administrative styles or methods should be followed in bureaucracies throughout the world? Essentially, the DATP staff has come to an intellectual "rest" which is based upon the answers given to us by our trainees when we have asked them: What right have we to educate you in these particular areas? Why do you come to us? Their answers are *not* to become "Western," and *not* take on our culture, and *not* to adopt. Rather, they wish to "modernize." The trainees know this is related to development and that development is related to change. Since we are supposed to be "modern," we are a place to come to learn the processes of modernization and the tools associated with being "modern." The skills learned here have values associated with them and these values the trainees are willing to incorporate *if* they will help their nations.

The days are past when American or Western technical know-how or behavioral managerial patterns are accepted without question. Possibly the upheavals which we are having in North American society have contributed to this temperance and caution on the part of administrators and political leaders from the developing nations. Nevertheless, the participants are fully aware of the technological gap that exists between the United States and Europe, and, therefore, the immense gap that exists between them and the United States. However, they now enter the program with more of a sense of national dignity and pride based upon a belief that they will be able to do the job just as well as others.

Learning Methodologies

A concerted effort is being made to relate the technical content of DATP's programs to managerial and development processes. For example, rather than viewing personnel administration as an unconnected series of skills and functions (classifications, wage and salary analysis, recruitment), DATP places human resource management within the context of public goals and the implications for development objectives.

Formal lectures and "talking at" participants have been greatly reduced. Emphasis in all DATP programs is focused on practicing techniques and concepts of management and behavioral science through workshops, group- and team-centered management games and simulations, case studies, individual exercises and assignments, videotape demonstrations, and other trainee-centered learning methods.

Through a synthesis of technical skills and managerial/behavioral concepts, the DATP trainee should be better able to relate the technical "know-how" that he has acquired to on-going public management functions and processes. Furthermore, he has had the opportunity to utilize his new knowledge and skills *before* he returns to his country and organization, because through team and individual exercises and on-the-job training, he has had an opportunity to test these management applications.

On-The-Job Training

DATP is the only university training center in the United States that provides on-the-job training (OJT) in a unified management program for development administrators. The staff is able to tailor the OJT placement to the individual's needs, and thus each trainee has an opportunity to observe private companies and public agencies engaged in work that relates to that which his organization performs in his country. The ideal work placement toward which DATP strives is one in which the participant can test what he has learned in the classroom, and utilize skills and ideas which are beneficial for himself and for the organization to which he is attached.

On-the-job training provides an unusual opportunity for professional and personal growth. During this part of the program a triangular relationship is established among the trainees, his supervising counterpart, and the area of mutual professional concern. OJT "frees" and expands the learning situation. It promotes communication and permits a sharing of experience— verbal and non-verbal—which is not possible in the classroom.

Originally New England oriented, on-the-job training sites are now located throughout the country, and this is necessary to obtain the specialized placement that the trainees require. For example, over the past two years, DATP participants have been placed at the Marine Research Laboratory in Rhode Island; with regional community development teams in Georgia and North Carolina; with the Acheson, Topeka and Santa Fe Railroad; in various offices of the Michigan, Pennsylvania, and Wisconsin state governments; with the Federal Reserve Board of New York City; and, of course, in numerous public and private organizations in Connecticut.

Evaluation of Training Effectiveness

The DATP is consistently engaged in evaluating its training efforts. We are trying to judge if, over time, DATP training programs have had any effect upon the trainees. This we are doing by administering questionnaires that measure attitudes and by obtaining performance ratings which relate to skill level. We are trying to see if there is any relationship among attitudes, skills, performance in the program, and performance when trainees return to their country.

Once this process is started, the problems of evaluating training effectiveness are narrowed, and the training institute, the involved organization, and the individuals involved can develop the needed criteria of effectiveness. This may somewhat narrow the cost/benefit analysis problem that Professor Colin Leys has justifiably emphasized.[7]

To empiricalize problems associated with the evaluation process, in a cooperative program with the Institute of Administration in Nigeria, we have attempted to avoid such broad measures of training effectiveness as "210 government officials will be trained," and have specified that "210 government officials shall be trained, returned to their jobs, utilize the concepts and techniques learned during the course, and shall receive, as available, follow-up consultative services from the institute staff."

Concern for the Complete Man

The DATP has continually stressed programing the "complete trainee"—that is, assuming responsibility for his training and his personal well-being. Any approach which separates professional education from the personal experience of the participants in the United States may be courting trouble. The trainees are here under extraordinary conditions—separation from family, different and strange language and customs, exposure to American wealth, materialism, discrimination, and religion, and extreme pressure to learn due to the personal and organizational goals of the participant and his country. Because of these conditions, the participant frequently lacks incentive, attention, and ability to concentrate, and frequently there is a general refusal to accept, appreciate or incorporate the training. The DATP training procedures and goals are therefore directed toward meeting these needs.

New Programs and Perceived Needs in DATP's Educational Programs

Development Administration Workshop

In September 1971, the new development administration workshop was presented. This is a multidisciplinary management program which aims to bring together various professionals from such disciplines as population control, education, health, welfare, agriculture, and engineering. The participants were placed in a common management-oriented seminar for a two week period. The curriculum covered such topics as the development process, management concepts and tools, staff development, budget administration concepts and skills, and communication and organization development processes. An original simulation/country game was developed by the DATP staff and used. The seminar's central purpose was to provide an action-oriented learning laboratory in which the participants who are trained in particular professions, such as health, education, engineering, or agriculture, can learn management/development-oriented techniques and concepts and apply them to relevant development problems in their professional sectors.

The development administration workshop, with simulated cross-sectoral development problems exercises and cases, provided immediate demonstration of the worth of management skills and concepts. Of equal importance, various sectoral objectives were placed in the context of the participants' overall societal goals and the appreciation of the interdisciplinary impact that a single project may have upon other professional/technical areas.

Training of Trainers

DATP was selected by the Agency for International Development to train trainers for state and municipal training centers in Northeast Brazil. Two programs have been completed and over 100 public officials from Brazil are expected to enroll in two more training administration programs over the next two years. The men and women enrolled in these programs will be non–English speaking, and course materials have been developed in Portuguese. Portuguese-speaking instructors will be used and simultaneous interpreters are available for the English-speaking staff.

It is believed that this training of trainers program could serve as a model for other countries interested in a human resources multiplier strategy that increases managerial talent. A central tenet of this approach is that a team of trainers, who are capable as consultants, can improve the management of program sectors and can help to institutionalize a process of continuous organizational change and renewal. This training of trainers strategy has applications to governmental training units and public administration institutes who wish to utilize more effective educational means to develop their nation's managerial manpower.

During this project DATP is implementing the "action plan" described above. In conjunction with the Brazilian agency (SUDENE), and the Agency for International Development, a DATP staff member assisted in the development of the training program's goals, the criteria for selection and the means to be used to achieve the training goals. A pre-arrival assignment was developed and a simulation exercise of a Brazilian municipio (county-city hall) was designed and implemented. After two groups are trained, a follow-up will occur and the DATP trainer who participated in the problem definition/goal setting stage will work in Brazil with returned participants to implement those changes that were identified by trainees as most likely to succeed and gain acceptance within their training institutes. Because a core of lead trainers will be selected to continue the implementation process, it is expected that the follow-up stage can become self-generated, and thus the goals of the "action plan" will be achieved.

Project Analysis and Management

The intent of this revised program was to apply the team-centered approach of the N.E. Brazil "Training of Trainers" effort to a specific development project and to follow this approach throughout the complete management cycle of a project. This approach is being applied in Nigeria (see below for more details), and there, the "action plan" incorporates selection of a team, utilization of DATP consultants, curriculum development and execution, materials development and follow-up with the team on the project's progress. A modification of this approach in project analysis and management is also being done with the Government of the Philippines in a regional approach to improving local government's delivery systems through specific development projects.

Consortium

As a training center, DATP seeks ways to cooperate with and assist other training centers in the development of their management educational programs. One such venture has already begun in a consortium among the University of Connecticut, the University of Massachusetts, and the University of Ife's Institute of Administration, located in Ibadan, Nigeria. Faculty members from the Universities of Connecticut and Massachusetts will share the teaching of courses in project analysis and management at the University of Ife. In addition, they will conduct action-type research, prepare case studies and provide consultative services to various Nigerian ministries. At the same time, a Ford Foundation team, teaching development economics at the University of Ife, will share teaching assignments with the University of Connecticut and University of Massachusetts staff members in an effort to maximize manpower resources in the four year program. While the American faculty members are teaching at Ife, six Nigerian faculty members will study for graduate degrees.

Professional Needs

Every year DATP acts as the secretariat for a management analysis conference of government administrators throughout the United States and those organizations that express an interest in other nations. This is a budding professional organization; it has met for the past eight years and has resulted in a series of conference papers. Being responsive to unmet needs is an important function of a public service educational center.

An Approach to Developing an Institute's Staff

The following section is an attempt to identify:

1. those characteristics which a training institute should attempt to develop in its staff members,
2. those strategies which the staff members might follow to insure that their organization is a responsive and action oriented training institution.

One major goal is to stop the perpetuation of "training for training's sake." One major purpose of a case study is to share those attitudes and experiences that our staff has found to be most successful in making what could be a routine job into a continuous growth experience for those concerned individuals and organizations.

Staff Development

Stress should be placed on the preparation of the individual and the development of his ability to teach and consult. The factor of experience can be developed through consultation in the organizational improvement process. This management training and organizational development system avoids the mental and physical distances between practitioners and training staffs. If successful, a symbiotic relationship is formed between the training institution and the organizations with whom it works.[8]

It is not suggested that *any* staff person can do this type of organizational training and consulting work. Some of the key attributes of such a staff member seem to be the following:

1. an open personality that understands and responds to organizational, group, and personal needs.
2. an ability to center attention on the *learner* and his organization's needs.
3. an ability to utilize a variety of learning methodologies that emphasize managerial behavior (process) more than administrative techniques (skills). However, his problem-centered style includes the capacity to bring technical skills into the management/organizational process when these techniques seem to solve the topic under discussion.

   Some specific methodologies would be:

   a. simulations centered on familiar experience
   b. role playing under stress
   c. case studies
   d. workshops
   e. exercises that elicit data on the attitudes and behavior found within the organization.
4. the ability to shift teaching and consultative approaches as circumstances require.

5. an ethical and open approach to the organization.
6. the ability to know when an organization, through the institution's staff and the organization's efforts, has developed an internal management and human resources improvement system. It is as important to know when the climate for organizational improvement is poor and any further efforts would lead to no results, or worse, negative achievement.

Some Training Strategies

In Table 16.2, the strategy delineations are sound guidelines, but since they are not mutually exclusive, a mix of training strategies can be developed. Again, an eclectic, dialectical and pragmatic approach is preferred rather than a one-solution method. However, the training strategy that Lynton and Pareek and our DATP staff propose and utilize would place emphasis on a *total program within an overall organizational improvement effort*. If adopted this would mean that most training institutes, as we presently find them, would need to be revitalized. This observation, if accepted, would apply equally as well to the United States as it would throughout the rest of the "developing" world.

Some Implications of a TS/OD Approach

My preference for a Training Strategy/Organizational Development approach has further implications for the training of an institute's staff. The time needed to train the training consultants is lengthy *not* because the content mastered is difficult, but because the process involved goes to the heart of an organization's operations and raises basic policy and procedural questions that leadership may not wish raised. If this is so, then the consulting training institute should not begin to expend its resources on such an organizational client.

During the course of involvement with organizations, there will be a mixed variety of clients—some development-oriented and some not-so development oriented. I would *not* recommend that the "not-so's" be excluded from an institute's list of clients. One contribution may be to open the organization's decision-making system to permit consideration of alternative goals and actions other than "business as normal."

Before any such teaching/consulting projects are accepted, the concerned institute must reform *itself,* and go through the process it recommends for others. Furthermore, if a management and/or public administration institute accepts the training strategy as discussed above, it decreases the dichotomy between the "what should be done" and the "what is done" approaches to teaching, research, and consulting. The charges by practitioners of "non-practical," "academic," and "fuzzy thinking" are more difficult to maintain. Therefore, rather than being on the periphery of governmental activities the training institution and its staff are closer to the actions and problems of government. This does suggest a more independent organization, but does not necessarily mean affiliation with a university.

Basically, this means that a team of trainers from an institute can, within an action-research mode, act as teacher/consultants to help work teams to identify and solve an organization's problems. However, they are like farmers in a cooperative—they are *not* the soil, the seed, and the environment—but hopefully they may see some fruit from their cooperative relationship with the vital elements.

Conclusions and Implications for Senior Managers in Developing Nations

National leaders have said that this is a time to collect ourselves and to decide on the direction that we wish to adopt in the future. Technical assistance to developing countries and development administration are also at such a point. Milton Esman indicates a need to make such a choice, when he poses the question, "Has the study, teaching, and practice of public administration anything to contribute to the mitigation of these frustrations, the resolution of conflicts, and the sustained achievement of a greater measure of dignity and well-being?"[9] The best answer is clearly affirmative. Public, comparative, and development administration—whatever it is called—has something substantial to contribute to developing and developed nations.

The following are very likely the major factors affecting international management development programs in the 1970s:

1. Multilateral aid will increase, but this will not prove to be a panacea. Essentially we are going through an important dialogue on foreign aid, the outcome of which is not clearly visible.
2. One should expect an increase in teaching teams overseas. There will be a decrease in reliance upon American schools of higher education to provide training for administrators in the United States.
3. There will be a greater utilization in the United States of development administration concepts, especially in domestic programs that concern rapid social change. Paradoxically, a general decrease among universities and colleges providing institutional support for overseas-oriented programs is likely to occur. Those programs that survive are likely to depend upon the forbearance of administrators and the presence of bilateral and multilateral aid administrators who are willing to "suffer through" this portion of the dialectic with interested and dedicated universities and colleges.
4. There will be a general disinclination on the parts of developing nations to place their faith in the prescriptions of the West. There will be an increased awareness of the interrelatedness of problems and the similarities of these problems in all nations. Already we can see a total system or international approach to such problems as pollution control, population control, and social and physical problems associated with industrialization and over-urbanization. Although these problems were known when the first Development Decade began, their existence will become part of the cognition map

Table 16-2. Comparison of Six Training Strategies.

Strategy	Emphases	Characteristic Methods	Assumptions	Action Stops
1. Academic	Transmitting content and increasing conceptual understanding	Lecture Seminar Individual reading	1. Content and understanding can be passed on from those who know to those who are ignorant. 2. Such knowledge and understanding can be translated in practice.	Builidng a syllabus to be covered in the program Examination to test retained knowledge and understanding
2. Laboratory	Process of function and change Process of learning	Isolation Free exploration and discussion Experimentation	1. It is useful and possible to pay attention to psychological factors for separate attention. 2. Understanding of own and others' behavior helps in the performance of the jobs.	Unfreezing participants from their usual expectations and norms Helping participants see and help others see own behavior and develop new habits
3. Activity	Practice of specific skill	Work on the job under supervision Detailed job analysis and practice with aids	1. Improvement in particular skill leads to better performance on the job. 2. Production and training can be combined rather simply.	Analyzing skill and dividing it into parts Preparing practice tasks, standards, and aids

4. Action	Sufficient skills to get organizational action	Field work, setting and achieving targets	1. Working in the field develops people. 2. Individual skills and organizational needs will fit together.	Preparation of field programs Participation according to schedule
5. Person-development	Improved individual competence in wide variety of tasks and situations	Field training, simulation methods, incident and case sessions, and syndicate discussion	1. Training in job requirements with emphasis on process will help a participant develop general skills and understanding. 2. Organization will support the individual in using understanding and skills acquired.	Identifying training needs Preparing simulated Data
6. Organization-development	Organizational improvement	Study of organizational needs Work with small groups from the organization	1. Attention to organizational needs as process develops understanding. 2. Organizational change will result in individual's change.	Survey of organizational needs Determining strategic grouping for training Working on organizational requirements

Source: R. P. Lynton and V. Pareek, *Training for Development* (Homewood, Illinois: Richard D. Irwin, Inc. Exhibit 3.2, pp. 51–52. Reproduced with permission.

of the average citizen. Therefore, because these problems are no longer the possession of an elite, we will finally put more effort to the solving of these problems.

5. There will be a tendency among training programs, such as DATP's, to emphasize the organization development and personal and work team commitment portions of their programs' curricula. This will be done to strike a balance among the "scientific management" and the "behavioral science" approaches to organizational and personal effectiveness and achievement. Motivation and its relationship to management objectives, goal setting and problem solving will take a turn toward the work team and a flexible creative organization that accepts change as necessary and links change to personal, organizational and national development.

6. Top level administrators and their subordinates will profit a great deal from an organizational centered training effort. Needs would be determined jointly. Participation in the training/organization improvement process could be physically done within a ministry and/or at an institute—the nature of the problem would seem to contribute to the determination of the training location.

Such a process should also increase the opportunity for and appreciation of needed management development programs because:

a. administrators should become more sensitive to personal and organizational training needs through the process of jointly setting an organization's objectives and/or the means to reach those objectives;

b. senior level and all other management training would be directed at *their* personal and *organizational* needs and problems, and not to a general unprescribed goal;

c. the pressure induced from other staff members' behavior, intra-organizational pressures, and self-awareness should lay a secure base of support for a management development program for top level administrators.

A management training "convert" who has seen the benefits of the training, is a prime factor in organizational improvement. Therefore, as a means of developing a top level clientele group that supports organizational change and development through management training, the obvious place to begin would seem to be the top and/or with a unit sufficiently independent so that it can make decisions and implement actions to change its organizational style. However, though obvious, this should not be accepted as *the* criterion for deciding if and when this process should be started. Targets of opportunity and a cooperative environment make excellent subjects for the demonstration effect and the necessary momentum for change —the mass that produces a chain reaction effect. The abandonment of a familiar position is a prerequisite for human development involved in organizational improvement.

Finally, we should note two critical standards by which to select those training programs that should survive and receive support. These promote a management educational service that:

1. provides the world with administrators more imbued with a social consciousness and who are responsive to their citizens and political leaders, and

2. creates and executes learning designs with which the learner/manager can increase his capacity to solve problems and to motivate the necessary changes with and within the personnel of his organization.

Notes

1. R. P. Lynton and U. Pareek, *Training for Development* (Homewood, Illinois: Richard D. Irwin, Inc., 1967), pp. 8–9. Emphasis is mine.

2. Milton J. Esman, "The CAG and the Study of Public Administration: A Mid-Term Appraisal" (CAG Occasional Papers, *American Society for Public Administration,* 1966) p. 24.

3. Fred W. Riggs, *Administration in Developing Countries: The Theory of Prismatic Society* (Boston: Houghton Mifflin, 1964), p. 348.

4. Robert T. Golembiewski (ed.) *Perspectives on Public Management, Cases and Learning Designs* (Chicago: F.E. Peacock Publishers, Inc., 1968), pp. 1–3.

5. Esman, op. cit., pp. 13–14.

6. Ibid., p. 30.

7. See Colin Leys, "Recruitment, Promotion and Training," in G. Hyden, R. Jackson, and J. Okumu (eds.) *Development Administration: The Kenyan Experience* (Nairobi: Oxford University Press, 1970), p. 150.

8. Lynton and Pareek, op. cit., p. 325 ff. In this section I have liberally drawn from chapter 10 of their book because it complements my experience and my value system.

9. Esman, op. cit., p. 40.

17 Views on Administrative Training Strategies in Africa

John H. Smith

Concern for new approaches to training in administration were strongly fostered when localization of the bureaucracy of the former British Colonial administration became a key part of the independence movement in several of the African countries. In this process, people involved in training were fortunate enough to be able to draw upon the United States experience and even more fortunate, I think, to have the cooperation of United States administrative agencies.

The account of the training that has taken place during the last decade in Africa has been written up by numerous writers.[1] It is not the purpose of this paper to simply relate what has or has not been achieved, but rather to place in perspective and evaluate this last decade of experience. My qualifications for this task are six years engaged in training, including two at the Institute of Administration in Zaria, Nigeria, which became a model for so many other institutes around Africa, and four years establishing and directing the Kauduna Staff Development Center. Other years were spent working in the bureaucracies in which I had my former students, first as subordinates and colleagues and then, with the pace of change in Africa being so rapid, as masters.

Misapplications of Training Emphasis

Being involved in the training process and having studied the results, I feel that there are four areas where the wrong emphasis has been applied. In identifying these areas it is appropriate to suggest what currently should be done about the difficulties.

First, in the context of rapid localization where there was extreme urgency, we attempted to teach people to run before they could walk. In practice—in Anglophone Africa at least—the generalist administrator still has a fundamental place, though he is becoming less essential. Training for this type of post was neglected in several ways. As a result there is only a small foundation on which to build specialist functions. In attempting to produce specialists we have overlooked the necessity to keep the basic machinery of administration functioning.

The second area of wrongly applied emphasis was in concentrating too heavily at high levels and neglecting lower and middle levels of administration. This produced two unfortunate results. The tendency was to train high level managers who later found they had none of the executive support at a lower level, which one would expect in a developed society. This is a frustrating and bewildering experience. Much more unfortunate was that we tended to reinforce a new kind of elite. Just as the British, with their notions of indirect rule, tended to crystalize traditional authority and permit a position of political stagnation during the colonial period, so in our post-independence training programs we have been in danger of crystalizing a new educated elite. This can only result in stagnation in administration. The gulf between the elite and the masses rose daily in a very frightening way in Africa, and the training emphasis tended to widen this gulf.

The third area where I think the emphasis has been wrong is that, just as bureaucrats of an earlier generation have been deluded by ill-digested concepts of economic take-off, so, I think, the African successors are being deluded by ill-digested concepts of modernization. Bureaucrats, of course, are always alleged to be trying to implement what academics were teaching a generation ago. In many ways the "new elite" aims to discard the whole of traditional society without really examining what values it possessed. Certainly there are very distinct human qualities of life in traditional so-cieties, which perhaps we are beginning to find again in the more techno-logical societies of the West. In the last three years of military governments in Africa there is far less contact and feedback from the masses than there used to be under the earlier political governments. A very real danger exists now of overconcern with the whole process and excitement of mod-ernization to the neglect of the worthwhile things of the past. Although attempting to treat some of these issues, one of the most fruitless programs in Africa has been the Human Relations Workshops of the late 1950s and early 1960s. They seemed to fulfill a pressing need for the organizers but left the participants untouched or unmoved in most cases.[2]

The fourth problem area where I think emphasis has been wrong is that we have expected technology alone, by and in itself, to be the major agent of development. It is clearly not sufficient to teach technology alone. We must get behind this fantastic technology and managerial exactitude which put man on the moon; we must use it for the commonplace needs in the developing world.

Suggestions for Possible Strategies

Having identified what to me seem to be the problems of wrong emphasis in training, I would like to suggest what should be done about them.

First, we should eliminate from our training programs—in Africa cer-tainly—the first academic degree in public administration. By all means include administrative training programs, but conduct them in social science programs.

For several reasons "entry requirements" for public administration de-grees have usually been set lower than those for other social science degrees. Furthermore, the content of programs has frequently been outmoded in terms of current research in development administration. There is a great danger of not making public administration training adequately respectable training, just at the time when it will be needed most. There is, in my experience, no evidence whatsoever to suggest that the bureaucrat who has had a first degree in public administration makes a better bureaucrat than the man who had a first degree in some other social science or discipline. There is an urgent need, on the other hand, to update post-graduate training in development administration.

To handle the problems of lower levels of administration we need to establish institutions such as technical colleges, which can handle both the public and private sectors. Training needs are great in both sectors. Within government there is probably a need for institutions which can keep people learning, so as to upgrade them and to hand on new skills. There are considerable advantages in operating training programs with complete flexibility and with a limited range of studies as determined by current demands. Filling the curriculum with nonessential techniques, because there are opportunities to do so or because the institution feels it has to justify itself, is a wasteful use of valuable educational resources. My view has been that students do not come to learn, but that they come for a major experience. Because the absence of necessary administrative help is very costly in terms of scarce high-level administrative time and talent, many more institutions for training these administrative assistants and office personnel are needed.

I think we will also have to create some kind of partial moratorium on higher education, on post-graduate studies, and on higher degrees. There is absolutely no question of being able to afford, in the developing world now, the system of education in the United States. The returns on investment in higher education are delayed too long to be of greatest value to developing countries. Rather than graduate and doctorate programs, what is required at the higher level are further training experiences.

There are great advantages in well-designed staff colleges, especially on a regional basis. These further training experiences should cover both the public and private sectors. In terms of what is happening politically in the developing world, it would be desirable to insure that the military staff colleges are combined with the administrative staff colleges. Staff colleges are vital, but they are never going to be successful until they make the directorship a post as prestigious and financially rewarding as the top post in the bureaucracy itself. A completely new look at training right through the bureaucracy can be achieved by this means. As many know only too well, the problem in training is getting the highest level of the government interested.

Sabbaticals for bureaucrats is a good notion. It works in academia and I think it should be used in the bureaucracy. Many think it is impossible to do this. However, the basic problem is in initiating the practice. Directed reading, research, and tutorial contact seem preferable to organized courses for this experience.

Another activity worth attempting is to assign senior and middle level bureaucrats to work situations in official organizations; for example, some time could be spent in a good city manager's office in the United States, not as an observer, and not to take a course or program, but to do a job. From my experience, this is the only possible way to attempt any attitudinal training. Attitudes, of course, are not learned in the classroom and are difficult to engender. Nevertheless, in adult life attitudes can be modified in certain circumstances, such as by working in a different environment, or by working in an efficient organization or in a dynamic department. There is much need for a rapid change and transfer of attitudes, and people in the developing world placed in suitable work situations would stimulate change.

Conclusions

These varied suggestions for change must be seen within a particular time dimension. It is not always easy for the developing world to jump a whole series of stages of change. If it is not possible to avoid certain stages then the series can be compressed into shorter time spaces.

The notion of counterparts has been disasterous and if continued can be harmful to effective development. The notion claims that we can set a cut-off time on a training program which might be supported, say, for five years. During this period experts will be engaged, usually for only two year periods. Thus there will be at least two experts who must find suitable counterparts able at the end of five years to take over the operation. This notion has not worked the way it should.

Africa is full of dying institutions from which support has been withdrawn. The reason for this is that we have had the rigid idea that something could be accomplished in a set period of time with this unwieldy counterpart relationship. Teams are far more preferable than counterparts. We should get people back into a group where they are partners. In this way we can keep the influence and the experience of the developed world far longer than we ever will when all we do essentially is repeat the colonial pattern of a master and pupil relationship. Rather than trying to teach, very rapidly, how to do a job, and then leave, what is needed is a very definite partnership of learning interactions. Our practices of technical assistance and training have not been effectively applied, especially in Africa where social and political change has been most rapid and where sound management and administration are extremely scarce in supply.

Notes

1. See especially, United Nations, *Handbook of Training in the Public Service* 66.II.H.1; African Conference of Directors of Central Personnel Agencies or Civil Service Commissions and Directors of Public Administration Institutes, Addis Ababa, May 1964 (E/CN. 14/UAP/21); Donald

C. Stone (ed.) *Education in Public Administration: A Symposium* (Brussels, IIAS, 1963); B. L. Jacobs, "Uganda: In-service Training of Senior Civil Servants," *International Review of Administrative Sciences* (Brussels), 30, 2 (1964): 206–209; Brian G. Weinstein, *African Schools of Public Administration: A Report* (African Studies Center, Boston University, 1965); A. Adedeji (ed.), *Problems and Techniques of Administrative Training in Africa* (Ife: University of Ife Press, 1969).

2. Note D. Nylen et al., *Handbook of Staff Development and Human Relations Training; Materials Developed for Use in Africa*, National Training Laboratories, N.E.A. (Washington, D.C., 1966).

18 The New Design of Development and Administrative Change

Milton J. Esman

Macro Planning and Development Administration in the 1960s and 1970s

My concern is with administration in the context of the Second Development Decade. My view is that the "bloom" is off comprehensive planning. The emphasis of the second decade is going to be on *action*, on administration, and on implementation. The test will be in getting things done that move resources and develop people.

In the first decade of development, the emphasis was on the total economy, the idea being that you manipulate policy instruments that would fill up a savings gap, or a foreign exchange gap needed to achieve target levels of economic growth. If you manipulated the total economy, somehow all the parts would respond in a kind of harmonious balance; economic, social, and political development would be the response to judicious economic management.

I think that in the second decade of development, the emphasis is going to be more on sectors of activity, on specific programs and projects—closer to where the action is; it will be less concerned about the process of balance and overall development within the society. In the first decade, the emphasis was on economic growth; there was a painful infatuation with economic measurement which was assumed to constitute the only indicator of progress and effective change. In the next decade, the emphasis will be more on employment—even at the risk of slowing down the rate of economic growth —and on equity, especially on a more equitable distribution of benefits of growth and change. Thus, a political dimension will be explicitly introduced into development planning and policy.

During the first decade the emphasis in foreign aid circles was on resource flows, the idea being that if enough economic resources flowed in the *right way* to the *right place* there would be an *immediate* response, just as in the Marshall Plan. The Development Assistance Committee of the O.E.C.D. anxiously measured the net transfer of resources. If it was a good year, transfers would be about 1 percent of GNP; and if it was a bad year the net resource flows would be much less than 1 percent. These flows were always in terms of financial or dollar denominated resources. I think that during the next decade, intellectual flows, technological and related knowledge-based transfers are going to be much more important. There will be much more concern with the use of indigenous resources, with the problems of managing human, natural, and organizational resources available to society, and with building and reforming institutions. One cannot look at many developing countries without being painfully aware of the enormous wastes and terrible mismanagement and dysfunctions in many activities which consume considerable resources, especially through the public sector.

Looking at the educational systems in one country after another, one sees an unbelievable waste of resources. Many of the products provided to society by their school systems are neither needed nor used, while acute needs are unfilled. Health, welfare, and agricultural services modeled on Western patterns are often dysfunctional to the societies that they are serving, and extremely costly as well. My impression is that most developing countries receive a low rate of return on a high investment in administrative services of various kinds. I once estimated for a certain country that in an average district, if 90 percent of the civil servants, exclusive of teachers, were just eliminated, there would be no difference in the levels of welfare or in productivity or in any activity that could be associated with developmental objectives. It would not be surprising if this were true of one country after another.

There is obviously an enormous need for building and reforming public service institutions, but this is irrelevant to whether the flow of external resources in dollar terms is seven-tenths of 1 percent or a full 1 percent of GNP. These purely financial flows, unfortunately, are considerations of the kind that still obsess the macro-economists. In the decade of development in the 60s the macro-economists were really determining much of international development policy. They were close to the summit of the power structure and very much in control of the intellectual doctrines of the time. Though it may be painful to them, this is not going to be as true in the next decade. I think that the professionals concerned with sectors of society, such as agriculturists, educators, and engineers, the administrators, and particularly the applied social scientists, are going to have a much more prominent role in development policy and development assistance than they had in the first decade of development. In the first decade of development they were almost disregarded as having little that was useful to say about the processes of growth and change. The coming emphasis will be on action and on knowledge transfers, and thus there will be considerable concern with administration during the second decade.

Transforming Administration

For the rest of this paper I plan to focus on countries, mainly in Asia and Latin America, which, since the beginning of technical assistance two decades ago, have built up very substantial institutional infrastructures. They have developed a very respectable supply of trained and sophisticated professionals and administrators in a wide variety of fields. I think it is in such countries that we are likely to see a new approach to development and to development assistance. In the African context, on the other hand, developing countries still need the traditional Point Four type of technical assistance oriented to the development of basic skills and institutions. The kind of administration which I shall focus on emphasizes action programs, those that deliver outputs to society. These are large scale action programs that mobilize substantial resources and convert them into a wide variety of services. These are the major concern of developmental administration.

For analytical purposes, we can classify the administrative activities in developing countries into two types. These two types of administrative program call for different kinds of action strategies. I am not dealing at all with regulatory administration or programs of control or systems maintenance, but only with developmental activities.

The first type of program would include those incorporating a high technological component, in which powerful technologies are essential to and determine the conduct of the program, in which there is very considerable consensus both on goals and means, and in which there is reasonably high predictability concerning the responses both of those within the administrative system and of the affected publics. This type of program would include such activities as telecommunications systems, power generation and distribution, transportation and highways, railroads, certain kinds of water and water control systems, and many kinds of industries where there is a fairly closed system, a predictable set of responses, and a dominant technology. Such activities, of course, are precisely those which have been the major beneficiaries of development loans from the World Bank, the IDB, AID, and similar financing agencies. Such projects will continue to be important. Significantly, this type of developmental activity calls for administrative practices and management technologies which have been developed and used successfully in the industrialized countries. Not only are the intermediate management methods, such as those associated with "scientific management," applicable in these projects, but also the more sophisticated administrative technologies, such as PERT, and even computerized information systems, are relevant to the management and control of these activities. The adaptation of such well-established administrative technologies to the needs of developing countries is called for in the 1970s.

No technology can ever be transferred from one society to another without significant modification. Technologies have to be adapted to the local interpersonal status relationships and to methods of communication. My impression is that there exists a very valuable opportunity for the American business schools to involve themselves significantly in the application and adaptation of management technologies to activities with high technology components in developing countries. Of course, much work is already going on, and I think it will go further. The major problem is that Western management technologies have to be adapted considerably to cultural contexts different from those implicitly assumed by Western business schools. This is a challenge that business school might be eager to accept.

In the public sector, especially of developing countries, there are problems including political influence and accountability which differ from the institutional framework implicitly assumed in most American business schools with their emphasis on the private corporation. Nevertheless, with a serious commitment to research, experience, and adaptation I think there is much technology that can be transferred and adapted to improve the quality of administration in the developing countries. This applies to intermediate and even more advanced management technologies focused on activities with a high technology component and high consensus on goals and means. I think such a prospect is quite feasible in the decade ahead.

The second type of development administration problem relates to client-centered activities. These tend to require changes in behavior and in institutions. They are concerned with the balancing and the manipulation of different interests and thus have an important political dimension. Conflicting forces and uncertainty about the responses of clients to government initiatives may impinge upon administrative activities. Here the cultural and social change dimensions are significant, as, for instance, in a family planning program.

Delivery Systems for Effecting Transfers

Known technologies cannot be transferred without an effective delivery system. But a delivery system that would be effective in one society may not be readily transferred and adapted to another.

Take as an example the establishment and management of rural credit institutions. It will not be easy to overcome the suspicion of the farmers, to enforce the discipline of repayment, to distribute the credit equitably among rich and poor farmers, or to solve the problems of competing sources of credit from money-lenders. Reforms in rural credit, in turn, implicate the whole system of agricultural service programs. These activities are not amenable to advanced command and control technologies. Other examples are in promoting curriculum changes in school systems which would motivate students and still produce outputs desirable to society; or in developing urban small works programs to deal with the unemployment in a manageable way; or, as previously mentioned, family planning programs. The whole series of activities which I call client-centered are essential to economic and social development; they involve institutional, behavioral, and cultural changes and engage administration under conditions of high uncertainty.

Even in such situations of high indeterminancy there are resources available to the administrator—access to well-established technologies, some knowledge of the context and clients, and comparative experience. Yet there is usually insufficient knowledge in the social sciences and inadequate practice that can be readily brought to bear on such problems. There may, moreover, be very limited information which is predictive of the motivations of the clients involved or their capabilities of responding to alternative policy measures, programatic incentives, or sanctions. We do not know what is likely to work in a particular situation.

This kind of problem suggests two types of action. First, they may require, and in many cases *do* require, changes in the organization of the client system. The development of improved capabilities on the part of the clients is needed in order that they may use public services more effectively and productively. The capacity of the administrative system does not depend merely upon the capabilities and motivations of administrators, important as that is; it also depends very much on the external environment, particularly on the ability of the clients to use public services. In the case of a passive clientele, which is not able to define or articulate its needs and cannot bring pressures to bear on the administrative system, administration is likely to yield a low output for its investment in resources and energy. I think that the problem of activating clients is an important research area in the field of development administration. There are some hypotheses about this and actual experience even in the United States where administrators have gone out and organized their clienteles. A prime example is what the Agricultural Adjustment Administration did with farmers in the early 1930s: they organized a clientele which then virtually took over the administration. That need not necessarily be the result for all programs or in all countries, but to develop desirable give-and-take between the administrators and their clienteles, a guidance-response relationship, is an important priority in development administration for client-centered programs.

It is difficult to administer programs that have a high degree of indeterminancy and unpredictability with a clientele which is passive and is not organized to use public services effectively. Even though administrators in developing countries may not perceive it this way, I think that an increase in the power of clients need not diminish the relative power of administrators. Quite the contrary: it actually increases their capacity to deliver public services effectively. It is not a zero-sum game situation. Enhancing and activating the clientele may actually increase the capabilities and the outputs of administration enormously. This is part of the strategy of development administration which we must look at very seriously in the decade ahead.

The New Approach for Technical Assistance

There is an important technical assistance implication to this problem. We need a new approach to technical assistance, which is more collegial than it has been before and which recognizes that in the developing countries there are now quite competent and sophisticated people in professional fields among administrators and social scientists. We do not have a reliable body of knowledge about specific practices and strategies which determine the effectiveness of delivery systems. Therefore, the situation calls for considerable experimentation, social innovation, and a kind of technical assistance which involves the joint identification of problems by foreign advisors and local specialists, and joint development and testing of hypotheses in real life situations, using the applied social science research capabilities not drawn upon in earlier foreign aid programs. These experiments should involve collegial and team relationships aiming to develop and test delivery systems which can be effective in a particular context.

I think that we shall move in the direction of learning strategies for the joint development of delivery systems. One sign of this trend was mentioned by Professor Tinbergen when he noted that the industrialized countries ought to devote a larger percentage of their research and development budgets to problems that affect the less developed countries, not only in terms of pure technology, but also in terms of the development of delivery systems which make these technologies effective. A second sign is the recommendation in the Peterson Committee report for a United States International Development Institute, one of whose main functions would be to sponsor research and experimentation jointly and collegially with Americans and experts from developing countries to make social actions programs more effective.

There is a growing demand for improved government action capabilities in developing countries, and thus a need to maximize the quality and effectiveness of available administrative resources. Because these resources are indeed scarce, strategies have to be improvised to maximize their effectiveness. First is the possibility of relying on more than bureaucratic instruments for the development and conduct of action programs. That does not mean that I denigrate the fundamental importance of improving bureaucratic institutions and performance, except that there are other resources that ought to be mobilized wherever possible: voluntary organizations; private sector enterprises where feasible; political parties having useful contacts with clients; local government authorities; and other kinds of action capability which can help to channel and deliver services and influence the attitudes of clients. These have to be mobilized in a coordinated strategy to deliver services that are required in areas of high indeterminacy.

The second strategy is to expand and improve the training of middle-level and other administrators who contact the public. My observation is that administrators dealing directly with the public are frequently the least competent in their role. The last link in the chain is often the weakest. As I said earlier, many could be eliminated and nothing would be changed. Improving the training of people concerned with delivering specialized services on the technical side, on the attitudinal side, and even in terms of values is a means of strengthening all the links. There must be a radical modification in the role-orientations of bureaucrats operating essential public service programs in many parts of the world. Improved training of administrators plus more activated clienteles can help produce that effect. We cannot wait for the activated publics, however, because very often the administrators themselves have to get the clienteles moving.

Many opportunities exist for more relevant training. I think people ought where possible to be trained in separate sectoral groups, because problems of administrators in the telecommunications service are simply not the same as those in a development bank or a family planning system. Sector-ally-oriented training is likely to be more useful than general administrative training for persons in service delivery programs. Although training is expensive, I think it is an indispensible need and requires greater attention and expansion.

A third approach is to recognize the need to build organizational centers of strength for social innovations, similar to the patterns which have been developed by the Institution Building Research Program. Critical institutions should be selected for further growth or remodeling as viable centers both internally and in terms of the systems of linkages which enable them to interact with their relevant environments. This is a strategy which should be promoted in the next decade. There is now a body of knowledge emerging from the Institution Building Research Program which is potentially powerful and significant and which will be available for wide application during the next several years.

A fourth objective is to work for the improved integration of specialized services at the level of clients, who are frequently overwhelmed by the chaotic competition of uncoordinated agencies presumably serving their needs. The need to integrate these services would bring local government agencies into closer liaison with specialized service provided by national and provincial agencies and might be enhanced by the organization and activation of client groups which might help to rationalize these competing and frequently ineffective services. The establishment and maintenance of patterns of cooperation would represent a far-reaching administrative reform in many countries where lateral interaction would seem to threaten entrenched patterns of hierarchical authority.

Conclusions

I am sure there will be an expanded interest in administration in the next decade of development. However, we must avoid the temptation to consider administration as a panacea for all the problems of development. We must acknowledge that there is no glamorous arsenal of administrative technology which can have the same transforming effect on developing countries as was falsely claimed for comprehensive planning during the past decade.

Although much emphasis should be given to development administration, it must not be conceived in terms of a transforming system of technologies which has the aura of magic about it. The simplistic slogan of a "management gap" is a great misrepresentation of what exists. Administrative development involves building the capabilities of human beings and of social institutions and reforming well-established practices—which means that time and sustained energies are needed to effect deliberate progress. The organization and establishment of improved links with clients will not take place instantaneously. A 5 or 6 percent net increase in national income a year denotes growth, but not necessarily development. Far more important would be a comparable growth in administrative capabilities in any developing country. For this would demonstrate increased capacity to combine and use resources more effectively, to respond to new opportunities, and to distribute the benefits of growth more equitably.

About the Contributors

David J. Ashton is Professor of International Business and International Program Coordinator, Boston University, College of Business Administration.

Wayne Broehl, Jr. is Professor of Business Administration, Amos Tuck School of Business Administration, Dartmouth College.

Allan R. Cohen is Associate Professor of Administration, University of New Hampshire.

Milton J. Esman is Director, Center for International Studies, Cornell University.

Vinton D. Fisher, Jr. is Director of the Development Administrators Training Program, University of Connecticut.

Ida R. Hoos is a research sociologist, Space Sciences Laboratory, University of California, Berkeley, California.

Jack Koteen is Deputy Director, Office of Development Administration, Agency for International Development.

Arne F. Leemans is Professor of Public Administration and Director of the Institute of Public Administration, University of Amsterdam.

Jan F. Glastra van Loon is Professor of Philosophy and Methodology of the Social Sciences, Institute of Social Studies.

David C. McClelland is Professor of Social Relations, Harvard University.

Walter G. O'Donnell is Professor of Management, University of Massachusetts.

Gustav F. Papanek is at the Center for International Affairs, Harvard University. He was formerly Director of the Harvard Development Advisory Service.

Fred W. Riggs is Director of the Social Science Research Institute, University of Hawaii.

Kenneth J. Rothwell is Professor of Economics, at the University of New Hampshire, and Visiting Professor at the Institute of Social Studies, The Hague.

William J. Siffin is Director of the Office of Development Administration, Technical Assistance Bureau, U.S. Agency for International Development.

John H. Smith is currently Financial Secretary, British Solomon Islands Protectorate. Previously he was Director of Kauduna Staff Development Center and Visiting Professor, Duke University.

Jan Tinbergen is Professor of Development Planning at the Netherlands School of Economics.

Chi-Yuen Wu is Director of the United Nations Public Administration Division.

Author Index

Ackoff, R.L., 113
Adedeji, A., 251
Alexander, Tom, 113
Almond, Gabriel, 34
Ansoff, H.I., 81
Apter, David, 36

Bakke, E.W., 191
Bailey, S.K., 132
Baron, George, 179
Bauer, Peter, 89, 93
Beer, Stafford, 225
Bennis, W.G., 34, 204
Berna, James, 92
Birkhead, G.S., 131
Blau, P.M., 35
Bobbe, R.A., 227
Braibanti, Ralph, 35, 131
Brandenburg, R.G., 81
Broehl, W.G., 93

Caiden, Gerald, 130
Carmichael, W.D., 36
Chandraknant, L.S., 15, 35
Chapman, W.L., 93
Charlesworth, J.C., 225
Chattopadhyay, P., 36
Churchman, West, 100, 114
Cloward, R.A., 114
Cohen, A.R., 131, 204
Coleman, J.S., 34
Cooper, D.H., 179
Crozier, Michael, 7, 34, 131
Culbertson, J.M., 36

Dayal, Ishwar, 203
Delion, A.G., 225
Dickson, Paul, 113
Doornbos, M.R., 34
Downs, Anthony, 132
Dror, Yehezkel, 37, 130, 214
Duke, R.D., 114
Dunn, E.S., 116
Durstine, R.M., 179

Easton, David, 36
Esman, M.J., 65, 234, 245
Ettinger, K.E., 192
Etzioni, Amitzi, 35

Farmer, R.N., 192
Fisher, R.A., 111
Foster, C.C., 116
Friedrich, C.J., 76, 81, 226

Gallas, N.M., 226
Gallati, R.R.J., 115
Glaser, George, 114
Greenberg, D.G., 113
Groves, R.T., 131
Gorvine, Albert, 131

Haire, M., 191
Hall, R.H., 8, 34
Harbison, Frederick, 35, 65
Havighurst, C.C., 116
Head, R.V., 113
Heady, Ferrel, 35, 225
Hershman, Arlene, 114
Hoek, F.J. van, 179
Hoffman, L.J., 116
Hoffman, Michael, 191
Holt, R.E., 21, 36
Hoos, Ida, 113
Huntington, S.P., 34, 179

Jacobs, B.L., 250
Jacoby, N.H., 192
Jacqz, J.W., 179

Kaplan, Abraham, 100, 114
Katz, S.M., 11, 35
Kaufman, Herbert, 225
Kaysen, Carl, 116
Kruskal, W.H., 115
Kuhn, T.S., 179

Landau, Martin, 116
Lee, Hahn-Been, 130
Leemans, Arne, 131
Leibenstein, Harvey, 88, 93
Leys, Colin, 245
Levine, Robert, 70
Likert, R., 15, 35
Lipton, Michael, 34, 179
Loon, J.G. van, 179
Lynton, R.P., 230, 243

McClelland, D.C., 74, 86, 204
Malik, C.H., 191
Marschak, Jacob, 101, 114
Mazumdar, D.L., 36
Mee, J.F., 191
Miller, R.F., 37
Miller, W.F., 116
Milne, R.S., 131
Moharir, V.V., 131
Montgomery, F.D., 65, 131
Morris, J.D., 115

Mosher, F.C., 131
Mouzelis, N.P., 132
Muhammad, Faqir, 36
Myers, C.A., 35
Myrdal, Gunnar, 34, 226

Nylen, D., 251

Olsen, M.E., 35
Organski, A.K., 34
Ostrom, Elinor, 36
Ostrom, Vincent, 36

Packard, Vance, 36
Packenham, R.A., 6, 34
Pareek, V., 230, 243
Pearson, L.B., 11, 35, 179
Piven, F.F., 114
Ponsioen, J.A., 15, 35
Price, J.L., 226
Pye, Lucian, 6, 34, 132

Richman, B.M., 192
Riggs, F.W., 34, 132, 225, 245
Robinson, R.D., 192
Rogers, D.C., 179
Rosander, A.S., 115
Rosenblaat, D., 115
Rothwell, K.J., 179

Samonte, A.G., 131
Schaeffer, R.H., 227
Schumpeter, Joseph, 84, 93

Scott, W.G., 227
Selznik, Phillip, 14, 35, 81
Sharpe, W.F., 114
Simon, H.A., 35
Solo, R.C., 81
Spencer, D.L., 36
Spengler, J.J., 35
Stigler, G.J., 101
Stone, D.C., 250

Terninko, John, 204
Thomas, John, 203
Thomas, Uwe, 114
Thompson, J.D., 76, 81
Thompson, V.A., 204
Tobin, A.W., 192
Turner, J.E., 36

Waldman, J.M., 36
Waldo, Dwight, 36
Walker, W.G., 179
Waterston, Albert, 227
Wedell, E.G., 178
Weiner, Norbert, 225
Weinstein, B.G., 251
Westin, A.F., 116
Wheeler, Stanton, 115
Wildavsky, Aaron, 210
Winter, D.G., 71, 74
Wood, M.K., 115
Wu, Chi-Yuen, 227, 228

Yamey, Basil, 89, 93

Subject Index

Achieving Societies, 70
Administrative Change, 12, 23-25, 117, 205-214, 219
Administrative Obstacles, 13
Administrative Reform, Defined, 118, 119
  Failures, 119, 120
  Feasibility, 120
  Initiation, 122-124, 254
  Macro Approach, 126
  Objectives, 124, 125
  Scope, 25, 118
  Strategies, 125-128
  Structuralist, 126
Administrative Role
  Planning, 207
  Salaries, 140
  Tactics, 12
Administration: Management compared, 3, 20-23, 33, 211
Afghanistan, 56, 136
Algeria, 223
"Alternative Futures", 134
Argentina, 57, 91

Behavioral Approach, 8, 70, 199, 202
  and Administrative Reform, 119, 126, 212, 213
Bureaucracy, 7-9, 142, 203, 226n, 248
  contemporary meanings, 7, 202
  and reform, 127
Bureaucratization, 8
Brazil, 57, 121, 222, 237

Capacity for Local Action, 61-65
Capacity for Training, 59
Chile, 56
China, 136, 141, 147, 185
Community Development, 65
Comparative Management and Administration, 42
Conflict Theory, 127
Constitutive System, 143-145
Contact Points, 173
Convergence, 3, 40
Convincing Model, 16

Data Bank, 100, 108
  and Invasion of Privacy, 110
  National Data Bank, 110-112
Development Administration, 47, 49-53, 232, 241, 253

Ecological View, 135, 145
Economic Management, 11, 15, 210

Economic Planning, 9-12, 27, 208, 253
Educational Planning, 154, 164, 168, 254
Entrepreneur, Defined, 69, 83-85, 194
Ethiopia, 70, 138

Growth Rates, Compared, 21, 152

Imposition Model, 15
India, Civil Service, 37
  Economic Planning, 9, 17, 163
  Management Training, 29, 193-203
Information, as Interpreted Data, 102
  Entrepreneur, 88, 90
  Explosion, 101
  Technology, 95
  also see MIS
Institution Building (IB)
  Concepts, 53, 67, 75-77
  Limitations, 80, 81
  Problems of, 55-58, 77-78, 259
  Research, 53, 58, 259
Interaction Model, 16
Interdisciplinary Studies, 4, 11, 60, 171, 220-222
Intermediate Training Institutions, 52

Japan, 21, 138

Korea, 56

Linkages, 54, 57
Local Government, 61, 62

Management Dimensions, 14-17, 184
Management Education, 28-31, 43, 49, 66, 216-217
Management Information System (MIS)
  Concept, 96
  Design, 100
  Development, 96-98
Managerial Capacity, 64, 181, 199
Managerial Manpower
  Planning, 54, 66, 190
  Shortages, 48-51
Military Management, 52
Mock Innovator, 92
Motivating Economic Achievement, 71
Multipliers, 222

Need for Achievement (N/A), 70, 86
  and Minorities, 70
Nigeria, 56, 238, 247

Organic Organization, 202, 203

Organization Development, 212, 240
Organizational Adaptation, 128
  Capability, 75
  Roles, 182, 195
Organization and Methods (O & M), 27, 140
Organizations and Management, 188, 195

Pakistan, 56, 122
Participant Training, 51, 174, 231
Participation Model, 16, 64, 206, 213, 227n
Pearson Commission, 11, 164, 169
Performance Budgeting, 139
Programs for Senior Executives, 51
Promotion Systems, 69
Political Development, 6, 7, 142, 159, 163,
  171, 208
Political Input-Output Analysis, 22
Project Management, 17–20, 58–61, 215
  Sponsorship, 18
  Implementation, 59
Public Sector and Private Sector, 39

Quantitative Analysis, 210

Risk Taking, 91

Soft State, 3, 34, 226n
State Direction of Economy, 10
System Building V System Improvement, 75
Systems, Approach, 4, 11

Criminal Justice System, 106–107
Delivery System, 256
Information and Larger Systems, 105–107
Transportation Information, 102

Tanzania, 220
Technical Assistance, 26, 157, 160, 164–166,
  241, 255
Thailand, 56
Tolerance for Ambiguity, 198
Training, – N/A Training, 72–74
  Strategy, 229, 231, 248–250
  see also Management Education and
    Training and Participant Training
Training and Education Compared, 30
Transfers to Developing Countries, 158–161,
  170
Transfers of Skills, 26–28, 189, 201, 256–
  257
Turkey, 56, 138

United Arab Republic, 121
United Nations Development Decade, 151,
  205
  Performance 1960s, 152–155

Venezuela, 220, 223

Westernization, 133, 189
World Solidarity Contribution, 157